BASIC AUDIO-VISUAL
MEDIA

Basic
Audio-Visual Media

*[For Degree/P.G. Diploma Courses in Journalism
and Media Communication]*

By
Shipra Kundra

ANMOL PUBLICATIONS PVT. LTD.
NEW DELHI - 110 002 (INDIA)

ANMOL PUBLICATIONS PVT. LTD.

4374/4B, Ansari Road, Daryaganj

New Delhi - 110 002

Ph.: 23261597, 23278000

Visit us at: www.anmolpublications.com

Basic Audio-Visual Media

First Published, 2005

ISBN 81-261-2452-0

PRINTED IN INDIA

Published by J.L. Kumar for Anmol Publications Pvt. Ltd., New Delhi - 110 002 and Printed at Mehra Offset Press, Delhi.

Contents

Contents

Preface

"Basic Audio—Visual Media" as a paper is being taught at the various diploma, graduate and post graduate level in 'Media Communication and Journalism' at various universities and institutions. This book is designed as an introductory text to the above paper, encompassing vital information on all pertinent aspects. Thus the material presented here would be of interest as well as of great use to the students, teachers and professionals of Media Communication and Journalism. This book will provide complete knowledge of the evolution of radio, its impact on society, various radio programmes, educational radio and T.V., development of T.V. and its impact on society, satellite and cable T.V., Indian cinema and other means of entertainment etc. to the students.

The major topics dealt in this book are—Brief History and Evolution of Radio; Impact of Radio on Society; Radio Programmes; Educational Radio; Brief History of Television; Development of Television in India; Educational Television; Impact of Television on the Society; Satellite and Cable TV Invasion; Future of Television; Brief History of Indian Cinema; Cinema After Independence; New Trends in Cinema; The Foreign Entertainment; The Control Over Cinema; etc.

It is hoped that all those will benefit from the contents of this book for whom it is meant. The author will feel amply rewarded, if motive is achieved.

Author

1

Brief History and Evolution of Radio

In 1894, an Italian Guglielmo Marconi concluded that the Hertzian waves could be used for telegraphing without wires and in 1895 secured a patent for wireless telegraphy. In 1901, working in Newfoundland Marconi picked up the Morse letter "s" transmitted by wireless telegraphy from England, leading to headlines in the New York times, "WIRELESS SPANS THE OCEAN." The main technical hurdle in the way of wireless voice broadcasting was overcome by the discovery of a means of high frequency alternating transmission, John Amblose Fleming, Professor of Electrical Engineering at Imperial College, London, invented the vacuum tube in 1904 and two other scientists, the Canadian, Regionald Fessenden and the American, Dr. Lee De Forest developed its refinements. De Forest using his invention the audion tube, projected speech by radio on December 31, 1906, only five days after Fessenden accomplished the same thing with his heterodyne system. In 1908, De Forest broadcast recorded music from the top of the Eiffel Tower in Paris and was heard five hundred miles away.

In July 1897, the first commercial company for the manufacture of radio equipment, the Wireless Telegraph and Signal Company Ltd. (England) was set up. Later it became Marconi's Wireless Telegraph Company Ltd. A subsidiary of the British Company, the American Marconi was incorporated in the United States in 1899 and soon came to control almost all of American commercial wireless communications, then limited to ship-to-shore transmissions and special point-to-point broadcasts. In 1910, the U.S. Congress passed a law requiring passenger ships to have radio equipment and operators. Two years later in 1912 the Titanic, on her maiden voyage struck an iceberg and sank, but thanks to this legislation a prompt wireless call for aid made it possible to save the lives of more than 700 passengers. David Sarnoff the wireless operator who received the distress calls from the sinking Titanic later became major figure in the development of broadcasting. Some American companies such as General Electric, Westinghouse and the Western Electric Company, the manufacturing subsidiary of the American Telephone and Telegraphy Company (AT&T) won several important radio patent after considerable research in the field. However, each manufacturer needed patents controlled by his competitors but each refused to licence others or to exchange patents, resulting in a deadlock.

During World War I the US government took over all the wireless stations and asked all the companies to pool their inventions in the hope of devising practical radio-telephone transmitters needed by the Army and Navy, In return the companies were assured legal protection against patent suits. After the end of War wireless stations were returned to their owners and things went back to square one. The confused patent situation prevented any extensive radio manufacturing, and to add to it, there was a clash of interest between the United States and Britain as the American Marconi company a subsidiary of the British Marconi still controlled a substantial part of the wireless industry in the U.S. In 1919 British Marconi negotiated with America's General Electric for the exclusive rights to the Alexanderson alternator, a device considered of critical importance in long distance radio transmission. But Admiral W.H.G. Bullard, Director of naval communications for the U.S. Navy appealed to General Electric not to sell the alternator to British Marconi, because the British would then have a monopoly on worldwide communications for an indefinite period. Negotiations, virtually concluded, were dropped and under Admiral Bullaru's guidance, General Electric evolved 'a plan by which a new company controlled entirely by

American capital, the Radio Corporation of America (RCA) was formed. This company bought all the patents and assets of American Marconi, Westinghouse and Western Electric. These agreements gave General Electric and Westinghouse the exclusive right to manufacture radio receiving sets and gave RCA the sole right to sell the sets. The AT & T got to the exclusive right to make, lease and sell broadcast transmitters, From 1919 to 1921 the RCA was concerned with ship-to-shore communications, trans-oceanic point-to-point radio service, and sales of radio parts to amateurs for construction of crystal receivers.

Thus, the early development of radio revolved around the perfection of point-to-point broadcasting as a substitute for transmission by cable or telephone lines. The main commercial criticism of radio was its lack of secrecy making it unsuitable for private service since unauthorised persons could overhear a broadcast conversation. In due course however, this very factor became its major strength. In 1916 David Sarnoff, the then contract manager of American Marconi and later the Chief Executive of RCA recommended that transmission stations be built for the purpose of broadcasting speech and music, and radio music box should be manufactured for general sale. He said it could become a household utility in the same sense as the piano or phonograph, being used not only to transmit and receive music, but also to broadcast lectures, special public events, baseball scores and various other subjects of popular interest. But by 1920 there were still only a few individuals who could grasp the radio's real potential. At the University of Wisconsin, an experimental station, later called WHA was operated by the University's Physics Department to broadcast weather and market reports. Willian E. Scripps of the Detroit News also appreciated the real virtues of broadcasting and started his experimental station, now WWJ, in the summer of 1920. In Pittsburgh, H.P. Davis Westinglu vice president and Dr. Frank Conrad, a research engineer, opened the first commercially licenced radio station, KDKA in November 1920, broadcasting the returns of the Harding-Cox presidential election as its first programme. By World War II radio had emerged as major mass medium and was used for war propaganda and mobilising the masses for war effort. From 1920 onward radio made phenomenal progress in America, Europe and Asia. The invention of electron tube and later the transistor (1948) made possible remarkable development.

EVOLUTION OF RADIO IN INDIA

In India, as early as August 1921, The Times of India in collaboration with the Post and Telegraph Department broadcasted a special programme from it's Bombay office. This was at the request of Sir George Llyod, Governor, who listened to the programme in Pune.

The first radio programme in India was broadcast by the Radio Club of Bombay in June 1923. It was followed by the setting up of a broadcasting service that began broadcasting in India in June 1927 on an experimental basis at Bombay and Calcutta simultaneously under an agreement between Government of India and a private company called the Indian Broadcasting Company Limited. After that the development of broadcasting in India proceeded with many ups and downs and in climate of much uncertainty. Improvements in technology also supported the change. The transistor was invented during World War II. This made hand sized radio and on the go listening possible and an important car radio for driving listeners. In 1930, Indian Broadcasting Company handed over Bombay station to the Government and it was renamed the Indian State Broadcasting Service (ISBS). It was renamed as All India Radio on 8th June, 1936.

When India became independent the AIR network had only six stations located at Delhi, Bombay, Calcutta, Madras, Lucknow and Tiruchirapalli with a total complement of 18 transmitters. Six on the medium wave and the rest on short wave was confined to urban limits of these cities. As against a mere 2,75,000 receiving sets at the time of Independence, today there are about 180 million estimated radio sets in the country. Now the broadcast scenario has drastically changed with 177 broadcasting centres, including 65 local radio stations, covering nearly cent percent country's population. According to AIR 1995, there are 104 million estimated radio households and 111 million radio sets.

Until now AIR has been fully owned, controlled and run by the central government but now with the implementation of Prasar Bharti Bill All India Radio will operate independently having different nature of control by the government. Before 1976, television constituted a part of the All India Radio. After that, it was separated from AIR and constituted into a new body and under a new banner Doordarshan. Now All India Radio is also called in the name of Akashvani like television is called Doordarshan. Radio is one of the media units of the Ministry of Information and broadcasting. Today AIR has 105 regional stations, 65 local stations, three Vividh Bharti broadcasting centres, and 3 relay centres and one auxiliary centre.

The important point to be noted is that while AIR made a substantial contribution to the popularisation of Indian classical music and light-classical music, brought literature in various Indian languages to the people's doorsteps and promoted an Indian consciousness and national unity, it has remained a state monopoly. There has never been a radio station in India other than an AIR station since independence. AIR was the one and only radio medium.

The phenomenal growth achieved by All India Radio through decades has made it one of the largest media organisations in the world.

Radio Considers as Mass Medium

Radio is widely used mass communication medium and has a great potentiality in dissemination of information as radio signals cover almost entire population. More than 177 radio stations are there across the country. About 97 percent of the population is reached by the radio.

Radio being a convenient form of entertainment caters to a large audience. With the advent of transistors this medium has reached the common man in urban and rural areas of India, though the utilization of radio is more among rural elites. It has advantages over the other mass media like television and newspapers in terms of being handy, portable, easily accessible and cheap. It is the most portable of the broadcast media, being accessible at home, in the office, in the car, on the street or beach, virtually everywhere at any time.

Radio is effective not only in informing the people but also in creating awareness regarding many social issues and need for social reformation, developing interest and initiating action. For example, in creating awareness regarding new policies, developmental projects and programs, new ideas etc. It can help in creating a positive climate for growth and development. It widens the horizons of the people and enlightens them, thereby gradually changing their outlook towards life. Research have shown that radio is an effective medium for education when it is followed up with group discussion and question-answer session.

In India, radio with it's penetration to the rural areas is becoming a powerful medium for advertisers. It gets 3 per cent of the national advertising budget. Radio is still to cheap alternative to television, but is no longer the poor medium in advertising terms. Because radio listening is so widespread, it has prospered as an advertising medium for reaching local audiences. Moreover, radio serves small highly targeted audiences, which makes it an excellent advertising medium for many kinds of specialised products and services. As far as commercials are concerned, no one is able to tune out commercials easily as is possible with remote control devices and VCRs. It is thought that radio's ability to attract local advertisers hurts mainly newspapers, since television is less attractive to the small, local advertiser. As far as audience is concerned radio does not hamper persons mobility. As a vehicle of information for masses it is still the fastest. For instance, it would take less time for a news reporter for radio to arrive on the spot with a microphone and recorder than the same for TV along with a shooting team and equipment.

Another important feature of radio as mass medium is that it caters to a large rural population which has no access to TV and where there is no power supply. In such places, All India Radio's programmes ccntinue to be the only source of information and entertainment. Moreover, AIR broadcasts programmes in 24 languages and 140 dialects.

"Radio should be treated akin to newspapers in view of the fact that it is local, inexpensive, linked to communities, has limited band width and operates through simple technology". Feels Arora (1997 : 5).

The economics of radio does allow tailoring programme content to the needs of small and diverse audiences. Thus it is economically viable to recast a programme for broadcast to audiences in different sub regional, cultural and linguistic context. This enhances the value of radio as a medium in networking developmental programmes. Thus, it offers many possibilities in networking, from locally or regionally co-ordinated broadcasts and interactive exchange of queries and data.

It can serve as a stand alone medium of information dissemination or a support medium for curricular learning, jointly with print material or with fieldwork.

Kapoor, Director General of AIR (1995) said, " Radio is far more interactive and stimulating medium than TV where the viewer is spoon-fed. Radio allows you to think, to use your imagination. That is why nobody ever called it the idiot box".

THE OBJECTIVES OF AIR

The All India Radio aims at providing information, education and wholesome entertainment, keeping in view the motto" Bahujan Hitaya, Bahujan Sukhaya." *i.e.* the benefit and happiness of large sections of the people. It strives to

1. Uphold the unity of the country and the democratic values enshrined in the constitution and promote national integration.

2. Present a fair and balanced flow of information of national regional, local and international interest, including contrasting views, without advocating any opinion or ideology of its own.

3. Produce and transmit varied programmes designed to awaken, inform, enlighten, educate, entertain and enrich all sections of the people.

4. Produce and transmit programmes relating to developmental activities in all their facets including extension work in Agriculture, Education, Health and Family Welfare and Science and Technology.

5. Promote the interests and concerns of the entire nation ensuring that the programmes reflect the varied elements which make up the composite culture of India.

6. Serve the rural population, minority communities, women, children, illiterate as well as other weaker and vulnerable sections of the society.

Current broadcasting policy is based on the AIR code of 1970, which sets down that "broadcasts on All India Radio will not permit:

1. Criticism of friendly countries

2. Attack on religion or communities

3. Anything obscene or defamatory

4. Incitement to violence or anything against the maintenance of law and order.

5. Anything amounting to contempt of court.

6. Aspersions against the integrity of the President, Governors, and Judiciary.

7. Anything showing disrespect to the constitution or advocating change in a constitutional way should not be debarred.

8. Attack on a political party by name

9. Hostile criticism of any state or the centre, or

The code allows an objective discussion of policies pursued by a government or political party. The broadcasting of the news of the death of high dignitaries such as the president, the vice-president, the prime minister and a few others can be done only after it has been cleared by the Home Secretary. Since 1977 air time is allotted for to political parties for broadcasting prior to national and state elections. (Kumar, 1989).

The following are some of the conventions observed by All India Radio and Doordarshan.

1. Appeal for funds are disallowed except in national emergencies.

2. Exclusion of trade names in broadcasts which amount to advertising directly (except in commercial service); and

3. Direct publicity is not permitted for or on behalf of an individual or organisation which is likely to benefit only that individual or organisation.

Audience Research Unit

All India Radio has Audience Research Unit, which has it's headquarters in New Delhi. It has six Regional Audience Research Units in Delhi, Bombay, Calcutta, Madras, Shillong, Allahabad and 38 units of AIR stations. This unit started in 1946. In the beginning it mainly concentrated on studying the audience characteristics.

The activities carried out by these units are:

(i) Providing research support to broadcasts at formative stage.

(ii) Evaluation of programmes and to provide qualitative and quantitative feedback to programme planners and policy makers.

(iii) Preparation of Audience profile

(iv) Preparation of popularity ratings of programmes.

(v) Maintaining Data bank on the activities of AIR and bringing out Annual compilations.

The methods employed to carry out these activities are sample surveys, observation, case studies, experimental researches, content analysis, quick feedback weekly studies etc.

Audience Research units compile the surveys/studies conducted by them. For example, listnership survey on four FM channels, Quick Feed Back studies on National programmes, studies on IGNOU Broadcasts, etc.

VARIOUS ALL INDIA RADIO SERVICES

AIR has a three tier system of broadcasting through which it caters to the information, education, and entertainment needs of the people. These are as follows:

National Service. The National channel of AIR started functioning on May 18, 1988. It covers nearly 76% of the population and 64% of the area of the country. It provides a judicious blend of information and entertainment to programmes, including news, high quality Hindustani, Karnataki and western music; investigative reports and features, magazines, plays, sports, on order segment and Vividha a causerie of people, men, matters and music.

Regional Services. The regional services cater to major linguistic and cultural groups. This service is offered by each state and union territory to the groups living in these areas. Except for news and national programmes of folks and music which are relayed from Delhi, the other programmes of each regional station directed at different groups such as farmers, workers children, women, youth are produced at the regional stations/centres. The national service programmes are broadcast over short wave transmitter which makes it possible for regional centres to relay them.

External Services. The external services of All India Radio act as a bridge between India and the world. The External Services Division (ESD) broadcasts programmes for 69 hrs. per week, every day in 24 languages-General overseas service in English, 15 other foreign languages and in 8 Indian languages for our listeners in different parts of the globe.

External broadcasts project the Indian point of view on world affairs and acquaint the overseas listeners with the developments in India along with the information on the Indian life, thought, culture, tradition and heritage. It also broadcasts in Indian languages for Indian people settled abroad. The programmes generally comprise news bulletins, newsreels, current affairs, review of the India press, sports, folk music and so on.

Vividh Bharati. The Vividh Bharati was started on 2nd October 1957, as a service of 'light entertainment' to compete with Radio Cylon, which had begin directing a commercial service to India on powerful short wave transmitters.

At present there are 30 Vividh Bharati and commercial Broadcasting stations in the country. Sixty per cent of the time of the stations is devoted to film music and the rest is earmarked for devotional music, light music and spoken word programmes in the form of short plays, talks interviews, etc. Sponsorships are also accepted for these programmes. Vividh Bharati service increased the popularity of radio as a mass communication medium. At present this service is on the air for 12 hours and 45 minutes everyday with an extra hour and a quarter on Sundays and holidays.

The Verghese Committee found that it has become a repetitive film-disc programme and there is a need to develop a genuine radio originated light entertainment programme along with film music.

News. The News Services Division (NSD) produces 89 bulletins in 19 languages which emanate from Delhi and are relayed by several AIR stations. In addition to these bulletins, the Regional

News Units, 41 in all, located in different parts of the country, produce as many as 134 regional and 7 external news bulletins. The News Service Division produces bulletins for listeners abroad in 24 languages.

Radio presents news in a dissimilar pattern. People hardly sit down for extended periods of time to listen attentively to a lengthy radio news broadcast. They used to before television was available, but today they listen to radio while driving car, before going to sleep at night, while preparing meals or while doing something else. Thus radio listening is often a secondary activity but is more convenient than newspaper reading because it can be done while doing other important things. Therefore, radio newscasters present their reports frequently and in brief 'bursts'. A radio news report offers few details. Thus radio news presentations touch on the main points.

Radio is relatively ineffective compared to newspapers when it comes to audience comprehension of the news. On the other hand, it has the factor of immediacy.

TYPES OF AIR PROGRAMMES

The three main pillars of AIR programme composition are:

1. News

2. Music programmes

3. Spoken word programmes.

News programmes constituted 22.49% of the total radio programme composition. Music programmes include classical, folk, light, devotional, film and western music programmes. Talks, discussions, interviews are regularly arranged to provide a forum for all shades of opinion on outstanding national and international issues.

Radio drama figures both in AIR's general programmes as well as in the programmes for specific groups. Radio features and documentaries are the formats which use the entire range of audio formats in a single programme, *e.g.* narration, music, drama, interviews, poetry, sound effects, etc.

Rural programmes are broadcast from almost all AIR stations in different languages and also in local dialects to provide educational and infonnational support to agriculture and rural development programmes. Special programmes for rural listeners are broadcast from almost all AIR stations.

The programmes for children are broadcast for tiny tots and also children up to the age of 14 years.

Educational programmes of AIR cover a wide spectrum, primary, secondary, tertiary and university levels. Enrichment programmes are also broadcast for teachers.

AIR is now giving more emphasis on the planning and production of science programmes in both the formal and non-formal spheres of educational broadcasts. Special science cells have been set up in most of the major stations of the country to improve the quantity and quality of science programmes.

All important sports events are also given due coverage by AIR. Apart from these, programmes for youth, Senior Citizens, industrial workers are being broadcast by AIR.

Radio went through two changes in its transformation. They were the localization and specialization of program content. More of local programs were offered using local content. This helped in reaching out to their local audience. As radio programmes included local content, many special interest audiences were attracted to radio programs such as programs on folk songs, local or regional music programs, programs for women, youth, teen-age, children, religious groups, industrial workers, rural masses, and so on. As an advertising medium also, it proved cheaper in reaching many of a time.

The effectiveness of a radio broadcast increases when the program writers take into account, vocabulary of the target group,

and if organizers encourage listeners to participate in a post broadcast
session, particularly if the broadcasts themselves are so designed as
to draw the listeners to a participatory programme in the form of
filling in checklists and other academic exercises".

It also included programmes such as talk shows, weather
reports, music, news summaries and many other entertainment
programs. Thus, in its various formats radio is surviving the challenge
of television.

AIR programme sources could be:

1. In house production by AIR stations.

2. Programmes obtained through, Programme Exchange
   Service of AIR.

3. Programmes obtained from foreign broadcasting organisation under cultural exchange or similar arrangements.

4. Co-production with specialised Institutions or Foreign
   broadcasting organisations.

5. Software projects—production of financially viable programmes (in home and outside).

7. Sponsored Programmes—in house as well as outside
   productions.

6. Programmes available on commercial records/CDs. etc.

8. Programmes obtained from SAVE (SAARC Audio-visual
   Exchange).

A wards for excellence in radio programme production and
technical excellence are given by AIR annually in all the categories of
programmes. Such as radio play, radio documentary, musical
productions, programme for national integration, innovative
programmes, youth programmes, farm and home programmes, choral
singing and family welfare programmes.

Radio Broadcast for Education

Educational technology in India has come a long way from the use of simple audio visual aids to that of electronic media. The history of radio broadcast for education can be traced back to the year 1932 when the All India Radio started offering programmes for schools for the first time. At present, several stations regularly produce programmes for the schools and a large number of auxiliary stations relay these programmes to reach children and teachers in remote areas. Based on numerous experiments and studies, the broadcasts have been made as self sufficient as feasible to ensure that the message of the broadcast is communicated to children even when the necessary assistance is not provided by the teachers. The radio programmes have also been made relatively independent of the pre and post broadcast activities of learners.

Recent Innovations in AIR

Frequency Modulation (FM) Broadcast. In FM radio signals from transmitting station travel into space without hindrance. There is no reflection of signals by the upper atmosphere. It is just sufficient that the reception set is within the area of the station. It. is often called FM radio station. Some stations are referred to as clear channel stations, which refers to powerful station broadcasting to wide area without any interference (Rayudu:373).

It is essentially a local channel with a reach of 70 Km. radius from the place of transmission. Owing to it's crystal clear reception it has traditionally been used for broadcasting music, often intercepted with local news and weather forecasts. FM was introduced in 1977 but it was not really activated. It was activated in 1992. The hours of FM broadcast increased from 6 to 12 hours a day. All MetrosDelhi, Bombay, Calcutta and Madras have a 24 hours FM service.

FM has chatty, interactive style of programming and thus radio substitutes as a friend. This is the key to the comeback of radio. The local music talents, who have earlier been wholly dependent on music festivals and new year parties now have FM to turn to for promotional help. It brings local artists to the fore. Thus, with FM, radio has scope for its growth as a powerful medium.

Voice-Mail. This is a service facility where people can telephone and record their requests, complaints, suggestions and appreciation, etc. These messages are later retrieved and played back in a special voice Mail Programme with suitable replies to their queries.

Radio Bridge. This is programme on special occasions and is broadcast live by uplinking AIR stations through satellite. It represents a live interaction among the participants including listeners in different parts of the country. Presently 20 AIR stations have uplinking facility.

Radio Paging. A major application of the additional data service injected in the FM broadcast channel known as RDS is radio paging. It would provide alert signals, emergency calls, valuable information etc., the service will be highly useful for medical professionals, business executives, commercial applications and emergency services. AIR has FM transmitters at 17 centres.

Phone-in-Programme. This provides simultaneous communication. People telephone to the broadcasting station on a given telephone number at the time of broadcast and ask questions and the experts at the station reply to their queries immediately.

Prasar Bharati (Broadcasting Corporation of India)

The year 1997 was a 'land mark year' which saw far reaching measures to ftee the broadcast media. from the shackles of Government control 50 years after independence. It was the first instance of a government voluntarily bringing legislation to free the media from its control which may set in motion a chain of events in the country bringing in revolutionary changes in the field.

For over three decades beginning with Chanda committee report in 1966 and continuing through the reports of the Verghese

Committee (Akash Bharti) in 1978 and the Joshi Committee in 1985-expert committees set up by the government made a case for organisational restructuring of broadcasting, so as to give it greater autonomy.

As a result, the Prasar Bharati Act (1990) was formed by the government. It was kept idle for seven years. In July 1997, it was activated after being notified and came into force on September 22, 1997. Then came the amendments to the Act which were widely seen as ushering in a regime of full autonomy to All India Radio and Doordarshan. The Prasar Bharati Board has been formed with an executive member and Six part-time members, paving the way for granting autonomy to Doordarshan and All India Radio.

The amendments were expected to be incorporated during the winter session of 11th Parliament but due to the dissolution of the House it was delayed.

The objectives of the Prasar Bharati Bill are:

1. To confer autonomy on Akashvani and Doordarshan, thereby ensuring that they function in a fair, objective and creative manner.

2. Upholding of both unity and integrity of the country.

3. Upholding of the democratic and social values enshrined in the constitution.

4. To look after the safeguarding of the citizen's right to be informed freely, truthfully and objectively.

The Bill has triggered a lively debate on controversial provisions such as cross media holdings, the extent of foreign equity allowed, uplinking facilities and the cosmopolitan and powers of the Broadcasting Authority of India.

Mehta points out that, the Bill has to be in harmony with the basic approach of the broadcasting policy as laid down by the

Supreme Court, which stated in a recent judgement that "air ways or frequencies for transmission of electronic communication are public property and should not be the monopoly of the government or anybody else. It should offer a plurality and diversity of news and views". Also, the policy has to take cognisance of the rapid changes in electronic media technology (1989:9).

ADVANTAGES OF RADIO

Like other electronic media radio duplicates one-to-one communication thousands of times. A large section of receivers can be communicated quickly through radio. In case of emergencies, for examples, warnings of floods and other weather disturbances can be repeated every 15 or 30 minutes on radio. It can convey the message with speed and immediacy.

Due to many local radio stations as compared to television stations, radio is the major source of local news for many people. Local radio stations are targeted at specific audiences youth, rural, housewives, ethnic groups and so on. Thus, it becomes a valuable medium for development workers.

Radio needs relatively low infrastructure and overhead costs. It is easier to get on radio than television since radio programme is cheaper to produce and not much preparation is required. News, programmes and advertising for radio need little preparation. It can accommodate the last minute news story and sudden change in advertising messages. Radio can stay ahead in all message areas. This is also not possible with time consuming procedures.

It has greater audience reach. Even in the physical sense of 'reach', radio lends itself to a greater diversity of receiving situations. It does not demand undivided attention. It permits receiver mobility. A radio broadcast can be followed while going about various activities and chores, indoors and outdoors. It is inherently versatile medium, as it offers wide range of programme and frequency choices to its audience. It offers variety of programming slots. Transistors can continue to communicate even in case of power failure. In India, radio caters to a large rural population which has no access to TV and where there is no regular or limited power supply.

In such places, All India Radio's programmes continue to be the only source of information and entertainment. Moreover, radio brings programmes in 24 languages and 146 dialects.

LIMITATIONS OF RADIO

Radio has many inherent limitations. It provides one way channel of communication. Therefore, no feedback regarding the messages can be received. Since the listener's attention is held only by the sound, messages communicated through radio can reach only those people who listen carefully and intelligently. One has to be very attentive to receive the messages from radio otherwise he misses a part of the message. Radio lacks the pictorial quality provided by television and motion pictures. Moreover, no visuals can be used with radio to support the messages. Radio is not suitable for all types of commercials as some require illustration or demonstration.

Since radio conveys messages through sound only, it demands a habit of skillful listening which generally people lack. Mohanty (1992) rightly pointed out that radio may broadcast a well developed lesson, but cannot develop a lesson with the audience. With many people to receive a complete detailed lesson or a programme through radio becomes very taxing or boring as it tends to become monotonous at times.

Rahman (1977) said, "Radio broadcast is evanescent, impermanent and rarely sufficient in itself for the case of illustration. intended in educational broadcasting. It cannot be turned to, studied or re-read at leisure".

A wasthy has aptly said that in radio the artist and his audience are nowhere near each other. In the physical sense they are non-existent to each other.

Suggestions for the Betterment of Radio

1. To take the challenge of television, radio format must be distinctive and competitive. The programmes should be interesting enough to hold the audience.

2. To ensure local level need based production of radio programmes radio needs to be made a localised medium.

3. Independent agencies interested in radio programme productions should be encouraged.

4. Radio stations and programme producers need to have collaboration and co-ordination between agencies like home science colleges, women's welfare agencies and broadcasters for producing programmes that are intelligible, interesting, and educative to target groups.

5. To strengthen the use of radio in networking developmental activities is necessary to promote listener's forums in institutional and community contexts. Such feedback mechanisms provide data for audience research and lead to meaningful programming.

6. To overcome language barriers, an infrastructure can be set up to transcreate radio programmes in the variety of cultural contexts existing in the region.

7. Outdoor and field based programmes also should be encouraged which have been very limited so far due to technical and financial limitation.

8. There is a need to set up broadcast coordination centres across the region to serve as local, regional, national and international programmes exchange units. They can identify programmes of common interest and disturb them in areas to which they are relevant.

9. Experts should be engaged by the radio stations to process and analyse feedback and assist in the production of fieldbased development programmes.

CONTEMPORARY RADIO

Frequency Modulation : FM

FM (Frequency Modulation) radio did not come to public attention until the end of the War, though it had been known to the radio industry since its development during the previous decade by Major E.H. .Armstrong at Columbia University. Using a much higher band of frequencies than AM radio (from 80 to 108 megracycles), PM has many advantages over standard AM radio. It is ordinarily free from static, fading and interference noises. All stations' within reception range come in with equal strength, and sound is transmitted with much greater clarity than over AM radio. However, it has one limitation—its coverage is usually limited to the line of sight from the top of the transmitter. PM is better suited for community and metropolitan centres than for rural areas. But this limitation in coverage also makes it possible for many FM stations situated not very far apart geographically to share the same frequency.

Radio Frequency Spectrum

Scientifically, the term radio means the usage of radiation and detection of signals propagated through space as electromagnetic waves to communicate. Electromagnetic radiation includes light as well as radio waves and the two have many common properties. Both are propagated through space in approximately straight lines at a velocity of about 300,000,000 metres (186000 miles) per second and have amplitudes that vary cyclically with time, *i.e.* they oscillate from zero amplitude to a maximum and back again. The number of times the cycle is repeated in one second is called the frequency in cycle per second and time taken to complete one cycle is sometimes called the period. One cycle per second is called hertz in honour of the German pioneer Heinrich Hertz. Higher frequencies are called kilohertz

(1000 cycles per second), megahertz (1,000,000 cycles per second) and gigahertz (1,000,000,000 cycles per second).

Number of Bands

Very low frequencies (vlf)	3 to 30 Kilohertz (KHz)	Time signals Standard Frequencies
low frequencies (LF)	30 to 300 Kilohertz	Fixed, maritime, mobile, navigational, radio, broadcasting.
medium frequencies (mf)	300 to 3000 Kilohertz	Land, maritime mobile, radio broadcasting.
high frequencies (hf)	3 to 30 megahertz MHz	Fixed, mobile, maritime & aeronautical mobile, amateur.
very high frequencies (vhf)	30 to 300 megahertz	Fixed, mobile, maritime and aeronautical mobile, amateur, radio and television broadcasting, radio navigation.
ultrahigh frequencies (uhf)	300 to 3000 megahertz	Fixed, mobile, maritime and aeronautical mobile amateur, television broadcasting, radio location and navigation, meterological, space communication.
superhigh frequencies (shf)	3 to 30 gigahertz	Fixed, mobile, radio location and navigation, space and satellite communication.

Radio Wave

Radio wave will have an amplitude variation along its direction of travel similar to that of its time variation, much like a wave travelling on a body of water. The distance from one wave crest of the next is known as wavelength. There is definite relationship between wavelength and frequency. Dividing the speed, of the electromagnetic wave by the wavelength gives the frequency. Thus a wavelength of 10 metres has a frequency of 300,000,000 divided by ten or 30,000,000 hertz or 30 megahertz.

The wavelength of light is much shorter than that of a radio wave. At the centres of the light spectrum the wavelength is about 0.5 micron (0.0000005 metre) or a frequency of 600,000 gigahertz. The maximum frequency in the radio spectrum is usually taken to be about 45 gigahertz corresponding to the wavelength of about 6.7 millimetres. Radio waves can be generated and used at frequencies lower than 10 kilohertz.

The radio frequency spectrum has been divided into a number of bands from very low to super high frequencies. Sections of the radio frequency spectrum have been allocated by international agreements to various users;

CARRIER WAVE

A carrier wave is a radio-frequency wave that carries information which is attached by means of a modulation process that involves the variation of one of the carrier-frequency characteristics such as its amplitude, its frequency or its duration. In amplitude modulation, the information signal varies the amplitude of the carrier wage. Frequency modulation involves varying the frequency of the carrier in accordance with the amplitude of information. The amplitude of the carrier wave is unaffected except for its frequency which changes.

A radio broadcast normally consists of only one information signal. The listener hears what he could hear at the microphone position if only one of his ears was functioning. It is a monoaural-system. In such a system the instrument groupings in an orchestra cannot be judged, nor can lateral movement be indicated, though movement toward, or away from the microphone is conveyed by a change in sound volume. Stereophonic broadcasting on the other hand, requires two microphones, one to collect sounds from the left and one from the right; the two sets on information must be separable in the receiver and be fed to loudspeakers on the left and on the right at the listing position. For high-fidelity reproduction the full audiorange upto 15 Kilohertz is transmitted. This can only be achieved satisfactorily at very high frequencies with frequency modulation.

Another system of modulation, the pulse code modulation switches the carrier on and off in pulses, the duration on position of the pulse being determined by the information signal. It can provide better protection from noise and a number of separate speech channels can be combined by allocating specified groups of pulses for each information channel and then interweaving these pulses in a process called time division multiplex. A comparatively wide tansmission channel is needed and the carrier must be an ultrahigh or superhigh frequency. The radio waves are returned to the earth when projected skyward because electrified (ionized) layers of air above the earth, (the ionosphere) reflect or refract (bend) them back to the earth, thus extending the range of a transmitter far beyond line of sight. The three layers-of the ionosphere are called D.E. and F layers. The D layers is approximately 80 Kilometres high and exists only during daylight hours. Because it absorbs medium frequencies and lower frequencies of the short wave bands, it limits the range of such stations during daylight.

❐

2

Impact of Radio on Society

So far radio has not enjoyed high credibility because of its being a government controlled medium but with the implementation of Prasar Bharati, it is expected that radio will not have to face such comments of critics.

According to Malhan, "AIR is considered by media authorities and researchers to have proved its worth and utility both as an informational channel and a development and cultural activist. It has provided healthy entertainment through its various light and humorous programmes. Extension research and other field surveys have already given great credit to radio as a credible promoter of a suitable climate for development and progress as also for having advanced form educational and cultural renaissance. Its contribution in the form of transmitting useful and timely information, motivation and suggestions for rural development is conceded. Its sponsors claim that radio is helping to create a climate of opinion in which social change can take place and people could be involved in the process".

It was pointed out at one of the seminars organised by AIR, that while AIR may have lost its primacy in metropolitan cities and big towns, it is still the main source of news and entertainment in rural areas and this position is likely to continue for many years for obvious reasons like cost considerations, unavailability of electricity and high rate of illiteracy. The large number of under privileged people in rural areas still stick to radio.

Various research experiments have proved that radio is an effective medium to address adequately a particular problem of our society. Radio, if used effectively, can help agencies, governments and the people in general to solve the problem of illiteracy and ignorance in our country.

In south and South East Asia region in its several languages, extensive programming on development and environment issues, packaged as information, education or entertainment is offered on radio. Radio played a significant part in transforming the public opinion and behaviour of an entire America by defining the noble purpose of IInd World War, and altered the lives of the people to Willingly contribute to the joint effort. Radio network as an instantaneous news medium unified a divided nation in to one that saw the war as a moral cause.

In India, at present local radio stations broadcast development programmes for rural masses, called farm and home programmes. There is a move to expand local radio stations. These stations can broadcast area specific programmes keeping in mind the needs of the local people. Thus, radio can become one of the powerful medium for development. The main problem in broadcasting developmental radio programmes is that most of the AIR stations are single channel ones so, they are not able to fit all the programmes of development in their schedule as there are demands for entertainment programmes also. Even today, the provision of radio sets in schools, adult or non-formal education centres is inadequate. There is lack of co-ordination and co-operation among the AIR officials, development practitioners, educationists and other key persons for tapping the potential of radio for development.

Moreover, radio programmes mostly focus on specific target groups. Such as programmes for children, women, youth, tribals, industrial workers programmes and so on. Audience research of AIR have shown that these special programmes have high listnership.

Every medium of communication has cultural identity and away from this, it tends to lose its effectiveness. Over the years radio has created for itself an image of being an important source of education and development. This has been possible because of its history of putting out programmes related to social and civic problems, agricultural programmes, health, family planning, and nutrition related programmes and on formal and non-formal education broadcasts. Television, on the other hand has evolved for itself an image of being essentially an entertainment medium and even as an extended arm of the film industry.

Rao (1992) found villagers' exposure to radio was significantly high with as many as 50 percent having access to the radio and getting the benefit of exposure to broadcasts as far as reach and utilization of the media and villagers' exposure to other informational channels was concerned. It was also found that agriculture or rural programmes were high on the priority of listeners. The local radio stations are very effective in reaching the people and ensuring their participation. As far as rural development is concerned, it is possible to broadcast need based agriculture programmes. Moreover, it provides scope for the use of local expertise and talents.

Audience researches conducted all around the country has shown that many radio programmes have fairly high percentage of listeners. The letters received from the listeners by AIR, Vadodara eliminate firmly the wrong notion of radio being "not listened to". These include feedback and suggestions on popular as well as special programmes such as Yuvvani, film songs, rural based programmes, farmer's programmes, expert's talks and question answer format programmes.

Many were attracted to radio and there was a time when "Chhaya Geet" on Vividh Bharati and "Binaca Geet Mala" were listened to religiously by one and all. Radio commercials have been very popular. In a country like India with different languages, commercial radio has been effectively used by the advertisers, especially at local level, to carry the product messages to the prospects. The main reason for the success of radio commercial in India is high percentage of illiteracy, where print media of newspapers and magazines are not effective advertising media.

Radio has helped in creating a positive climate for growth and development. India has had a rich tradition of the use of radio for non-formal education programmes, rural development and also for providing various types of learning opportunities and information to the people. The Pune Radio Rural Forum Project in India is cited as the most celebrated use of radio in development. Although the project was subsequently discontinued, yet the experience demonstrated that the radio rural forum can be cost effective in bringing about community development.

AIR's "Yuvvani" programme has provided a forum for the self expression of the youth between the ages of 15 to 30 years.

The evaluation of the AIR's farmers' programmes have indicated that the audience find them extremely useful. It is interesting to learn form the record projects of agricultural universities that AIR's rural programmes are not only useful to the villagers but command credibility and acceptability. The imprint of AIR is best known by the terms radio seeds and radio fertilizers. Community listening scheme was introduced by the government in Sixties. Assessment of this scheme revealed that the discussions in community listening and deliberations were excellent or good and participants learnt a 'great deal' or 'quite a lot'. Also these farmers developed rapidly in to decision making bodies capable of speeding up common pursuits of the village.

Other developing countries have also found using radio successfully in reaching "hard-to-reach" rural audiences quickly and quite inexpensively.

Vyas (1989) tapped the effectiveness of radio to enhance maternal and child health care in the rural areas of India, women were organised into listening groups who met regularly to listen, discuss and decide on action under the supervision of the trained personnels. Evaluation and review of the programme revealed that 97.19 percent of women in Haryana showed significant gain in knowledge regarding child survival and development issues. The knowledge retained on different topics ranged from 20.81 percent to 95.18 percent depending on the topic. In Tamil Nadu, more than 75 percent of the listeners indicated their strong desire to use the radio broadcast information with regard to the behavioural changes, nearly half of the listeners in Tamil Nadu had shown their willingness to add more milk and vegetables to their diet after listening to the programmes, while 16-32 percent of the respondents had consulted medical practitioners on immunization, nutritive food for children, care of children and health of pregnant women. This project was carried out with the co-operation of the Ministry of Information and broadcasting. It promoted services for material and child health care and fostered community participation in the child survival and development programmes.

Indian Broadcasting Company

Organised broadcasting in India was started by the Indian Broadcasting Company (IBC) in 1927. Bombay and Calcutta stations were inaugurated in July and August, 1927. The first radio programme journal India Radio Times was started on July 15, 1927. Its name was later changed to The India Listener and again to Akashvani.

IBC was a financial failure in spite of a loan from the government. It went into liquidation and was closed down in March, 1930. Under pressure from the radio-set dealers, programmers and the general public, the government took over the Bombay and Calcutta stations in April, 1930. The Indian Broadcasting Service was formed.

Those were the days of world wide depression. The government too faced financial difficulties. Even otherwise, it was not very enthusiastic about broadcasting. So, it ordered the closure of the Indian Broadcasting Service on Oct. 10, 1931. Representations and agitations compelled the government to reverse the orders on November 23, 1931. The Government doubled the duty on radio sets.

In. 1932, the British Broadcasting Corporation (BBC) started an Empire Service: The number of receiving sets, which were all imported, doubled in less than two years. This resulted in an increase in the government's income from license fees. The increase in import duty on radio sets and components of the radio sets also enhanced the government's revenue. Broadcasting now became financially viable. It was decided to start a radio station in Delhi. It actually went on the air on January 1, 1936.

The BBC loaned the services of Lionel Fielden who became the Controller of Broadcasting. (Today the radio chief is called Director General). He persuaded the government to realise the potential of broadcasting and allot more money to the service. In his autobiography, The Natural Bent, he writes about financial problems and red-tapism. He also gives an interesting account of how he could persuade the then Viceroy to adopt the name All India Radio for the broadcasting service. The name was adopted from June 8, 1936.

Fielden got together a group of devoted young people. With the help of these and of Goyder, his Chief Engineer, he started short-wave service in 1938, to cover the entire country. Lucknow station went on air on April 2, 1938, and Madras on June 16; 1938. In 1939, the Tiruchi station came into being. The same year the External Service Division at Delhi was started.

A.S. Bokhari, another dynamic administrator, took over from Fielden to become the first Indian Director General. He was the chief during all the war years and thereafter till the partition. A new Broadcasting House was built on Parliament Street, New Delhi. On June 3, 1947, Lord Mountbatten (the Viceroy), Jawaharlal Nehru and Mohd. Ali Jinah made historic broadcasts on the partition of India. In the midnight on August 14-15, 1947, Nehru broadcast his famous speech "Tryst 'with Destiny". It is preserved in the AIR archives.

First Three Plans

Following the country's partition, six radio stations came to the share of India (Bombay, Calcutta, Delhi, Tiruchi, Lucknow and Madras). When the princely states became a part of India, five more stations (Hyderabad, Aurangabad, Baroda, Mysore and Trivandrum) were taken over by AIR.

First Five Year Plan. During the First Five Year Plan (1951-56) much development of broadcasting took place. In 1952, the first National Orchestra was set up with Pandit Ravi Shankar as its conductor. Regional news bulletins in Hindi and Marathi were started in 1953 from Lucknow and Nagpur respectively. The first National programme of Talks too went on the air in 1953. In 1955 the first Radio Sangeet Sammelan was broadcast. The same year the Sardar Patel Memorial Lectures and Radio Newsreel were started. In 1956, the first National Symposium of Poets was broadcast and also the National Programme of Plays, Operas and Features. By the end of the first plan, the number of radio stations had increased to 26.

Dr. B.V. Keskar, the Minister for Information and Broadcasting (1953-61), did a lot for Indian classical music. He also brought eminent writers, poets, musicians and playwrights on contract as Producers.

Second Five Year Plan. Finances for broadcasting for the Second Plan (1956-61) were increased four times as against finances in the First Plan. In 1957, Vividh Bharati, an All India Radio Variety Programme Service, was started at Bombay. It provided light entertainment with a generous dose of film music. Over the years. it has become a very popular service. The service was started to counteract the increasing popularity of Radio Ceylon's commercial service. It has succeeded very well in its aim.

1957 also saw the start of an Inter-station Programme Exchange unit at Delhi. An annual folk music festival, "Songs of Nation Builders", was started in 1958 but it was short-lived. The scheme of Radio Rural forums was implemented in 1959, for two-way communication with rural listeners. In 1960, Jawaharlal Nehru's speech at the U.N. was directly relayed from New York. By 1961, radio covered 55% of the population and 37% of the area.

Third Five Year Plan. The Third Five Year Plan (1961-66) saw much expansion of medium-wave broadcasting. As many as 26 transmitters were added to AIR stations for broadcasting Vividh Bharati Programmes. In addition, two independent transmitters were installed at Chandigarh and Kanpur. By 1966, 54 stations covered 70% of the population and 52% area.

Chanda Committee

A committee on Broadcasting and Information Media was set up in 1964 under the Chairmanship of A.K. Chanda. It gave its report in 1966. It recommended separation of radio and television with two independent corporations. It was not accepted by the government then. The separation ultimately came about in 1976 and the TV setup was called Doordarshan. Another recommendation was for the starting of a commercial service. Commercial service was started from Vividh Bharati in 1967.

Code for Broadcasters

A 9-point code for broadcasters, introduced in 1969, prohibits the following:

* Criticism of friendly countries

* Attack on religion or communities

* Anything obscene or defamatory

* Incitement to violence or anything against maintenance of law and order . Aspersions against the integrity of the President, Governors and Judiciary.

* Attack on a political party by name

* Anything amounting to contempt of court

    * Hostile criticism of any state or the Centre

    * Anything showing disrespect to the constitution or advocating change in the constitution by violent means, but advocating changes in a constitutional way should not be debarred.

In 1969, a new channel "Yuva Vani" was started at Delhi. The sponsored programmes on the commercial service were introduced in 1970 and the Sanskrit news bulletins were introduced in 1974. Earlier, in 1971, the highest AIR station was set up at Leh. In the same year, the first satellite link was established.

Verghese Committee

In 1977, the Janata government appointed a Working Group headed by B.G. Verghese, to suggest an autonomous set-up for AIR and Doordarshan. The Group recommended in 1978 the creation of a National Broadcast Trust or Akash Bharati to look after both radio and TV. A bill to create the recommended Trust, was introduced in 1979. The recommendations of the Working Group; however, were much diluted in the Bill. Eventually the bill lapsed when the Janata government went out of power.

The Janata government also introduced party election broadcasts for the first time in 1977, on the eve of assembly elections in several states.

The Present Status

By 1980, radio covered about 90% of the population and over 78% of the area in the country.

Expenditure on radio broadcasting in the first plan (1951-56) was just over 2 crores. By the 7th Plan (1985-90) it increased to 700 crores.

In 1991, we had 102 full-fledged radio stations which were production centres. The number of broadcasting centres, which included relay centres, was 205. The population covered was 97.5%.

Area covered was 91%. The number of transmitters was over 300. This number included short wave, medium wave and VHF (very high frequency) or FM (frequency modulation) transmitters. National AIR channel via satellite was started in May, 1988.

Vividh Bharati

Vividh Bharati programmes are broadcast from 32 centres including two short-wave transmitters at Bombay and Madras. They are relay centre with low-power transmitters. They broadcast taped or pre-recorded programmes. The tapes are sent to the various centres much in advances.

External Services

The External Services Division broadcasts programmes in 24 languages (17 foreign and 7 Indian) for a total of 75 hours daily. A special weekly programme is prepared and is broadcast through foreign radio stations in U.K., U.S.A. and Canada. These programmes are meant for a large number of Indians living in these countries.

Educational Services

Several stations broadcast educational programmes for schools (school broadcasts), twice or thrice a week. The duration generally is 30 minutes. Unfortunately only about 20 thousand schools out of 7 lac schools have their own radio sets. Only about 40% schools actually listen to school broadcasts. They too do not have the listening period in their regular time-table.

Some stations help the Directorates of Correspondence Courses with University broadcasts. "Yuv Vani" provides the youth (15-30 years) with a channel to express themselves and for their talents to blossom.

Audience Research

Communication process is a two-way process. Unless there is feedback, the quality or effectiveness of broadcasts cannot be known.

For this purpose AIR started an Audience Research Wing in 1946. But in 1952, just after six years, the Wing was closed. Some critics say that it was closed because the findings of the Research Wing were not very pleasant for the bosses.

In mid-sixties the Audience Research Cell was set up again. Unfortunately it does not have adequate staff. The staff is also not very well trained. Some other means of getting feedback are letters from the listeners, staff meetings (daily) of stations and newspaper media columns.

Radio now covers almost the entire population of India. It has a great ability to inform, educate and entertain the people. It can be made effective as an agent for development, especially in the rural areas. Rural areas do not have as many facilities for information, education and communication as the urban areas have. It remains a very relevant medium in India, like in other developing countries. This is so because about 40% people in India are below the poverty line. Many are able to afford only a radio set or a transistor. TV sets are out of their reach. That is why, in a poor country like India, TV is called an elite medium which only the rich can afford.

Here, about half the population is illiterate. Radio, being a medium of the spoken word, uses conversational, simple and direct language. This can be easily understood even by illiterate folks. The effectiveness of radio can be guaged from the fact that its Rural Programme has been able to help the farmers in agricultural work. Varieties of grain or fertilizer popularised by the radio are commonly known as "radio seeds" or "radio khad".

But, to be fully effective, our radio must come out with new categories of programmes and new styles of presentation. It should encourage the formulation of Radio Forums or Clubs. Through these, radio should associate the people, the target audience with every aspect of Programmes. In this way, there will be audience participation which surely leads to the success and effectiveness of radio.

Radio stations should also go local. There should be at least one radio station in each district. The station should take care of the felt needs of the local communities. Small stations can involve the local communities in the total production process. That way the local people will have a sense of belonging to the radio and its broadcasts.

FM (frequency modulation) should be strengthened to provide reception without noise and disturbance.

Feedback needs to be strengthened. Fair and systematic research alone can yield truthful findings. Feedback for external services broadcasts should also be obtained in a more meaningful way. These services are important for our nationals, sitting far away from home. Their thirst for home news and cultural needs to be adequately satisfied. External services are also important for projecting the Indian culture and situation correctly and effectively in foreign countries.

New Role and Innovativeness of Radio

Known as Akash Vaw since 1957 AIR in its reach and impact is now the biggest media organisation of the Union Government, with its programmes received by over three crore radio receiver sets in India. As a fast and instantaneous communication medium, it has an inbuilt advantage of overcoming the country's formidable literacy, linguistic, cultural and physical barriers. It could also involve different types of people and integrate various kinds of cultural, musical, dance and folk art forms that obtained in India. During the British period this was not possible because the alien Government had little respect for national aspirations 'as also for indigenous forms of entertainment. After Independence this attitudinal obstacle ended.

Luckily, AIR had experienced personnel and "its innovative zeal was unbounded". For example in 1948, AIR Bombay arranged to interview the Hollywood star Greer Garson through an intercontinental link arranged by the P & T Department. In fact that spirit had infused largely the software policy of AIR. Accordingly the main thrust of its programmes was on putting out need-based innovative programmes. And that was the requirement of the time after the communal blood-bath of Partition, the urgency of emotional integration after the re-organisation of States and the initiation of the process of integrated planning.'The programme advisory committees set up at various stations and guidelines evolved in August 1980 too have sought to inject a high spirit of professionalism. in broadcasting programmes and to make them more receptive to constructive criticism. To this end listeners' letters, regular feedback surveys, and analysis of listener's reactions by audience research units to the programmes broadcast have also contributed their bit.

The manifestation of the spirit of innovativeness was evident when AIR covered sports events during Asiad 1982. In fact the coverage was a landmark. AIR broadcasted the various events to listeners all over the country. It also furnished facilities for dubbing and relaying the events to foreign broadcasting organisations. A team of nearly 550 people consisting of programmers, engineers and technicians were placed on duty in different stadia to catch the events in sound and convey them to listeners. All the technical infrastructure required for this historic event was provided internally.

Diversified Programmes

AIR's programmes have been diversified over the years. Today its Home Service programmes are transmitted for 3.91 lakh hours every year, excluding 1.76 lakh hours of Vividh Bharati programmes. In addition there are also external service transmissions which present programmes in 17 foreign languages and 8 Indian languages for over 56 hours daily to present India's viewpoint on important'issues to listeners abroad.

Radio is known as a popular music box especially of the common man. Formerly music and particularly classical music was largely'the privilege of the princely families or music enthusiasts. Now all kinds of music-classical, tribal, devotional, light, vocal, orchestral, folk and film based can be enjoyed by anybody possessing the set. In all radio stations about forty per cent of the total broadcasting time is devoted to music, music appreciation programmes and music lessons. As a result AIR is helping to preserve and develop the musical heritage of the country. Its musical programmes also- go a long way in acquainting the younger generulation with our classical tradition and help them to learn music through radio. AIR is seeking to scout new talents continually through regular music auditions as well as annual music competitions. Young and promising artists of higher grades are regularly featured in public concerts as well as in zonal hook-up programmes. Classical music programmes comprise a weekly national programme of music which presents to the nation music by leading practitioners of both Hindustani and Karnatak schools of music. As a promotional measure, a festival of music, known as Radio Sangeet Sammelan is also organised every year. The recordings of these concerts are broadcast on AIR's network in the country. One of the significant achievements of AIR's national programmes in music as also of Radio Sangeet Sammelans is integration through the interaction of the two major styles of Indian music—the Hindustani and Karnatak. Eminent artistes as well as the more promising younger talents in both styles are presented in these programmes which are beamed on the national network.

Since 1973 it also broadcasts a national programme of regional music, which brings to the listeners the rich tradition of folk and light music of the various regions. Besides this, AIR stations put out sizeable chunks of folk and light music in their programmes. 1n 1952 it started the orchestral programme called 'Vadya Vrinda' consisting of both Hindustani and Karnatak instrumentalists. The Delhi unit has done remarkable experiments in orchestration of Indian music and has a wide repertoire of a variety of compositions based on traditional ragas and folk tunes. The Madras unit comprises mainly Karnatak musicians. AIR is also paying equal attention to the development of folk, light and choral music.

Discerning people still like to listen to radio news bulletins, for they attempt to give comprehensive and speedy coverage of news and views in addition to commentaries and discussions on current affairs. Besides focussing on major trends in political, economic, social, cultural and scientific fields, they give adequate attention to rural development, parliamentary proceedings and sports activities. News is broadcast daily through 254 bulletins. Of these, 68 bulletins in 19 languages are beamed from the home service from Delhi, 123 regional bulletins in 60 languages and dialects and 63 bulletins of external services in 24 languages. Specialised news, sports' news, State and development news, slow-speed bulletins in English, Hindi and Urdu, a weekly bulletin of human interest stories, constitute other important bulletins of AIR covered by its own correspondents. In days when Parliament is in session, daily commentaries in English and Hindi review the day's proceedings in the two Houses. Since 1977 a weekly coverage has also been introduced. A similar coverage of State legislatures are broadcast for State capitals in the languages concerned.

The external services broadcasts are designed to project a true and objective image of the country to listeners abroad. They explain the country's point of view on matters of national and international importance. They also seek to acquaint foreign listeners with the ideas and achievements of India as an open society, as also its secular ideals. These broadcasts are equally meant to serve as a link with the people of Indian origin living or settled abroad.

AIR beams programmes for special audiences and occasions. Specific programmes are relayed for the Armed Forces, women and children, youth, students, industrial workers and rural and tribal people. Fourteen stations broadcast daily programmes for the Armed Forces. Fifty-five stations present programmes twice a week in regional languages for women with the objective of providing entertainment and imparting information on household topics. Programmes on family welfare, a very important sector of human progress, are planned and produced by 36 family welfare units at various stations of the broadcasting network. These programmes are integrated with the general programmes as well as those meant for special audiences like rural, folk, women, youth and industrial workers.

The early sixties saw a vast growth in rural broadcasting. Auxilliary transmitting centres were installed to extend the coverage of existing stations. Farm and home units were created at several stations. By 1965 every station of All India Radio started broadcasting special programmes for rural areas. Today all the stations broadcast programmes specially for rural listeners for about 30 to 75 minutes every day. Besides, a daily programme on hard-core agriculture and weather reports are broadcast for 45 to 55 minutes from 64 farm and home units, located in different AIR stations. These programmes aim at providing educational and informational support to the intensive agricultural and rural development programmes. They also seek to disseminate new agricultural technology to farmers in their local languages or dialects, besides covering other subjects like rural co-operation, animal husbandry, poultry, fisheries and cottage industries. Thirtyone stations present specially conceived and cooperatively devolved programmes called the 'Farm School of the AIR' where instructions and guidance on farming is provided to listeners. In this programme lessons on subjects like rice and wheat cultivation, use of fertilisers, dairy, poultry, fisheries and nutrition are given. The evaluation of these programmes have indicated that the audience find them extremely useful. It is interesting to learn from the record projects of agricultural universities that AIR's rural programmes are not only useful to the villagers but command credibility and acceptability. The imprint of AIR is best known by the terms radio seeds and radio fertilisers.

In order to provide a forum for the self-expression of the youth between the ages of 15 to 30 years, AIR puts out a programme for youth called 'Yuvavani' from 74 stations. This service provides an opening for the talents of this age group to present their viewpoints by participating in a wide range of programmes, talks discussions, interviews, plays, features and music. Under this programme a youth news bulletin is also broadcast by the youths.

AIR is an extension arm of India's cultural activities. Its programmes include at least two plays a week. Besides, original plays, radio adaptations of outstanding stage plays, novels and short stories are also broadcast. Since 1956 outstanding plays from Indian languages are being transmitted in the national programme of plays. Other important links in this chain of programmes include monthly serial plays, humorous skits, etc. The national programme of features which commenced in 1956 focuses attention on matters of national importance or interest in political, economic, social or cultural spheres. In fact, many people with a literary bent of mind lay great store on AIR's literary and cultural progerammes and draw mental exhilaration from them. AIR is becoming a good aid in school education. Most AIR stations broadcast programme based on the cool curriculum to reach students in interior areas. Radio support to university correspondence degree courses is also provided by several stations.

Sports events in India and abroad are covered by reviews, running commentaries and voice despatches. In metropolitan centres a daily Sports service is put out for 95 minutes covering all important sports events. In addition, two news bulletins, one in English and the other in Hindi, of five minutes duration, and weekly sports newsreels are also broadcast.

There are special occasions which attract special programmes on the national hook-up of AIR. These include the Republic day, Independence day, anniversaries, visits of foreign dignitaries or the visits of Indian dignitaries abroad.

Radio is a popular entertainer too. Vividh Bharati, a popular broadcast for the purpose, is transmitted from 31 centres, including two shortwave transmitters at Bombay and Madras. The total duration of Vividh Bharati is twelve hours and forty-five minutes on week days and thirteen hours and fifteen minutes on Sundays and holidays. The programmes which are generally acclaimed are music, humorous skits, short plays and features.

AIR introduced broadcasting of commercials on 1 November 1967. That is a part of marketing service, though it brings revenue too. Today the service is provided by twenty-eight centres. Advertisements are accepted in any language as tape-recorded spots of 7, 15, 30 and 60 seconds duration.

Radio as a mass media and the concept 'radio for all' will be roughly measured in terms of the number of radio receiving or transistor sets in the country. Since Independence these sets have increased manyfold to an aggregate of around 3 crores. The number may increase with the lifting of licence fee this year. In terms of diffusion rate it means nearly 4.4 sets for one hundred persons, still a figure below the minimum UNESCO norm of 5 sets for hundred people or one set for each family. In the Indian context, however, the redeeming situation is that one set can be used to serve a larger number of people beyond the household. In addition there are about 1.6 lakh community sets which operate in rural areas. Although the transistor revolution which has swept every part of the country has reduced the importance of community sets, some recent studies have underlined the need of continuing to have community receiver sets at least in selected areas. In the sixties when the community listening scheme was in full swing and assessed, it was revealed that the discussions in community listening and deliberations were excellent or good, and that participants learnt a 'great deal' or 'quite a lot'. Also, these forums developed rapidly into decision-making bodies capable of speeding up common pursuits of the village.

The Government's interest in radio and its concern about us growth was reflected in the allocations to broadcasting in its successive five-year plans. As a result AIR grew in size and status. Today this national service comprises 86 stations (supported by 162 transmitters) including two Vividh Bharati commercials centres, one at Chandigarh and the other at Kanpur. In addition, the network includes two auxilliary studio centres at Bhubaneswar and Shantiniketan.

AIR's programmes are beamed from 162 transmitters, of which 126 are medium-wave. Speaking broadly we may say that AIR now serves about 90 per cent of the population and about four-fifths of the total area of the country. More than any other media, its sweep includes far flung areas like Leh in Ladakh, Tawang in Arunachal Pradesh and the distant islands like the Andaman, Nicobar and the Lakshadweep. One may hope that it is not in the distant future that

AIR may reach its fullmoon day by claiming to cover all the areas of the country and its entire population.

Simultaneously AIR has also staged a leap forward in its software and research development aspects. Today it does face occasional fireworks or adverse comments of critics. It also has an intrinsic weakness of not enjoying high credibility because of its being a government controlled medium. Yet, AIR is considered by media authorities and researchers to have proved its worth and utility both as an informational channel and a development and cultural activist. Still more, it has provided healthy entertainment through is various light and humorous programmes. Extension research and other field surveys have already given great credit to radio as a credible promoter of a suitable climate for development and progress as also for having advanced farm educational and cultural renaissance. Its contribution in the form of transmitting useful and timely information, motivation and suggestions for rural development ilt conceded. Its sponsors claim that radio is helping to creat a climate of opinion in which social change can take place and people could be involved in the process. That is the crux of the problem. One can safely presume that along with TV, documentaries and farm journals, AIR will provide an adequate communication umbrella to the integrated rural programme. This it can do through its rural broadcasts, feed back interviews, 'meet the activists and innovators' and critics series, impacts studies, etc. Thus, AIR has an activising roll in furthering India's culture, education, music and other practising arts. The increasing number of walkman transistors and the growing popularity of listeners' letters are obvious indications, though one may concede that improvements and innovations know no bounds in this very challenging spoken word medium.

❐

3
Radio Programmes

Radio programmes may be classified into two broad groups:

(1) Spoken word programmes, which include news bulletins, talks, discussions, interviews, educational programmes for schools and colleges, specific audience programmes directed at women, children, rural and urban listeners, drama, radio features and documentaries.

(2) Music programmes which include disc jockey programmes, musical performances of all types and variety programmes (called 'magazine programmes'). It is obvious that a good number of programmes like drama, features and documentaries need both the spoken word and music. This is true in particular of programmes broadcast on Vividh Bharati.

News Bulletins. News bulletins are put out by AIR almost every hour of the day in English and the various regional languages. The major bulletins are of 15 minutes' duration, while others are of only five minutes' duration. They present summaries of news stories in order of importance and interest-value. National and international happenings get-pride of place, while regional and local news is read out if time permits. Human interest stories and sports news generally round off the major bulletins. AIR's news bulletins are much to formal in language, structure and presentation, suitable more for a lecture than a talk across the table which news reading really is.

Newsreels. Newsreels, generally of 15 minutes' duration, present 'spot' reports comments, interviews, and extracts from speeches. A much more complex and expensive format than the news bulletin, it calls for skilled tape editing and well-written link narrations.

Documentaries/Radio Features. Documentaries or radio features are usually factual, informational in character and sometimes educational in intent. They bring together the techniques of talks and drama to tell the story of events, past or present or those likely to happen in the future. They may sketch the biography of a great leader, or merely offer an interpretation of the world around us, or teach us about peoples and cultures unfamiliar to us, or even inquire into social, political, economic or cultural problems. Indeed, any subject of interest is grist to the mill of a feature writer.

The use of a narrator interspersed with voices of real people or/ and actors and of appropriate background effects and music bring a documentary/feature to throbbing life. In Fielden's words, 'a feature programme is a method of employing all the available methods and tricks of broadcasting to convey information or entertainment in a palatable form.'

Radio Plays. Radio drama is a story told through sound alone. The sound is of course that of dialogue and voices of people, background or mood effects, musical effects, atmospheric effects and the like. Radio drama, like stage drama is based on conflict, uses characters and has a beginning, a middle and an end. Movement and progress, generally to a crisis or climax, must be suggested in radio drama through sounds. The voices of characters must be sufficiently distinguishable, one from the other, lest the' listener gets confused. They must sound natural, speak true to character and above all, be interesting.

Radio listeners would be confused by the presence of more than three to four characters. In fact, the shorter the drama (the average duration is 30 to 60 minutes) the fewer should be the major characters. In the early years of Indian broadcasting, the radio play book is the characteristics of the theatre as it existed on the stage in a particular region. Radio plays were broadcast then for three hours at a time. In Bombay, Parsi, Gujarati and Urdu play were frequently put on the air: in Madras, mythological plays proved very popular. It was Fielden who introduced the present norm of the 30-minute radio play on AIR.

Music Programmes. Music programmes enjoy much greater popularity than talk shows, as is evident from the popularity of Vividh Bharati programmes. We enjoy music for its rhythms, melodies and harmonies and above all for the relaxation it provides. Like any talk show, a music programme must have unity and form. Disc jockey programmes of 'pop' or 'disco', therefore should not be mixed up with classical or light classical music. Variety is the keynote to any music programme; the different items should be linked together with interesting comments, announcements and narration.

Talks. Radio talks are not public speeches; rather, they are chats with a friend who does not see you, but is nevertheless close and attentive to you. Radio talks should give the impression to a listener that the speaker is addressing him or her alone in an. informal manner.

The words of a radio talk need to be kept simple and familiar, yet descriptive and powerful, and the sentences short and without dependent clauses and awkward inversions. Care should be taken to keep close to the rhythm of ordinary speech when writing the talk, and also when recording it. Radio talks have no definite structure. All that the listener expects from them is that they should be interesting and informative.

Movie Trailers. Vividh Bharati's movie trailers are sponsored programmes usually of 15-30 minutes' duration. They are fastpaced, and packed with extracts of dialogue and songs from the film being advertised. The narrator links the elements with dramatic appeals and announcements. The names of stars, of the producer, director, playback singers and musicians figure prominently in the trailers.

Quiz Shows. Largely studio-based and inexpensive to produce, the quiz show is easily one of the most popular programmes for the family. It's the sense of participation and involvement in the quiz questions that makes the programme very enjoyable family fare.

Programme Composition of AIR. The major sources of AIR's programmes are in-house productions, outside productions, sponsored programmes, and programmes obtained under the Cultural Exchange and Programme Exchange Service, apart of course from those programmes available on commercial records, CDs, etc. A small number of programmes are obtained from SAVE (the SAARC Audiovisual Exchange). However, for its news bulletins AIR is dependent on PTI and UNI for national and regional news, and to Reuters, Associated Press, AFP and other multinational news agencies for its foreign news coverage. The multinational news agencies route their copy via the national news agencies.

Music takes the lion's share of time (39.73%) on the Home Service excluding Vividh Bharati, with Spoken Word programmes claiming 37.78%, and News and Current Affairs the remaining 22.49% of the time.

AIR's mode of classifying spoken word programmes is rather eccentric, but it is clearly a pointer to its programme policy, and the pressures under which it functions. Women and Youth are given adequate time on spoken word programmes, while children, industrial workers and tribals appear to be lower in its priorities. Dr. B. V. Keskar 's ghost continues to influence AIR's policy on music: Indian classical music dominates programming, followed by 'light music' (largely semi-classical), and 'film music.' Folk Music which is the popular music of the people is given the least attention.

Ownership and Control

Until September 15, 1997, AIR was fully owned, controlled, and run by the Central Government. But this is not what the founding fathers intended. Pandit Nehru believed that "we should approximate as far as possible to the British model, the BBC; that is to say it would be better if we had a semi-autonomous corporation under the Government, of course with the policy controlled by the Government, otherwise not being conducted as a Government department but as a semi-autonomous corporation."

The Chanda Committee on Broadcasting and Information Media said in its Report in April 1966 that 'it is not possible in the Indian context for a creative medium like broadcasting to flourish under a regime of departmental rules and regulations' and therefore recommended an 'institutional change' so that AIR can be liberated; and separate corporations for Akashvani and Doordarshan. In April 1970, four years later, the Indira Gandhi Government responded stating that the present is not an opportune time to consider the conversion of AIR into an autonomous corporation.' However, with effect from April 1, 1976, Television was separated from AIR and constituted into a new body, Doordarshan.

The Verghese Committee in February 1978 called for the establishment of a 'National Broadcasting Trust' called Akash Bharati as an "autonomous 'and independent public service." Accordingly, the Akash Bharati Bill, 1978 was introduced in the Lok Sabha by the Janata Government though it had some reservations about it.

Broadcasting Policy

Both radio (All India Radio or Akashvani) and television (Doordarshan) in India were 'media units' of the Ministry of Information and Broadcasting. It is this same Ministry that was the official policy-making body for the broadcasting system, assisted by the Secretary and a massive Secretariat divided into three wings (Broadcasting, Information, and Policy and Co-ordination), each under a Joint Secretary.

The Government's monopoly of broadcasting rested on Article 246 of the Indian Constitution which states that Parliament has 'exclusive' powers to make laws with respect to any of the matters enumerated in List 1 of the seventh schedule. Item 31 in this list includes 'posts and telegraphs, telephones, wireless, broadcasts and other like forms of communication.' The Indian Telegraph Act of 1885 and the Indian Wireless Telegraphy Act of 1933 (which were drawn up during the British regime) continued to be in force, and to give the Government the legal right to a monopoly in broadcasting, besides the right to intercept and to censor mail. This exclusive monopoly of the use of the airwaves was struck down by the Supreme Court in 1995 when it declared that 'the airwaves are public property and that the public is distinctive from the government. It therefore directed the Central Government to constitute an autonomous broadcasting authority to licence and regulate the use of the airwaves for broadcasting. In September 1997, the Prasar Bharati (or the Broadcasting Corporation of India) was established as an autonomous body to give effect to the Prasar Bharati Act (1990). The Prasar Bharati Board has been constituted by a Presidential Ordinance; the future of the Board and of independent broadcasting is now in doubt, with the new Government threatening to let the ordinance lapse. The Broadcasting Bill (1997) drawn up by the United Front government is also likely to be considerably revised before it is introduced in Parliament by the present Government.

Broadcasting Code

Current broadcasting policy is based on the AIR Code of 1970, which sets down that broadcasts on All India Radio will not permit:

(1) criticism of friendly countries;

(2) attack on religion or communities;

(3) anything obscene or defamatory;

(4) incitement to violence or anything against the maintenance of law and order;

(5) aspersions against the integrity of the President, Governors, and Judiciary;

(6) attack on a political party by name;

(7) anything amounting to contempt of court;

(8) hostile criticism of any State or the Centre; or

(9) anything showing disrespect to the Constitution or advocating change in the Constitution by violence; but advocating change in a constitutional way should not be debarred. The Broadcasting Code also forbids 'direct publicity of an individual or of a commercial benefit to an organisation', and the use of 'trade names amounting to direct advertising.'

The Code applies to criticism in the nature of a personal tirade, either of a friendly Government or of a political party or of the Central Government or any State Government. But it does not debar references to and/or dispassionate discussion of policies pursued by any of them.

The Code adds that 'if a Station Director finds that the above Code has not been respected in any particular or particulars by an intending broadcaster he will draw the latter's attention to the passage objected to. If the intending broadcaster refuses to accept the Station Director's suggestions and modify his/her script accordingly, the Station Director will be justified in rejecting his or her broadcast. Cases of unresolved differences of opinion between a Minister of a State Government and a Station Director about the interpretation of the Code with respect to a talk to be broadcast by the former will be referred to the Modern UGC Net: Mass Communication Minister of Information and broadcasting, Government of India, who will decide finally whether or not any change in the text was necessary in order to avoid violation of the Code.'

The Code and other restrictions on broadcasting are based on Clause 2 of Article 19 of the Indian Constitution. Other restrictions include the broadcasting of the news of the death of high dignitaries such as the President, the Vice-President, the Prime Minister and a few others only after it has been cleared by the Home Secretary. The AIR or Doordarshan Correspondent has to get the news from him, inform the News Room, before it can be broadcast. This explains the excessive delay in the announcement of the news of Indira Gandhi's assassination, though the BBC had made it known worldwide four hours earlier. According to an agreement arrived at by all political parties in 1977, air time is allocated for political broadcasting prior to national and state elections.

Ethics of Broadcasting

Radio and television were introduced into India to be the carriers of entertainment and education for the general public. Though introduced with 'public service' as the prime objective, both the electronic media have been widely used for government propaganda as well as for commercial interests. Non-broadcast media like video and cable are in the private sector and therefore know no control and no regulation. Attempts at regulating cable and satellite TV have not been very effective because of the large number of operators and sub-operators involved and also because of the corruptibility of the regulating authorities.

Where broadcast news is concerned, the ethics of broadcasting is very similar to those for the print media. These relate to questions of accuracy and fairness, of respect for privacy and the religious beliefs/practices of different communities, of the need for caution in reporting violence and communal disturbances, and in criticising judicial acts, of the right to reply, of respect for the confidentiality of sources, and of the need to eschew obscenity and vulgarity.

Take the coverage of Operation Bluestar by All India Radio and Doordarshan, for instance. Or, their announcement of the assassinations of Indira Gandhi and Rajiv Gandhi. What was the 'ethic' involved in their low-key coverage of the storming of the Golden Temple at Amritsar, and their rather late declaration of the news about the assassinations of the Gandhis? The professional journalist's view is that, irrespective of the consequences, news should be transmitted immediately after the event no matter what the event or who the persons involved. However, there is an alternative view that tragic news which affects an entire nation and which might lead to violence, may be withheld or delayed for a while till tempers cool down and the law and order situation is under control. This alternative view suggests that professional 'ethics' cannot take precedence as these professional journalistic ethics have been evolved in Western liberal democracies, and often have little relevance to the social and cultural needs of developing countries. However, the misuse of the air ways by government for blatant political party propaganda, or for criticism of opposition parties without representing their perspective, must be termed 'unethical.' Also 'unethical' is the false representation of rallies, strikes and bandhs to suit the ruling party's interests. The deliberate non-coverage of events of public concern and also the banning of programmes expressing alternative views on controversial issues (*e.g.* Anand Patwardhan's 'Ram Ke Naam', Saeed Mirza's 'Kashmir' and the documentaries on the Bhagalpur Windings, police brutalities, the Bhopal disaster, etc.) is also considered 'unethical' since broadcasting is not the private property of any political party or commercial broadcaster, as the 1994 Supreme Court declaration that 'the airwaves are public property' has made amply clear.

Listenership Surveys

The Audience Research Units of major All India Radio stations conduct 'listenership surveys' regularly to find out who its listeners are, which programmes they listen to, and how popular various programmes are. The marketing agencies that conduct National Readership Surveys also gather data about radio listeners.

But who is a radio 'listener?' If Vividh Bharati is on the whole day long in a household, does it mean that every member of the household is a 'listener?' Indeed, for most Vividh Bharati listeners, the music provided is background music while they go about their household chores.

Further, few members of a household listen very attentively to every programme, except perhaps to the news or announcements. So, most radio listeners, especially listeners to popular music programmes are in reality only 'secondary' and 'tertiary' listeners: not much attention is given to this musical wallpaper at home or in the office.

RADIO BROADCASTING IN INDIA

The discovery of radio added a huge dimension to the state of mass communication. Simultaneous broadcasting of the spoken and taped word and music to millions of people in far flung places became a reality and a single big step in the direction of evolving a global village. Because of its radiation potentiality it also helps to rush news to people on the move as also to distant audiences.

Reinforced by powerful transmitters on land and satellites in the sky, and availability of cheap sets or transmitters and cassettes operating as instruments of field and feedback communication, the radio has become the principal medium of mass communication, entertainment and distant education in developing countries. As a comparatively low cost spoken word medium, it has cut across the barriers of illiteracy. In the third world radio is being used signally where TV is not fully developed as the premier means of extension, education and entertainment. This portable box his become a constant companion for farmers, workers, travelers and sports lovers and for all those who are interested in news, music, drama or quiz programmes, farm bulletins or views of eminent persons on public affairs. Because of its low cost and easy availability, it is a common man's paradise and for poor people a symbal of social respectability as well.

Historically, radio is the result of many researches. In 1895, Marconi perfected wireless telegraphy, working on principles developed over the preceding decades. Twelve years later, Lee De Forest in USA invented the vacuum tube which made sustained radio transmission possible. Wireless telegraphy and the radio telephone made rapid strides in maritime and other uses and received great impetus as a means of military communication and propaganda during the First World War.

Wireless transmission of verbal messages alone however did not constitute radio broadcasting. It lacked music, an element which was lent by the construction of a radio music box by the Radio Corporation of America in 1916. With the package of these inventions, the word radio thereafter came to mean the sending of words, sound and music through the air by the radiation of electro-magnetic waves. With the coming of TV it came to mean in contrast, simple sound broadcasting, as distinct from the broadcasting of pictures. Combined, these two media are known are the electronic media—the principal channels of mass communication in advanced countries as also in developing countries.

It was not until a few years after World War I that the world properly entered the broadcast era. The first regular broadcasting station was set up in Pittsburg in 1920 in USA, followed closely by transmissions by the Radio Corporation of America. Two years later, the well-known British Broadcasting Corporation (BBC) came into being.

Although India was a dependency, she was among the earliest countries in the world to adopt broadcasting. Its manifestation was first in the form of an experimental broadcast of a 'special programme of music put out by the Bombay office of the Times of India in collaboration with the Posts and Telegraphs Departments on 1 August 1921. Then commenced the phase initiated by the radio clubs of Bombay and Calcutta and by YMCA at Labore. This type of adhoc broadcasting, however, lasted only up to 1927. Financial difficulties came in the way. Ultimately, on the request of these clubs, a new mode of broadcasting ensued in the form of a regular service initiated by the Indian Broadcasting Company Limited, a private concern. Even this venture couldn't last long and the Cempany went into liquidation in 1929 despite the fact that 7775 licences were in force and the radio stations especially of Bombay and Calcutta were functioning effectively. The Inchcape Committee suggested the closure of broadcasting but the government under the pressure of public and trade first agreed to continue the service and then took over in 1930 to continue broadcasting under the Indian State Broadcasting Service. In addition to Bombay and Calcutta stations which already existed, a third station was commissioned at Delhi. Encouraged by the experiment, the government decided to place broadcasting on a permanent footing in 1935. Mr. Lionel Fielder from BBC was appointed as the first Controller of Broadcasting. In 1936 the service was redesignated as All India Radio (AIR). Since then broadcasting made rapid strides and the number of licenses rose from 10872 in 1933 to 92782 in 1939, when World War II broke out.

Initially placed under the Department of Industries and Labour and later transferred to the Department of Communication, the administration of broadcasting was ultimately entrusted to the Department of Information and Broadcasting in 1941. Two years later AIR's headquarters moved to the beautiful building constructed at Parliament Street', New Delhi in 1934.

Notwithst anding many potentialities of medium AIR, during the early period of its history, operated essentially for entertainment. In that respect the programmes of Bombay and Calcutta stations had a cultural leaning and were qualitatively good, These programmes attracted some of the best talents, But without acoustics, the programming was more one of trial and error, though in the process the staff gained a lot of professional experience, In the Bombay station good programmes of dramas and Western and Indian music were tried. In course of time, the programmes were further diversified by the addition of school broadcasts and rural programmes. Reading from good literature had already come in vogue. In 1935, the broadcast of time signals was introduced and in the following year the famous Colaba pip.

War Publicity Arm

With the breaking out of World War II, AIR had to bear a huge burden of the war publicity. AIR was recognised as a vital source of news and views, covering events at home and abroad. This made the government set up additional transmitters including 200 shortwave transmitters, probably the first of their kind in this part of the world. The significant aspect of development programmes included the organisation of its second unit of broadcasting-the External Services-and the expansion of the news services and transmission hours. As a result, a wide variety of programmes like talks and features were introduced. Centralised news bulletins in various Indian languages also commenced from Delhi. These were initially in Tamil, Telugu, Gujarati, Marathi, and Pushto in addition to the earlier bulletins in English, Hindustani and Bengali, making a total of 27 news bulletins a day. By this time AIR gained popularity in all big towns.

Monitoring of foreign stations was another responsibility which came to be entrusted to AIR after World War II. The Monitoring unit worked from Simla for the most part.

Prior to Independence, some of the princely states also started running their broadcasting stations. At the time of partition of the country in 1947 India had 9 stations; 3 of which were located at Dacca, Lahore and Peshawar (places which were transferred to Pakistan in 1947. The total number of broadcasting receiving sets was 276000.

High Tributes

Tributes paid to the medium of radio by three eminent Personalities of India during the past speak eloquently of what Indians felt about radio even in the initial stages of its history. Pt. Jawaharlal Nehru enthusiastically hailed, "Forward Radio", when he wrote in the visitors' book at the Bombay Station at the time of Inaugurating the educational programme in 1933. Sarojini Naidu, the Nightingale of India, was rather more poetic in her entry a week later: "To harness the ether for the service of those who dwell Upon the earth is one of the loveliest services that the modern age can render to humanity So upward Radio". Rabindra Nath Tagore, our Noble Laureate, wrote a special poem entitled "Akashvani" for AIR in 1938 on the inauguration of the Calcutta shortwave transmission. The poem read:

"Hark to Akashvani upsurging

from here below,

The earth is bathed in Heaven's glory,

Its purple glow,

Across the blue expanse is firmly planted

The alter of the Muse;

The lyre unheard of Light is throbbing

With human hues.

From earth to heaven, distance conquered,

In waves of light.

'Flows the music of man's divining,

Fancy's flight.

To East and West speech careers,

Swift as the Sun,

The mind of man reaches Heaven's confines,

Its freedom won."

Despite these poetic overtures, the fact remained that broad-casting in India could not become a mass medium during the British period. Being organised, planned and run by the alien governmcmt with little respect for national aspirations and scant knowledge of popular indigenous forms of entertainment, this most cherished medium actually lost the prestige and credibility it deserved.

◻

Radio Programmes

Across the cities expalins to firmly planted

Hereafter of the Moses

The very unheed of fruit is dropping

With human face

be computed

4

Educational Radio

The radio is the cheapest and the most easily accessible of all these means. No doubt, its potential audience is very large in comparison to the audience of other mass media. It caters to the people of different ages and levels of maturity ranging from a primary school child to its grandfather. Besides the cost-factor and the wide-ranging appeal, another reason for its popular use it is the fact that is easy to handle. While all these attributes make it a wide-reaching means of mass communication, it has a pedagogically strong reason for its use in education and that is its versatility, leading itself to serve different purposes. For instance, while it provides learners with new joys of learning, it can develop their command over vocabulary, promote concentration and critical listening, and improve fluency and confidence in speech and discussion. It can be used for formal and non-formal education. Its broadcasts can be designed to supplement/ enrich the formal school subjects. These broadcasts may clarify a concept, or give additional views , on a theme, or provide further illustrations and case studies related to an issue, Broadcasts under non-formal education may comprise programmes such as children's programme, women's programme, adult education programme, rural development programme and social action programme, etc.

History of Educational Radio

It was a great invention that human voice could be transmitted by electromagnetic waves over long distance without the help of a wire. The radio which achieved it brought thereby a new age in the area of communication.

In India, as early as July 23, 1927, a radio station at Bombay was formally inaugurated by Lord Irwin. It was followed by the Calcutta Radio station (on August 26, 1927) and the Delhi Radio Station (in January 1936). Since then, there has not only been a remarkable expansion of the network in terms of the number of radio station, the number, of transmitters and the power of transmitters, but also a staggering technological development in the field of radio communication and electronics engineering. According to a 1984 report (Broadcasting in India 1984; I) The all India Radio (AIR) network, one of the largest in the world, consisted of 86 radio stations equipped with 162 transmitters. The radio network covered 89.69 per cent of the total population over different parts of the country (Broadcasting in India, 1984; I)

The AIR plans to effect total coverage of the country by providing a 3-tier service *viz.*, national, regional and local, so as to cater to a reasonable range of the needs of the whole population. The major emphasis of the AIR has been to extend regional services so as to make at least one channel available to everyone.

The development of educational radio has two sides to it:

(i) the establishment of the broadcast network and

(ii) the preparation and production of specific educational programmes.

As far as the broadcast network is concerned, the AIR as made a tremendous achievement having managed to reach as much as about 90% of the population of this large country. It is matter or pride that it is one of the largest networks in the world.

As for the educational programmes, the broadcast-projects that we discussed in this section suggest how efforts had been all along towards both formal and non-formal education. Broadcasts of formal education (as the discussion on school broadcasts and university broadcasts suggests) were too general to begin with, but have gradually turned to be 'more and more specific. The attempt to make school broadcasts more curriculum oriented and the attempt to make university broadcasts supplement the correspondence education have made the educational radio more purposeful and specific.

The broadcast programmes of non-formal education of the AIR have recorded tremendous success in achieving worthy objectives in the areas of agriculture and rural development.

The introduction of educational radio can be viewed in five types:

(1) School Broadcasts. Even before the AIR came into existence, there were occasional broadcasts for schools from Bombay and Calcutta. It was only in 1937 school broadcasting started in Calcutta. Funds were allotted to schools to buy radio sets. Out of enthusiasm, the AIR authorities embarked on school programmes from Delhi, Calcutta, Madras, and Bombay without waiting for schools to acquire radio sets. In the beginning, the school programmes were not strictly governed by the curriculum.

The AIR is assisted by various agencies in planning their educational programmes, particularly the programmes for the young-the primary and the secondary level students. For example, the Central Institute of Educational Technology (CIET), a wing of NCERT, regularly produces programmes for primary classes and these programmes are broadcast by Jaipur and Ajmer stations of the AIR.

(2) Adult Education and Community Development Project. In 1956, an attempt was made to communicate with the rural people and promote innovation through broadcasts. The programme was called 'Radio Forum' and was tried in 144 village in the vicinity of Poona. This kind of programme was originally designed and tried in Canada. With the help of UNESCO, India decided to try it in the Indian context. 'Radio forums' (defined as a 'listening-cum-discussion-cum-action group') of village of about 20 members each were organised in everyone of the 144 villages.

(3) University Broadcasts. Radio programmes on subjects of academic interest have been broadcast from the AIR stations from the very beginning of organized broadcasting. In 1965, an attempt was made to asses the impact of these broadcasts on students and it was found that there was little interest among students.

(4) Farm and Home Broadcasts. To improve the effectiveness of radio programmes in rural/social change, the AIR initiated the farm and home broadcasts in 1966. These broadcasts were designed to provide information and advice on agricultural and allied topics. The aim was to educate the farmers and provide them assistance in adopting innovative practices in their fields. The broadcasts, under this programme are of immediate local relevance. They are directly linked with the day to day agricultural practices of the farmers.

(5) Language Learning Project. In 1979-80, the AIR conceived and implemented an experiment to use radio broadcasts for language teaching. The experiment was conducted in collaboration with the Department of Education, Government of Rajasthan. Under this experiment an attempt was made to teach Hindi as first language to school going children. The experiment was called 'the Radio Pilot Project' and it aimed to cover 500 primary schools of Jaipur and Ajmer districts.

Use of Devices in Educational Radio

Some devices of independent and/or accessory function have come into use along with the radio in the recent days. These devices have become popular because they help use overcome some of the weaknesses of radio broadcasts-like the availability of broadcasts on scheduled times alone. Besides, these devices have also been cheap enough to be within the reach of a considerable large proportion of the population. There are two main devices *(1)* Audio-tape, *(2)* Radio-vision.

(1) Audio-Tapes. Audio-tape can overcome the limitations of educational radio broadcasts. It provides considerable freedom to the students. It can be used when the individuals need it and at any time and place convenient to them. The learner can review the learning materials by replaying the tapes, as often as needed.

For working adult learners, availability of spare time is very important. Their study has to be fitted into their leisure time outside their working hours. Furthermore, many adults desire to study at a place and time of their convenience. Audio-tapes can be the best device of such learners.

The audio-tape recorder is comparatively inexpensive, simple to operate, durable and portable. This technology is available at commercial level too.

(2) Radio-Vision. Pioneered by the BBC, the technique of radio-vision allows the subject matter to be presented through two channels, the audio and the visual. The visuals are presented in the form of still strips, charts, slides, models, etc., while the explanation is given through recorded narration. This is used by educational institution as a substitute for educational television, Radio-vision has its own advantages:

(a) it is economical.

(b) it can cater to different categories of learners.

(c) it is easy to produce such programmes at the institutional level or at the learning centres,

(d) it provides visual suppwt to the concept that is taught.

Types of Radio Programmes

Different types of radio programmes are in vogue. These types can be broadly categorised into two groups. One group of programme type relates to the mode of the programme and the other to the service. Thus, we have service-based types and mode-based types. A knowledge of these types is essential before one discusses the production process of radio programme. Hence, we present here below a brief account of different programme types under the two categories.

(1) Service-Based Types

From the service point of view, radio programmes can be categorised as under:

- *(i)* **Music.** The AIR devotes 36 percent of its broadcast time to music programmes (classical, folk, light, film and western music).

- *(ii)* **Spoken.** Work Programme: These include lectures, talks, discussions, features and play.

- *(iii)* **Programme for Special Audiences.**

  - *(a)* *Farm and Home Programme.* Farm and Home units set up at 64 stations provide specific programmes for target listerners. The development programme for improving the status of women, health and hygience, family welfare etc., are broadcast under such programmes.

  - *(b)* *Yuva Vani.* This programmes provides a forum for self-expression to the youth who constitute the majority with a view to give them a sense of partnership in the country's destiny and to ensure their involvement in the service of nation-building.

- *(iv)* **News Service.** News service of the AIR puts out 68 bulletins for a duration of 10 hours 8 minutes daily in 19 languages on national hook-up. In its external services, the AIR broadcasts 63 bullentins from Delhi, Bombay, Calcutta and Madras for a duration of 8 hours 28 minutes in 24 language.

- *(v)* **Vividh Bharti and Commercial Service.** A self contained service of popular entertainment of October, 1957 to meet the growing demand for popular music and songs. The commercials were introduced on the national on April 1, 1982. At present there are 29 commercial broadcasting centres in India.

> *(iv)* **External Service.** This service of the AIR is aimed to project the true and objective image of the country to listeners abroad. External services are available in 25 languages; 17 foreign and 8 Indian-for 57 hours and 15 minutes everyday. The service in each language comprises news, interviews, discussions, music etc.

(2) Mode-Based Types

On the basis of format, radio programmes can be grouped into different types. The most common among them are listed below:

> *(i)* **Straight Talk.** This format is very common on radio and it presents a well developed talk of an individual. This format is useful in presenting maximum information within minimum time.

> *(ii)* **Interview.** This is also a popular format. This helps in bringing outstanding personalities and experts to the public on radio.

> *(iii)* **Reality Broadcast.** On the stop events can be broadcast directly. The real events have emotional appeal such programmes can sustain interest for longer time.

> *(iv)* **Pane/Round Table.** This format is suitable for presenting conflicting views. Thinking process can be stimulated through such formats.

> *(v)* **Dramatisation.** Dramatisation makes the programme more attractive and appealing. A variety of subject-matter can be catered to through drama. The radio is relatively simple to produce and the participants do not have to memorise the dialogues as in the case of the television drama.

> *(vi)* **Forum Broadcast.** The subject experts express their views on a given topic. This format provides a good forum for adult learners.

Production of Radio Programme

The process of preparing radio programmes can be studied in two stage-preparing the radio script and producing the radio programmes.

(1) **Preparing The Radio Scripts.** Radio scripts are different from an article for publication or a speech. A radio script should be a mixture of' information, education and entertainment depending on the nature of the programme. The radio script should cater to the information needs of the audience, their learning characteristics etc.

Writing for radio is a difficult and technical task. It requires specific skills and creative imagination. The script-writer has to go through certain steps before he produces a formal script. First, he should set the objectives. The objective should be framed in behavioural terms specifying what the listener is expected to accomplish after listening to the programme. Having specified the objective, he should analyse the content, making an inventory of the themes and sub-themes and placing these themes and sub-themes in their relative positions of importance and relevance, Then he should, on the basis of his understanding of the content, choose an appropriate presentation made for the programme. The script-writer should then conceive a plot-line to suit the content, keeping in mind the need to make the programme 'tell a story'. He should decide on the length of the programme also.

Having accomplished these preliminaries, the script-writer should prepare a programme layout. The layout should list the segments and the sub-themes under each segment. It should also specify the duration for each sub-theme. Besides, the layout should also identify the kind of supportive around arrangements (in terms of, say, music) to accompany the sun-themes wherever found necessary. After the layout is written, the script-writer can write the final draft.

The final script may be developed in a 'descriptive' format of a 'columnal' format. In the descriptive format, the script may be written from the top of the page to the bottom. In the columnal format, the script is written in the form of two columns. (This format is more in use, while writing script for television programme. While one column presents information on shot numbers, sources and characteristics of visuals, the other gives details of music, narration, dialogue and sources of sound.)

The characteristics of a good radio script are listed below:

(1) The script should be easy to comprehend; the vocabulary and the structure used should be simple.

(2) The script should be precise. There should be proper use of words and the right model of delivery should be indicated clearly.

(3) A good script should have shades of humour and be able to arouse one's thinking and interest.

(4) The script should exploit the use of 'sound effect' properly.

(2) Producing Radio Programmes. The process of preparing a good radio programme begins with the conceptualisation of given idea and ends with its presentation in the form of a programme. The presentation is preceded by the three stage of planning, production and post-production.

(a) Planning Stage. The planning stage includes the following development steps:

(i) Select the Topic/Idea. The programme planners should know w^at course or subject-matter the radio programme belongs to. The scope of the programme should be defined in clear terms.

    (ii) State the Objectives. The objectives are set in terms of the expected behavioural changes.

    (iii) Analyse the Target Audience. The needs and interests of potential listeners should be analysed, Age, sex, professional experience, education, availability so spare time etc., need to be analysed to guide the making up of the programme.

    (iv) Analyse the Content. The content should be analysed into topics and sub-topics. The relevant information should be collected through specific research projects on the topic (s).

    (v) Write the Script. The content matter should be put in sequence following a systematic way. The format should also be decided at this stage.

    (vi) Select the Music and Sound Effects. The music should be attractive and should suit the nature of the given content. The sound effect should provide a background reflecting the period, the location or the mood of the content matter.

    (vii) Select the Voice. In radio, the 'talent' who gives the talk or lecture of participates in a programme is important. The 'talent' should be an effective 'communicator'.

(b) Production Stage. After the planning stage is gone through, the actual production *i.e.,* recording of the programme is undertaken. It involves:

    (i) Preparation of the Studio and the Equipment. The studio is kept ready before the recording takes place. Special equipment, if needed, is arranged to adjust music, sound effects, etc.

    (ii) Rehearsal. Before the final recording, 'production conference' (where everyone involved in the

production is briefed on that he/she is to do) and 'rehearsal' are helped to ensure the best possible quality, in terms of content and presentation. A rehearsal helps boost self-confidence of the participants and to ensure the quality of the final product.

(c) Post Production Stage. This is the final stage of programming. After production, the programme is reviewed and unwanted segments are edited to adjust the programme to an exact time length.

All the above stage facilitates a good production. But the creativity, imagination and sincerity on the part of programme planners, subject experts and producers play a more important role in producing a good piece. One, therefore, should not force the programme to strictly follow all these steps one by one. He should, when he is capable of handling the situation independently, be given enough freedom to break away from the formal production process.

Characteristics of Educational Radio

The potentials of radio broadcasting stem from two sources:

(1) Its low capital requirements, low operating costs and wide coverage.

(2) Its pedagogical values.

We identify here some characteristics that contribute to its potential:

(i) Easy Accessibility. In comparison to other media radio is accessible to the majority of our countrymen. Low cost transistors within the easy reach of even the economically weaker, people are available in the market. It can, therefore, be used as a home-based means of imparting education.

(ii) Wide Coverage. Today we cover a major portion of our territory by radio broadcasts as the broadcast facility is available

throughout the sub-continent. As such, the radio can extend learning at a distance as it can easily and quickly reach the isolated rural audiences. The AIR has many years of experience of combining the radio with correspondence and non-formal education.

(iii) Low Capital Investment and Operating Cost. Radio technology is comparatively cheap. In terms of installation and production of radio broadcasts, it is quite economical and needs less production facilities compared to other electronic media.

(iv) Easy Learning-Reception. Radio broadcasts can be listened to even while one is doing some manual work. Distance learners can listen to programmes from wherever they desire to.

(v) Motivation Supportive Facilities. Broadcasting can make education interesting and enjoyable, when it is used imaginatively. The feeling and motivation of listeners can be stimulated and directed by music and other sound effects. (By supportive facilities we refer to music, special sound effects and such other means that make a broadcast programme effective.)

(vi) Easy Production. Production of creative radio programmes is simpler compared to a TV or video programme production. No complicated mechanism, nor any sophisticated instruments are needed for such productions. It requires less man-power too, compared to the production of a television/video programme.

(vii) Effective Thought Promotion. Radio tapes, thinking process of the learner as listening is invariable accompanied by simulaneous information processing. It can also stimulate it listener's imagination with a tactful use of music or the technique of pause.

(viii) Feasible Mode of Learner-Enrichment. The most common function of media in education is 'enrichment'. This function is easy to materialise with the help of radio and with relatively little expense.

(ix) Effective Re-creationl Transmission of Reality. A powerful 'audio' version brings a scene into sharp focus and also establishes

'movement' effectively. A live broadcast can make listeners share the experience of a scene of reality taking place, say, some 100 miles away. It can also make listeners partake of an experience of a scene of the past that took place, say, some 100 years ago.

(x) Direct Instruction. The use of radio for direct instruction has been tried. This, however, demands intensive and systematic use of the radio. Under such schemes, syllabus based programme are broadcast for definite target groups.

Limitations of Education Radio in the Instruction

The radio has its drawbacks too. We can summarise the limitations of radio as a medium of instruction as follows:

(1) The radio is not a flexible medium. There is no face-to-face interaction, dialogue or discussions between the listener and the speaker/producer. In the absence of motivation, guidance and supervision, the atmosphere for learning is not very conducive and the teaching/learning process becomes a one-way transit of information.

(2) There is a dearth of adequately qualified personnel for producing worthwhile educational programmes. Radio programming demands experienced and creative personnel with both production and academic background. It is difficult to find the persons with experience along both the lines.

(3) The doubts/queries arising in the mind of a learner cannot be attended to immediately. Thus, there is no provision for immediate feedback to the learner; nor is there any feedback on the quality of the content.

(4) Educational radio programmes have not been given adequate and appropriate broadcast time-chunk. This phenomenon causes inconvenience to learners as they have to make themselves available during the schedule broadcast time whatever be their engagements then.

(5) It may not be an effective medium for all types of course materials; for example, the subjects which need demonstration/visual illustrations cannot be taught effectively through radio.

(6) The technical staff concerned with the planning and production of radio programme don't have adequate knowledge of the relevant pedagogical needs of the learners and their characteristics. The subject experts do not have any deep acquaintance with the complexities of programme production. So unless there is a perfect co-ordination and understanding.between the two groups, no good production could ever be achieved.

(7) The span of attention of a learner is short and thus, the retention of factual information given after first few minutes of the start of the programme is generally low unless some special efforts are made to reassure attention from time to time. Furthermore, educational broadcast is not a priority area of programming in the radio set-up.

(8) In a country like India, educators have to plan programmes for heterogeneous masses (such as the illiterate, school dropouts, the unemployed etc.). The more heterogeneous the audience, the more difficult it is to produce a radio programme of common utility/appeal.

❐

5

Brief History of Television

Experiments in television broadcasting were initiated during the 1920s in the United States and Europe. These experiments used a mechanical scanning disc that did not scan a picture rapidly enough. In 1923, however, came the invention of the iconoscope, the electric television tube. The inventions of the kinescope or picture tube, the electronic camera and TV home receivers arrived in rapid succession during the next few years and by the 1930s the National Broadcasting Corporation (NBC) had set up a TV station in New York, and BBC a TV station in London, offering regular telecast programmes. Germany and France too established television stations around the same time.

The World War put a brake on further developments in television, though in Nazi Germany television was widely used as an instrument of political propaganda. Nazi party conventions were televised, but the top event in the first chapter of German television history was the 1936 Olympics in Berlin which was staged as a gigantic propaganda show for the Third Reich. But by the late 1940s and early 1950s television had become a feature of life in most developed countries. In 1948, for instance, there were as many as T.V. stations in the United States covering 23 cities through half a million receiving sets. Within a decade, the figure jumped to 533 stations and 55 million receivers. Canada, Japan and the European countries did not lag very far behind.

The age of satellite communication dawned in 1962 with the launching of Early Bird, the first communication satellite. The two big international satellite systems, Intelsat and Intersputnik began operating in 1965 and 1971 respectively and from then on the progress was phenomenal. Today, almost every country in the world has earth stations linked to satellites for transmission and reception. Communication satellites nave literally transforated the modern world into what Marshall McLuhan, the Canadian media sociologist, liked to call 'a global village.'

In the 1970s more sophisticated transmission techniques were invented employing optical fiber cable and computer technology. Japan succeeded in designing a computercontrolled network to carry two-way video information to and from households. The audiovisual cassette and the video tape recorder, closed circuit TV, and more recently cable television, pay-television and DTH (Direct-to-Home) television have changed the course of the development of TV in new and unexpected ways. DTH and digital compression technology have enhanced the number of channels which can be accessed, as also the quality of picture and sound transmission.

But this rapid growth has been rather lopsided. Most of the poor countries in Africa and Asia have still to possess their own domestic satelliltes or to provide an adequate number of production and transmission centres and receiving sets. The World Communications Year (1983), sponsored by the United Nations, sought to narrow this gap in technology hardware between the rich and poor countries, but, with newer technologies of information and leisure (such as the Internet), this gap has indeed widened.

Indian Television

For more than a decade, the Ministry of Information and Broadcasting managed to hold out against demands from educational institutions, industrialists, politicians and indeed the middle-classes in urban areas for the introduction of television. But then in 1959, Philips (India) made an offer to the Government of a transmitter at a reduced cost. Earlier, Philips demonstrated its use at an exhibition in New Delhi. The Government gave in, with the aim of employing it on an experimental basis 'to train personnel, and partly to discover what TV could achieve in community development and formal education.' A UNESCO grant of $20,000 for the purchase of community receivers and a United States offer of some equipment proved much too tempting to resist, and on September 15, 1959, the Delhi Television Centre went on air.

The range of the transmitter was forty kilometers round and about Delhi. Soon programmes began to be beamed twice a week, each of 20 minutes' duration. The audience comprised members of 180 'teleclubs' which were provided sets free by UNESCO. The same organization concluded in a survey conducted two years later in 1961 that the 'teleclub' programmes had made 'some impact.'

Entertainment and information programmes were introduced from August 1965, in addition to social education programmes for which purpose alone TV had been introduced, in the capital. The Federal Republic of Germany helped in setting up a TV production studio.

By 1970, the duration of the service was increased to three hours, and included, besides news, information and entertainment programmes, two weekly programmes running to 20 minutes each for 'telcclubs', und anotller weekly programme of the same duration called 'Krishi Darshan' for farmers in 80 villages. 'Krishi Darshan' programmes began in January 1967 with the help of the Department of Atomic Energy, the Indian Agricultural Research Institute, the Delhi Administration and the State Governments of Haryana and Uttar Pradesh. The programmes could easily be picked up in these States, as the range of the transmitter was extended to 60 kilometers.

The number of TV sets (all imported) in 1970 stood at around 22,000 excluding the community sets. By the mid-seventies, however, Indian sets were in the market, and the number overshot the 100,000 mark in no time. By the early seventies the demand from the Indian cities, television manufacturers and the advertising industry as well as the Indira Gandhi Government's popularity contributed to the decision to expand the medium nationwide. By the end of the decade there were more than 200,000 sets in Delhi and the neighbouring states. The Bombay centre was opened in 1972, and in the following year, TV centres began to operate in Srinagar, Amritsar and Pune (only a relay centre). In 1975, Calcutta, Madras and Lucknow were put on the television map of the country. From January 1, 1976, 'commercials' came to be telecast at all the centres.

Another significant development during the same year was the separation of TV from All India Radio. Television now became an independent media unit in the Ministry of Information and Broadcasting, under the new banner-'Doordarshan.' Thus cut off from its parent body, hopes were raised about improvement of the quality and duration of its service.

In 1977, terrestrial transmitters were put up at Jaipur, Hyderabad, Raipur, Gulbarga,. Sambhalpur and Muzaffarpur, to extend television coverage to a population of more than 100 million. For the first time in the history of Indian broadcasting, political parties shared equal radio and TV time with the ruling party for their election campaigns.

Meanwhile, the success of the Satellite Instructional Television Experiment (SITE) brought India international prestige; the country appeared ready for satellite television. NASA, ITU-UNDP, Ford Aerospace were major foreign actors in this success; the minor actors were General Electric, Hughes Aircraft, the Massachusetts Institute of Technology, and representatives of Western nations at the ITU's World Administrative Radio Conference. The INSAT series of domestic communications satellites and microwave cable networks have provided the country the infrastructure for a national satellite hookup. However, as the table above shows, access is still limited, and as the Joshi Committee Report (1983) found, the development of indigenous software continues to serve the urban elite in the main.

The Asian Games which were held in New Delhi in 1982 proved to give further impetus to the rapid expansion of the national television network. In the mid-1980s, a second channel was introduced first in New Delhi and Bombay, and later in the other metros; this second channel was to evolve into the popular Metro Entertainment Channel (or DD-2).

With the success of Hum Log and other soap operas like Buniyaad and Khandaan, Doordarshan's revenue from advertising soared, and the sponsorship of indigenous soaps, sitcoms and other serials provided a spurt to production, sometimes taken up by the advertising agencies themselves (such as Lintas' production of a popular detective serial, Karamchand). The religious epics, the Mahabharat and the Ramayana, which followed the soap opera format, with a harking back to the magic of the early Indian cinema, proved to be phenomenal successes on the small screen. Advertisers discovered a new advertising medium and they gave it all their support. By 1987, over 40 serials had been produced; on average two were being screened each evening at prime-time; foreign serials were gradually edged out, and so were several prime-time talk shows, film-based programmes, and quiz programmes. In 1987-88, Doordarshan's revenue shot up to Rs. 136.3 million, and further rose to Rs. 256 million at the end of 1990, and to a whopping Rs. 490 crores (Rs.4900 million) in 1997-98. At the close of the 1990s, there were 58 million television sets in the country, with around 15 million connected to neighbourhood cable networks.

Social Objectives of Television

Public television in India has the following social objectives:

1. To act as a catalyst for social change

2. To promote national integration

3. To stimulate a scientific temper in the minds of the people

4. To disseminate the message of family planning as a means of population control and family welfare

5. To provide essential information and knowledge in order to stimulate greater agricultural production

6. To promote and help preserve environmental and ecological balance

7. To promote interest in games and sports

8. To highlight the need for social welfare measures including welfare of women, children and the less privileged

9. To create values of appraisal of art and our cultural heritage.

This, however, is official stated policy; a close examination of the programming and scheduling suggests very different priorities.

Educational Television (ETV)

The distinct advantage of using television for formal and non-formal education is that large numbers across the length and breadth of the land can be reached simultaneously. Experts in various fields of education can offer their services to the whole nation; The main disadvantage, of course, is the enormous expenditure involved not only in production and transmission, but for reception of programmes. Although television access is widespread, receiver-sets are still beyond the reach of the majority of the urban and rural poor who are in need of further education.

Visual demonstrations of rare and complex material markedly improve understanding of many aspects of the physical sciences, of medicine, of geography and of the elements of drama and history. England, Japan and the United States have a fairly well developed of educational TV service. The British Open University makes wide use of TV-time over BBC to beam its various faculty programmes. The United States' Public Television's School Programmes serve teachers and students in the classroom and at home. Besides, the National University Consortium consisting of seven U.S. Colleges, offers college credit courses on public television. An integral part of the courses of the Open University and the N.U.C. is the tutorial system under which students work with qualified tutors living in the same cities or towns.

Delhi TV took the decision in 1961 (when it covered only the twin cities and was still at an experimental stage) to broadcast curriculum-based lessons on selected subjects, particularly on science. The aim was to improve standards in the teaching of science at the secondary level. At the time, few Delhi schools had laboratory facilities, and further, there were few qualified science teachers. These disadvantages were sought to be overcome by the visual medium of TV.

Teachers and students responded with enthusiasm to the new teaching aid. The experiment was made possible by financial assistance from the Ford foundation. It was evaluated in 1969 by a UNESCO expert, Paul Neurath, and he concluded that ETV had amply proved its usefulness as 'an aid to the teaching of science subjects.' Though Delhi TV covers a much larger area now, and many more receivers have been installed in schools there has been no significant development in the educational programmes put out. Indeed, there has been a decline in interest. According to an NCERT (National Council of Educational Research and Training) survey on the utilisation of educational TV in schools under the Delhi administration, only 38% of the 500 schools provided with receivers in the secondary classes for which lessons are telecast every week, switched on to the programmes. Some of the reasons: poor maintenance of receivers, shoddy viewing conditions in the classrooms, indifference among teachers and students.

Doordarshan Centres in Mumbai, Chennai, Kolkata, Srinagar and other cities transmit educational programmes in English and Science for primary and secondary classes. The unfortunate part of these 'lessons' is that they provide little knowledge of general interest, adhering strictly to the school curriculum and the classroom format. The camera moves outdoors only for short periods. The English language lessons are well-planned, but presented by teachers and students using a variety of accents and pronunciation.

With the extension of satellite and micro-wave facilities to almost the entire country and the installation of many more studios and transmitting centres, Doordarshan will inevitably increase its educational telecast across the length and breadth of the land. But what needs to be done before this take-off stage is close co-ordination between the centre and the states on ETV. It must be noted that the broadcast media are under Central Government control, while education is a State Government subject under the Constitution. The way out could be the setting up of an autonomous board of educationists, social scientists and media experts at the state levels. This has been recently initiated by granting 'autonomy' to the SIETs (State Institutes cf Educational Technology).

Television and Higher Education

The Verghese Committee set up by the Janata regime in 1978 strongly recommended granting broadcast franchises to educational institutions. This would empower national institutions of higher learning to use low-power radio or television transmission solely for the propagation of quality education to large masses of students and others.

The UGC Higher Education Project launched in August 1984, serves this purpose. Known as Countrywide Classroom, and coordinated by the Consortium for Educational Communication (CEC), New Delhi, its ETV programmes are beamed across the country every weekday-morning and afternoon. 1700 colleges have been provided with free colour TV sets (few colleges have bought sets from their own funds), the number of community sets stands at 60,000. However, a good number of programmes telecast continue to be of foreign origin (mainly from Britain, United States, West Germany and Russia), though indigenous programmes, produced at seven EMRCs (Educational Media Research Centres) and eight AVRCs (Audio Visual Research Centres) set up in different parts of the country, are increasing their contribution steadily. According to a 1993 ADMAR study, the UGC programmes have a viewership of over 19 million. Of these, 12 million watch the programmes at least once a week, and around seven million are regular viewers, watching two-to-five transmissions per week, though only 45% of the regular viewers are students.

TYPES OF TV PROGRAMME

Television News: A TV newscast cannot match the wide coverage and in-depth report of radio news. The time taken up by visual material does not allow for a probe, or even for adequate background information. Indeed, a TV newscast cannot present the most interesting and significant news since the cameras just cannot be present where such events take place (*e.g.*, a coup, an invasion, a war, or a cabinet meeting).

A TV newscast is, however, the ideal medium for presenting ceremonial events like coronations, swearing-in-ceremonies, arrivals and departures of VIPs, signing of treaties, parades, inaugurations, and sports. Unfortunately, the hard-core news does not lie in these events-even if they are telecast 'live' and constitute only a small percentage of the daily fare of news.

The standard newscast in India employs the radio technique of reading out the news in a formal manner from a script (on cards or on an electronic "teleprompter"), interrupted with an occasional still, a map, or a moving picture. Frequently, the news is tailored to the visuals available. With the acquisition of ENG (Electronic News Gathering) and the latest computerised graphics equipment, the number of visuals has increased. Indeed, the news bulletins of Doordarshan's channels, as also those of the many satellite channels, have in recent years taken on the format of 'magazine' programmes.

News Bulletins and Current Affairs. News bulletins, general news magazines, and panel discussions of public affairs are some of the popular news programmes on Doordarshan. All these are either in Hindi or English, like most other programmes on the National Network. Visuals include slides, film clips, maps, diagrams, charts and other visual devices. PTI-TV and UNI are major sources for national and local news footage and reports. As Doordarshan has few correspondent, cameramen posted overseas it depends largely on Reuters and Asia-vision for film clips of foreign news. The Asian Broadcasting Union helps out with its international news exchange system. Yet another important source is the Asia News International (ANI).

TV Documentaries or Features. Television documentaries, like cinema documentaries can feature any subject of interest to a number of viewers, such as the state of pollution, poverty, famine, the cultural scene, or the plight of construction workers. The aims of documentaries are to enlighten, arouse, and motivate, or simply to entertain. The stress is on portraying real people and real situations, and on activity rather than on talk and commentary. In a documentary, it's the story that dictates film technique, not vice versa; film is exploited here as a tool to document reality, and not to display gimmicks of the cameraman or editor in shooting reality, even though the documentary is in essence a 'social construction' of reality.

The format of a TV documentary takes the form of a 'direct presentation' of the substance of a problem or an experience or a situation, by contrast with the 'discussion'in which a situation or problem may be illustrated, usually relatively briefly, but in which the main emphasis falls on relatively formal argument about it.

Interview Programmes. Interview programmes are of various types: Personality interviews such as those in 'Superhit Muqabla', in which the attempt is to probe well-known film personalities; 'In Conversation' and 'Vibrations' which focus on literary figures; Content Interviews, such as 'Parikrama' in which the message rather than personalities is of prime importance; and Group Interviews such as a Press Conference in which a group of press people hurl questions at the Prime Minister or a Cabinet or Chief Minister on sundry subjects of current interest.

Quiz Programmes and Game Shows. These are popular because of active audience participation, as quiz-programmes and game shows are studio-oriented. Advertisers provide their products as prizes for such shows. Examples of Quiz Shows are: 'Wild Encounters', and 'Kudrath Namah', while the popular Game Shows include 'Family Fortunes', 'Antakshari' and 'Close Encounters.'

Children's Programmes. These are defined as programmes specially made for and offered to children, at certain special times. Cartoons, puppet-shows, 'live' stories and plays, and educational items are some of the items that make up a children's show. Some children's programmes have been turned into quiz shows. Feature films in Hindi for children are screened occasionally.

Music and Dance Programmes. The National Programmes of Dance and Music have brought India's foremost performers to the TV screen. The standard format of these programmes is an elaborate introduction in Hindi and English of the performer and his or her style, followed by a 'live' recital of various items. Each item is briefly explained in the two languages so that appreciation of the performance is enhanced. The programmes focus on the classical and the folk forms.

Light music programmes like Aarohi, Sham-e-Ghazal and Bazme Quwali have also proved popular. They are compared by well-known figures and feature top-notch singers. Chhaya Geet, the film based music programme, has a format all its own, with film clippings of old and new song-sequences put together in a haphazard manner. Similar programmes in Marathi, Gujarati, Tamil and other languages are also extremely popular.

Programmes for Farmers and Industrial Workers. These cater to the special interests of urban and rural workers, and are largely instructional. Amchi Mati Amchi Manse and Kama Ishwa are two such regular weekly programmes.

TV Commercials. A TV commercial arrests attention immediately and holds it for a full 10 or 20 seconds. TV commercials take many forms: slides alone depicting pictures and words, slides with sounds such as a 'jingle' or a powerful message, a movie with sound effects and jingles well synchronised. The message presented is easy and simple to understand such as the 'Come alive' message of the makers of soft drinks. A simple idea with the minimum use of words makes for maximum impact. The structure of a TV commercial is varied.

A 'logical structure' rather than a haphazard jumble of visuals and words is easily understood. A 'story-line structure', based on a believable situation that can be identified without much effort is perhaps the quickest way of attracting attention. The opening sequence is of prime importance.

Then there is the 'problem-solution structure' which offers a product as a solution to a dilemma, or to a frustration. In the 'spokesman structure', a famous name is used to talk about a product. The demonstration structure, on the other hand, depends for its appeal on a meaningful and relevant demonstration of the benefits of a product. Commercials employing the 'suspense structure' are common. They tell a story with a climactic ending, at a rapid fire pace. Humour is often an important element.

Among the other formats of TV programmes are: reviews of films, recorded music and books, educational television (ETV) programmes, situation comedies ('Sitcoms'), soap operas, plays and talk shows. The most interesting of these formats are the 'sitcom' and the 'soap opera'. 'Examples of 'sitcoms' include Kakaji Kahen, The Flop Show, Zaban Sambhalke, Mr. Yogi, Dillagi, Kya Baat Hai and Tu Tu Main Main, where humour, slapstick and satire come together in a loose narrature structure. A critical analysis of the 'soap' genre on Indian television follows.

Soap Operas. Domestically-produced Indian-language television serials came into their own only in the mid eighties. For almost a decade since 1976 when the first commercials were allowed to be aired, Indian television was dominated by Hindi feature films and film-based programmes. But the only 'sitcoms', soap operas, detective or other TV genres telecast were from British, United States or German television. The British sitcoms shown during those early years of the national network were very regional in their humour and accent. Examples of these were To the Manor Born, Some Mothers Do Love 'Em and Sorry. However, British television also provided Indian viewers some of its foremost productions such as Bronowski's Ascent of Man, Kenneth Clark's Civilization, and nature documentaries by David Attenborough. American serials like I Love Lucy and Startrek, or German 'telematches' and detective series like The Fox, introduced Indian viewers to other kinds of foreign fare. Indian

programmes that proved popular were quiz shows like What's the
Good Word?, talk shows by Kamleshwar and Tabassum, and of
course, sports programmes.

Mexican 'Telenovela'. Indian television soap operas were
directly inspired (not by American daytime soap opera) but by the
success of Mexico's Televisa, a private commercial network, in
producing popular melodramatic series such as 'Yen Conmigo'
(Come with Me) which promoted family planning. The Mexican
'telenovela' (literally, a television novel) was in turn influenced by the
Peruvian telenovela, 'Simplimente Maria' which told the story of a
migrant girl who gets rich because of her skills in sewing with a
Singer machine. The' telenovela, as might be surmised, was sponsored
by the Singer Company, the manufacturers of the machine. It is
reported that the sales of the sewing machine in Latin American
countries shot up dramatically.

In 1983, David Poindexter, the President of the Centre for
Population Communications International, New York, who had played
a key role in popularizing the Mexican experience with development-
oriented soap operas, arranged (at whose expense we don't know)
for officials from India, Egypt, Nigeria, Kenya, and Brazil, to visit
Mexico City and confer with Miguel Sabido, the producer. The
Indian delegation was led by S.S. Gill, Secretary in the Ministry of
Information and Broadcasting, who was later to be appointed the first
Chief Executive Officer of the Prasar Bharati (Broadcasting
Corporation of India).

Hum Log. On his return to Delhi, Gill got together a producer
(Shobha Doctor, an ad person by profession), a director (P. Kumar
Vasudev), an executive producer (Satish Garg), and a script writer
(Manohar Shyam Joshi) to produce India's first indigenous soap
opera, Hum Log. 156 episodes of the serial were telecast twice a
week from July 7, 1984 to December 17, 1985. The soap opera was
sponsored by Maggi Noodles, a product of a Nestle subsidiary, Food
Specialities Limited. The product was launched with the serial, and
has today become a popular fast food in urban Indian households.

'Hum Log' told the story of the ups and downs in the life of a North-Indian lower nuddle class joint family with parallel stories which tackled the problems of smuggling, political corruption and underworld activities. Ashok Kumar, the highly respected film actor, wound up each episode with an authoritative exhortation on 'the message.' The family planning theme was first diluted and then almost dropped from the soap opera after the thirteenth episode. Several other revisions were introduced because of the feedback from viewers who made suggestions on the progress of the plot and the characterization.

Hum Log was proclaimed by the media and advertisers (the latter in particular) to be a phenomenal success. The Indian Market Research Bureau (IMRB), a unit of Hindustan Thompson Associates, a multinational ad agency, conducted a study which demonstrates that the soap opera registered its highest ratings in Delhi and Bombay, and the lowest in Calcutta and Madras. Moreover, it was much more popular among middle and lower income people than among the upper middle class who made up the large majority of TV owners. Doordarshan's Audience Research Unit also rated it a success. Singhal and Rogers of the Annenberg School of Communication, Los Angeles, surveyed 1,170 adults in 1987 and found that 90% of the respondents said they 'liked' the serial. But in Madras, only 48% of the respondents (much fewer than those from the North) reported that they had seen at least one episode.

The success of Hum Log, but more significantly, the success of Maggi Noodles in the market place, led advertisers to promote indigenous soap operas on the box, and to spend more on television advertising. Prior to Hum Log, few advertisers had much faith in television as an advertising medium; by the time the first soap opera came to a close, advertisers were forced to queue up for 'commercial slots' frequently having to wait for ten months at a time. Doordarshan's revenue from advertising soared; the sponsorship of Indian serials provided a spurt to production, which was sometimes taken up by advertising agencies themselves. Indigenous serials came off the production studios in quick succession; soap operas like

Khandaan and Buniyaad; sitcoms like Yeh Jo Hai Zindagi; televised adaptations of Indian and foreign short stories (by well-known filmmakers like Satyajit Ray and Shyam Benegal); children's stories (*e.g.* EK Do, Teen, Char; VIkram Aur Betaal); and women-oriented stories (*e.g.* Chehere). By 1987, over 40 'serials' had been produced; on average two were being screened every evening. Foreign serials were edged out gradually; so were several prime-time talk-shows, quiz programmes, film based programmes. Politically bolder news and current affairs programmes (such as Newsline, Janavani, and Sach Ki Parchiyan) were introduced, and then dropped without warning.

Influence of Cinema on Television

The entry of film directors and producers into the world of television was inevitable. low-budget directors like Basu Chatterjee, Ray, Benegal, Saeed Mirza, and Govind Nihalani went to television to express themselves. Chatterjee's crusading 'Rajani' did leave a mark on the new medium; so did Mirza's politically and socially challenging 'Nukkad', and Nihalani's story of partition, 'Tamas', though Benegal failed to draw the viewers to his Sunday morning 'Bharat Ek Khoj' (loosely based on Nehru's Discovery of India).

But it was the commercial box-office film-makers who succeeded in taking over television by storm. With their reverential and solemn versions of the religious epics, first the Ramayana, and later the Uttar Ramayana and the Mahabharata, television was returned to the mythologicals and the magic of early Indian cinema. In the early nineties the television viewer in north India was still in awe of the great religious epics, though ever So gently jolted into reality by hospitalbased experiences ('Jeevan Rekha', 'Doctor Saheb'), political satires ('Kakaji Kahen'), and little gems from the South ('Malgudi Days').

Video, Cinema and Television

Estimates of the number of video-cassette recorders (VCRs) and video-cassette players (VCPs) in India are hard to corne by.

Time was when flights to Singapore were known as 'VCR Flights'. In 1984, India Today put the estimate at close to three lakhs (300,000) with an average rate of growth at 20,000 every month. A study by the Indian Institute of Mass Communications, New Delhi, in 1985 put the figure at around five lakhs (or half a million). Video advertising agencies claimed that there were many more. In mid 1987, a survey by Mode Services for Prime Time put the number at 1.8 million; Contrast Advertising believed, however, that the number of VCR sets did not exceed one million. In early 1989, video companies claimed that the average figure for each film was 2.4 million viewers.

According to officials of the Film Federation of India, the video boom which followed the conclusion of the Asiad in 1982 in New Delhi, reached well over 400 towns in the country. The Study Team on Consumer Electronics reported in 1984 that 11 units in the organized sector and 60 units in the small scale sector have been granted licenses to manufacture 500 video-cassette recorders each per annum. However, despite the further liberalization of imports of electronic items, and the entry of several multinational manufacturers, recorders continue to be priced far above international prices. This gives a fillip to the illegal import and smuggling of sets. As regards video cameras, editing, duplicating and related technologies, the situation is very similar.

Video ownership is not the only means of access to video in India. Of the million or so viewers who watch video every day, the majority club together to rent video-players, or go to video-parlours, video restaurants, video clubs, or watch video while travelling on 'video buses.' It is estimated that a thousand video rental companies operate in each of the four metropolitan cities. In the other large cities, around a hundred to two hundred rental companies/shops operate. Besides, over 50,000 video parlours do brisk business. Of the number of video restaurants, video clubs and video buses it is impossible to calculate even the approximate number. Cable and satellite TV has however brought about a dramatic decline in the video business.

The video has taken over the function of permanent and mobile cinema theatres. Paucity of exhibition outlets has always been a major constraint on the expansion of the industry. By the mid-eighties, even remote areas in far-flung districts had access to video. In Madhya Pradesh, for instance, even tiny villages with a population less than 2,000 were equipped with videos. In the Chattisgarh region alone, 150 restaurants organize video shows regularly, with an admission fee of Rs. 5 per head. The Vindhya and Malwa regions too have easy access to video. Restaurant owners in Punjab, Orissa, Karnataka, Kerala and even remote north-eastern states have cashed in on the video craze. There has been a letup in the video boom of the mid-eighties because of the heavy hand of the law on video pirates. The whole video business even today is largely illegal as most tapes are transferred from film prints in a clandestine manner. Pirated cassettes reach India mainly from Dubai and Hong Kong. But Indian cinema producers and the NFDC, which has entered the video business in a big way, have banded together to have the Cinematograph Act amended to include films on videotape. The amendment has made it illegal to screen films on video or cable without certification from the Central Board of Film Certification. Further, video parlours and video restaurants in some states are required to pay entertainment taxes. And frequent raids conducted by the police on video parlours that screen 'blue' films or pirated versions, have deterred many an owner of video-parlours. Whereas earlier, cinema producers gave international video rights only to Esquire for distribution abroad, now they have began to offer video rights for domestic distribution as well. To counteract the video 'menace', producers frequently resort to 'saturation releases' in theatres, and later sell the rights to video companies at moderate prices.

Video for Social and Political Education. Video is widely used in India at the time of regional and national elections to propagate the campaigns of political parties. For instance, during the 1984 national elections, Rajiv Gandhi's speeches on videotapes were employed for electioneering: further over 500 copies of a 20-minute videotape of 'Maa' (on Indira. Gandhi) were distributed. The opposition parties too exploited the new medium; over a hundred prints of a video film of the Tamilnadu Chief Minister, M.G. Ramachandran, undergoing treatment in a hospital in the United States, made the rounds in the South. The BJP, the Congress, and the Shiv Sena have used audio and video cassettes extensively for their political campaigns. 'Video-raths' (video vans) have now become a common sight at election time. In late 1993, the JAIN TV channel was launched to provide 'infotainment' a mix of entertainment and politics.

Social service organizations like SEWA in Ahmedabad, and CENDIT in New Delhi are using the new medium for conscientizing marginalized groups. Besides, news and film magazines such as India Today, Hindustan Times and Stardust got into the video distribution business during the late eighties and early nineties. India Today's monthly Newstrack, Hindustan Times' Eyewitness and Stardust's Starbuzz, launched a new trend in 'video news magazines.'

Other film video magazines of the time were: 'Leheren', 'Chalte Chalte', Eknath', 'Movie Magic', 'Sitaron Ki Duniye', and 'Bush Film Trax.' Sportsweek introduced the sports video magazine, 'Sportstyle.' By late 1993, many of the video magazines had ceased production, owing to the explosion of cable and cross-border satellite channels on television. Some of the video news magazines like 'Newstrack' and 'Eyewitness' then managed to obtain slots on one of the many television channels.

CABLE TELEVISION

Until the arrival of cross-border satellite television, 'cable television' in India meant no more than the relay via cable of pirated video copies of popular Indian and American films from a central control room. In Cable Television, programmes are 'piped' to viewers' sets from an ideally placed common antenna, instead of each viewer individually receiving signals from his/her private antenna. Such 'rediffusion' systems have now become fairly common in urban and rural India.

In North America, where cable TV had its origins in the need for improved reception of television signals in hilly and remote terrain. Cable TV has the advantage of good reception from local transmitters and offers the possibility of relaying services from distant and foreign transmitters beyond the reach of domestic antennae. Further, cable TV facilitates access to multiple channels. In Canada and the United States, for instance, it is possible to hook up a television set to a dozen or more 'basic' and 'pay TV' channels. Some of the channels available are: the Disney Channel, MTV (Music Television), news channels, shopping channels, movie channels, community and educational channels. The installation and rental charges are minimal.

In India, the hotel industry, public and private sector companies housing colonies, highrise buildings and co-operative housing societies pioneered the distribution of cable TV Cable installations took off in the mid-eighties. Flats in skyscrapers, for instance, were wired up to central control rooms from where video players transmitted programmes taped abroad, and Indian and foreign films on video tapes. Numerous housing colonies in Bombay's suburbs and in other cities are now 'cabled'. Cable owners have been restrained by the Bombay High Court from screening Indian films for which they have not received permission from the holders of copyright. Film producers have argued that 'home viewing' is distinct from 'the public viewing' which cable facilitates. Cable networks across the country have installed satellite dishes to pick up the television channels of STAR-TV and Doordarshan and to re-transmit them via cable to around 20 million homes. At the close of the 1990s, there were over 200,000 cable networks in the country. Almost half of them were in. 'building clusters', and a third in 'single-building systems.' More than a third of the networks had from 250 to 750 subscriber homes, and 20% had from 1,000 to 1,500 subscriber homes. SitiCable (of the ZEE TV Network) and INCABLENET (of the Hinduja Group) are the two largest consortia in the cable business, and the majority of cable operators have joined one or the other group so as to keep up the competition. In Bombay alone, INCABLENET has 600,000, and

SitiCable 400,000 cable connections under their control out of a total of 1,200,000 connections. Small time cable operators control a mere 200,000 connections.

However, direct-to-home (or DTH) technology which takes cross-border satellite programmes direct to viewers' homes without the intervention of cable operators, threatens to ruin the cable operators' business. DTH television is digital and interactive, and offers up to a hundred subscription channels. Rupert Murdoch's NewsCorp is leading the DTB revolution, having already established the Bsky B in Europe, the JSky B in Japan, and now has plans to launch I Sky B on the Indian sub-continent, and A Sky B on the North American continent.

Advertising on Video and Cable TV. The early eighties saw the dramatic growth of the video industry in India. This followed close on the heels of Doordarshan opening up to advertising and sponsorship of soap-operas and other entertainment oriented programmes. Further, the switch-over to colour television, and the reduction of customs duties on imported television sets and VCRs/VCPs, paved the way for a video boom. By May 1985, there were about 5.5 million TV sets and at least half a million video-recorders/players in the country.

Indian advertising agencies were quick to transform video into a 'vehicle' for their business clients, despite the largely illegal and unorganised nature of the video industry. Indeed, the very fact that the industry was unregulated (like the advertising industry itself), made video attractive to advertisers. Rampant piracy forced many film producers to sell the video rights of their old and current films to Garwares, Bombino, Shemaroo, Super Cassettes, Esquire, Eagle and other companies.

The National Film Development Corporation (NFDC) too negotiated terms for video rights with Indian and foreign film producers. That the video rights would be misused to promote consumer products through advertising, was not expected.

"Ad concessionaires" then stepped in to peddle audiovisual space on video. Video advertising was first restricted to export order cassettes, but the expanding home market was much too large to be overlooked by advertisers. The introduction of cable networks in the late 'eighties, first in Bombay's skyscrapers and later in 'colonies' and neighbourhoods of metropolitan areas, expanded the video market further. Consortia of leading video distributors were established. Perhaps the largest is Cable Video (India) Pvt. Ltd., which controls the home viewing and cable rights for over 3000 movies. The company is the sole ad concessionaire for these titles. Showtime Communication, a Dalmia group company distributes the company's titles in Delhi. Others who have entered the cable industry include the State Video and Governments of Mizoram, Kerala and West Bengal, and Times Television.

The big spenders on video and cable include Nestle-India, Cadbury's, ITC, United Breweries and others. With over 50,000 cable operators across the length and breadth of the country, it is a free-for-all for advertisers, especially for those whose products cannot be advertised on Doordarshan. Such products are: alcoholic drinks, baby foods, pan masalas, cigarettes, under-clothes, etc. Over rupees one crore was earned from advertisements on Cable in 1991, as against Rs. 253 crores (Rs.2530 million) earned by Doordarshan. Advertisers are not deserting Doordarshan, but rather using cable as a supplementary medium. Cable offers the advantages of what is termed 'segmentation' of the market.

In all this frenzy to make easy and quick money from video and cable advertising, the greatest losers have been the film producers, Doordarshan, and video/cable viewers. Advertisements are seen to be a nuisance, especially when they are superimposed by 'crawlies.' The fast-forward button on the remote is of little use when almost every frame is thus appropriated by advertisers. But producers and viewers are fighting back. Organisations like INFACT and the Association of Video Rights Owners of India are putting pressure on Government to set up special 'anti-piracy cells' in each State to enforce the Copyright Act. A Copyright Enforcement Advisory Council has been established to consider effective ways of enforcing the Act. It has been suggested that a Copyright Council be established. It has also been suggested that the Indian Telegraph Act (1885), the Indian Wireless Telegraph Act (1933) and the Copyright Act (1957, Amended 1983) be revised to take into account recent developments in video, cable and satellite television.

Together with viewers, film producers are planning to form Viewers' Associations to fight the blatant misuse of video and cable by advertisers. Their demand is for a Code for Advertising on T.V. Video and Cable, so that viewers' rights are respected. They believe that the Code drawn up by the ASCI does not go far enough in dealing with Video and Cable. In 'November 1993, the Cable Operators Federation of India reached a consensus with the Ministry of Information and Broadcasting on the Cable Television Networks (Regulation) Bill. The Act, which was promulgated by an Ordinance in November 1994, made registration of cable companies with the Post Office obligatory. Further, all cable operators were obliged to transmit at least one Doordarshan channel, and to stop the relay of programmes and commercials of foreign satellite channels, which do not conform to prescribed codes and guidelines of the Indian Government. However, the Act has lost its relevance with the formation of the Prasar Bharati (Broadcasting Corporation of India) and the announcement of the Broadcasting Act.

Ownership and Control of Television

Like All India Radio, Doordarshan was until November 1997 a 'unit' of the Ministry of Information and Broadcasting. The Government of India, of course, always claimed that Doordarshan enjoyed 'functional autonomy' in its programming and administration, but no matter what the claims, the Ministry remained the real decision-making body. A fair amount of freedom was permitted in the selection and production of entertainment programmes. But news and current affairs programmes were closely monitored by the

Ministry. That remained the practice since Independence no matter
which political party was in power in Delhi.

The question of the ownership and control of India broadcasting
was first raised during a discussion in the Constituent Assembly.
Pandit Nehru, however, dismissed the issue with these words: "My
own view of the set-up for broadcasting is that we should approximate
as far as possible to the British model, the BBC; that is to say, it would
be better if we had a semi-autonomous corporation under the
Government, of course with the pobey controlled by the Government,
otherwise being conducted as a Government department but as a
semiautonomous corporation. Now, I do not think that is immediately
feasible." Though that was the first Prime Minister's personal view,
it remained the official position until 1964 when the Chanda Committee
was established to look into the whole issue afresh.

The Chanda Committee

The Chanda Committee recommended that a Broadcasting
Corporation should be established by an act of Parliament in which
its objectives should be clearly laid down. It emphasised that 'the
scope of Government's authority should be clearly defined and be
free of ambiguity. The right to require the Corporation to broadcast
certain programmes as also the right to veto broadcasts in certain
subjects may be reserved to Government. It must be understood that
such powers must be sparingly used and only when the national
interest so demands. These reservations would automatically define
the accountability of the Minister of Parliament. We also consider
that the Act itself should lay down the authority and powers of the
Governors to prevent possible encroachment.'

Accordingly, it recommended a Board of Governors (no more
than seven) to be headed by a Chairman. 'The Chairman should be
a public figure with a national reputation for integrity, ability and
independence, and the members should be drawn from diverse fields
of national life and enjoying a reputation in his particular field.' The
Committee left selection to the Government itself, and the term of
office of Governors was restricted to six years with two members

retiring every other year in rotation. It argued that conditions for creativity could only be fostered by decentralisation of authority down to the regional and local levels.

The Verghese Committee

The Verghese Committee recommended the setting up of a National Broadcast Trust (or Akash Bharati) under which a highly decentralised structure would operate. It did not see the need for autonomous corporations or even a federation of State Government Corporations. Neither did it support the idea of two separate corporations for radio and television. However, besides asserting that the Trust should be an independent, impartial and autonomous organisation', the Committee wanted 'the autonomy of the corporation and its independence from government control to be entrenched in the Constitution.

The Committee recommended that the Trust be supervised by a Board of Trustees (or Nyasi Mandal) consisting of 12 members who would be appointed by the president on the recommendation of the Prime Minister from out of a list of names forwarded by a nominating panel comprising the Chief Justice of India, the Lok Pal and the Chairman of the UPSC. The Chairman and three members would be full-time members while the other eight members would be part-time. It would be the responsibility of the Board of Trustees to appoint the Controller-General Broadcasting, the Directors and other senior personnel. The Controller-General would head the Central Executive Board and will be ex-officio Secretary to the Board of Trustees. The Central Executive Board, in co-ordination with Zonal Executive Councils, would be responsible for implementing the policies and directives of the Board of Trustees. Programming would necessarily be decentralised and producers down to the local levels would enjoy a significant measure of autonomy.'

Joshi Working Group on Software for Doordarshan

Though the Joshi Working Group was not asked to go into the question of broadcasting autonomy, it did stick its neck out in stating bluntly that 'functional freedom' did not exist at all in Doordarshan, despite government claims. However, it noted that the crucial issue is not 'autonomy versus government control but urgent reforms in structure and management styles for support to creativity. It, therefore recommended the creation of an institutional arrangement which provided co-ordination and interaction among political, administrative and communication spheres for policy guidelines and evaluation of software. Further, it recommended the establishment of a National Doordarshan Council to tender advise to the Minister on the broad social objectives and the modes of TV programming. The Joshi Working Group however, did not favour the freeing of broadcasting from the control of the I and B Ministry. It had no objection, to Doordarshan receiving directives from the Minister or his deputy.

Prasar Bharati Bill (1989)

The Prasar Bharati Bill (1989) is based largely on the Verghese Report (1978) and the Prasar Bharati Bill (1979) that was introduced by the Janata regime in Parliament in May 1979. There are some basic differences too. While the Prasar Bharati Bill favours the creation of a Broadcasting Corporation through an Act of Parliament, the Verghese Report clearly wanted broadcasting autonomy to be a part of the Indian Constitution. This would be necessary to ensure that no future government would tamper with the freedom and independence of the corporation. Further, a Trust in the service of the public was what the Verghese Report envisaged; the present Bill proposes a 'Corporation' which does not have statutory dignity and power. The objectives that the present Bill sets out for the corporation are taken almost verbatim from the Verghese Committee's objectives for the National Broadcast Trust. Yet it does not go as far as the Verghese Report which wanted the Ministry of Information and Broadcasting to shed its responsibility for broadcasting altogether. The bill manages to sneak in a representative of the Ministry as a part-time Governor. This is not the 'full autonomy' the Verghese Committee had in mind.

The Verghese Committee warned against 'copying blindly' the structure and organisation of western broadcasting institutions. The structure envisaged by the new Bill is patterned closely on that of the British Broadcasting Corporation; even the nomenclature is similar. Moreover, the Verghese Report underscored the need for a decentralised structure with powers delegated at regional and local levels; the present Bill says little about devolution of the powers of the Central Governing and Executive Boards. The Bill does not also go into the question of 'franchise stations' for educational institutions or of independent radio and television producing agencies. On the matter of the selection of the Chairman of the Board of Governors too, the Bill departs from the Verghese recommendations. Instead of the nominating panel consisting of the Chief Justice of India, the Lok Pal and the Chairman of the UPSC, the present Bill would rather include the Rajya Sabha Chairman, the Press Council Chairman and a nominee of the President. Similarly, it deviates radically on the composition of the Broadcasting Council/Complaints Council. Indeed, the current Bill is far closer in content, form and spirit to the Prasar Bharati Bill (1979) than to the Verghese Report's recommendations.

B. G. Verghese, Umashankar Joshi and other Committee members reacted strongly to the 1979 Bill. Both felt that the then Government had been 'distrustful' of the people and that the extent of autonomy provided in the Bill had been considerably diluted; there was no provision, they remarked, for any decentralisation of the functioning of the proposed broadcasting corporation. These objections can be raised against the 1989 Bill too. The Bill became an Act in 1990 with approval by all political parties in the Lok Sabha and Rajya Sabha.

Prasar Bharati Act (1990)

The first step the ruling Congress government took in response to the 'invasion' by cross-border satellite television was to set up the Varadan Committee (1991) to re-examine the Prasar Bharati Act (1990). The Varadan Committee suggested that Doordarshan should devote at least 20% of total broadcasting time on each channel to socially relevant programmes.' Further, 'no more than ten per cent in terms of time of the programmes broadcast should be imported.'

It also recommended that 'while dealing with any matter of controversy, the programmes shall present all points of view in a fair and impartial manner.'

The United Front Government went a step further. It sought to draw up a comprehensive National Media Policy which would take into account questions such as decentralisation of television, regulations, cross-media ownership, participation by foreign media houses, role of advertising, and up linking from Indian territory. The Ram Vilas Paswan Committee was set up for this purpose in 1995. It submitted a 104-page working paper with 46 recommendations on public and private electronic media, newspapers, news agencies, and film. The Committee had hammered out consensus on National Media Policy. Some of the recommendations were incorporated in the Broadcasting Bill introduced in parliament in May 1997. The Nitish Sengupta Committee (1996) was constituted in 1996 to have another look at the Prasar Bharati Act and to suggest amendments. It submitted its report in August of the same year.

Broadcasting Bill (1997)

In mid-May 1997, the Broadcasting Bill was introduced in Parliament. A Joint Parliamentary Committee headed by Mr. Sharad Pawar of the Congress (I) was constituted to have a second look at some of the controversial clauses such as cross-media ownership, licencing procedures, extent of foreign equity to be permitted, and uplinking services for private satellite channels.

The Bill makes it mandatory for all channels whether Indian or foreign to transmit their programmes from Indian territory. Licences for satellite channels will be granted only to Indian companies, and they would be allowed up to 49% foreign equity. No foreign equity for terrestrial channels would be allowed.

The Bill bans cross-media ownership (newspaper publishing houses can have no more than 20% equity in television or cable companies), and foreign ownership. Besides, no advertising agencies, religious bodies, political parties or publicly funded bodies will be granted a licence to own a TV company. Direct-to-home (DTH) services would be lincensed only to two companies after a bidding process.

The Cable Television Networks (Regulation) Act would stand repealed once the Bill came into effect. The Broadcasting Bill was introduced in direct response to the Supreme Court of India's direction to the Central Government in February 1995 'to take immediate steps to establish an independent autonomous public authority representative of all sections and interests in the society to control and regulate the use of the airwaves.' The Supreme Court was opposed to the privatisation of broadcasting, observing that private broadcasting, even if allowed, should not be left to market forces, in the interests of ensuring that a wide variety of voices enjoy access to it. The Court saw 'a potential danger flowing from the concentration of the rights to broadcast/telecast in the hands of (either) a central agency or of a few private broadcasters.'

SATELLITE TELEVISION

The satellite TV revolution in urban India was ushered in by five-star hotels in Bombay and Delhi which brought the 'live' coverage of the Gulf War to the small screen via the CNN (Cable News Network) of Atlanta, Georgia. STAR-TV (with four channels) was launched in 1991 when there were around 11,500 cable networks in the entire country. In Delhi alone, there were at the time around 45,000 households linked to cable TV (STAR-TV added a fifth channel-the BBC World Service, on October 14, 1991). The number of cable networks increased steadily as it became clear that only a dish antenna would be necessary to transmit STAR-TV channels to basic cable-linked households. Around 78% of the cable households get STAR-TV programmes.

Conducted in May 1992, the ARD's study covered ten cities and towns: Delhi, Bombay, Madras, Calcutta, Hyderabad, Bangalore, Lucknow, Nagpur, Jaipur and Cuttack. These cities and towns represent different sizes of population, different levels of cable penetration, and different levels of knowledge of English and Hindi. The study estimated that none of the satellite TV programmes have more than eight per cent viewing and very few programmes reach even five per cent. The programmes with higher than five per cent viewing were feature films, serials, cartoon shows and news. The study concluded: It appear that most of the satellite TV viewing is chance viewing. The programmes are yet to build up a loyal audience. The reasons are obvious. The programmes are in English and even for a majority of English knowing people the accent in the dramatic programmes is not easy to comprehend.

The study added that 'the VCR programmes of the local operator have good viewing which goes up to 24% at times. These are mostly feature films, some new and other popular hits of yester years. Generally, the local VCR peaks in the afternoons and after 10.00 p.m. when feature films in the local languages are put on the cable network.' An IIMC survey of 300 respondents in Delhi conducted in January 1992 arrived at a similar conclusion.

The major effect of the mushroom growth of cable and satellite television has been on the advertising revenue earned by Doordarshan and the print media. Advertisers of sanitary napkins, pan masalas, alcoholic drinks, jewellery and other products which are banned on Doordarshan have begun capitalising on Star-TV's five channels. Other advertisers too are taking advantage of the lower rates of STAR TV and Zee TV, especially in the area of premium brands of soaps, consumer items and consumer durables. Doordarshan has launched a metro channel and four other channels which are available via satellite in any part of the country, in a bid to win back the top advertisers. Doordarshan's efforts are bearing fruit since advertisers and ad agencies are provided opportunities to produce programmes on the Metro and the national networks.

The effects of satellite television on other mass media and such as the cinema, radio, recorded music and even the press have been equally remarkable. Though the production of films continue at the same rate as in earlier years (around 800 a year), several cinema theatres have been forced to close down, especially in Mumbai and other cities of Western India. The privatisation of PM radio in the metros is clearly a fallout of the widespread access to satellite and cable television, and an attempt to combat the popularity of the MTV channel on STAR-TV. The recorded music industry too has been forced to change its strategies to keep pace with the interests of the 'MTV-generation.'

The press has not escaped the onslaught either. With round the clock news on BBC World, CNN (Cable News Network), STAR NEWS, and Zee India News, Indian newspapers find that their reports cannot match the immediacy of satellite networks which present, as the claim goes, 'news as it happens.' In an effort to compete, Indian newspapers and magazines have introduced visuals and colour as well as interesting layouts to keep the attention of their readers. Besides, both newspapers and magazines now present news stories in the form of 'snippets' and 'briefs', and features that are investigative and analytical in nature. Several publications, such as Bombay (of the Living Media Group) and The Illustrated Weekly of India (Times of India Group) have fallen by the wayside.

Satellite television has had some influence undoubtedly on the socio-cultural environment of the urban and rural groups that afford access to the cable and satellite channels. The operas, sitcoms, talk shows and game shows of the American British and Australian networks often deal with subjects that are of little relevance to Indian society; yet they are eminently watchable. Zee TV's shows are pale imitations of the American genres. The openness with which topics related to sex and violence are discussed or enacted, is passed in affluent societies; it is not so in most Eastern cultures. Constant exposure to 'images' and ideas from dominant and powerful cultures give rise to media and cultural imperialism. During the seventie's and eightie's, the non-aligned countries brought up this issue in UNESCO and other fora, and pleaded for a New World Information and Communication Order (NWICO), wherein the flow of information between the countries of the North and of the South would be 'fair, equal and balanced', and not predominantly from North to South. The United States and Britain saw this struggle as a 'communist plot', and walked out of UNESCO.

The reporting of the BBC, CNN and ABC News on culturally and politically sensitive issues over the satellite channels has been far from commendable. Apparently, they have little concern for the possible repercussions of their frequently provocative visuals and reports. Some national governments have pointed out that this is tantamount to 'interfering in the internal affairs' of Asian nations under the guise of providing world news.

Perceptions of Viewers

In January 1992, the Indian Institute of Mass Communication conducted a survey in New Delhi of the 'perception' of viewers on the socio-cultural impact of Cable and satellite television. The following were some of the conclusions of the survey. (It must be noted, however, that 'perceptions' do not indicate 'impact' or effects).

(i)   While 84 percent of the respondents found the MTV programmes entertaining 60 per cent felt that they would have a socio-cultural effect on the younger generation. The reactions included the view that the younger generation will adopt the western life style, that MTV will hamper their studies and they will be more inclined to migrate to the West. However, some respondents felt that the younger generation will become smarter and more aware because of this exposure.

(ii) With regard to BBC, while 58 per cent of the respondents felt that it has "wide, in-depth and balanced coverage", surprisingly 42 per cent felt that "stories about India sometimes reflect bias and distortion of facts."

(iii) About 80 per cent of the respondents felt that foreign serials were entertaining. An equal percentage opined that "STAR serials are more imaginative and creative" (than Doordarshan). Yet, 35 per cent felt that foreign serials are 'not relevant to our culture history, region and society'; and 42 per cent said that the foreign serials "are always glorifying Western society and their culture, which will adversely affect our children and youth."

(iv) With regard to films shown on the "VCR Channel" of cable systems, the audience was almost exactly divided between those who felt that "the number of films shown is too many" and those who stated that "their number was just right. As many as 70 per cent felt that the moral and ethical values of our society will be affected by the onslaught of films. While there was concern about the depiction of sex and violence, some felt that there is already so much exposure to this (through other sources) that cable TV will not make much difference.

(v) A substantial proportion of respondents (between 45 and 62%) were worried about the negative effects of cable TV on children. A majority (57%) feel that "children will be adversely affected." The sports activities of children will be curtailed, felt 62 per cent, while 51 per cent felt that reading and other creative activities will be adversely affected.

Ethics of Telecasting

Television, cable and satellite TV producers have not drawn up any Code of Ethics for regulating practices in the profession. While television producers (and also 'independent producers' making programmes for Doordarshan) are required to follow the 'AIR Code' and other guidelines issued by the Central Government, cable and satellite TV producers follow a policy of crass commercialism. Any programme which attracts advertisers and brings in some viewers is telecast-worthy. There appears to be a certain indifference to questions of ethics and morality among professional media persons.

Even as STAR-TV imposes largely western-type entertainment and news programmes on Asian audiences, Doordarshan imposes a

North-Indian Delhi-centric culture on the whole country. It is very likely that the Metro channels and the five additional national channels will continue this 'unethical' practice. The pluralism of cultures in India will not be presented because of advertisers' influence on programming, and Doordarshan's unwillingness to take on a 'public service' role.

The staple fare on Doordarshan, cable, and satellite channels is mainstream commercial cinema. Even films and soap operas meant for adults are telecast at times when children cannot be kept from watching. Explicit scenes of sex and violence are the main ingredients of such films. How 'ethical' is such telecasting?

Further, how 'ethical' is the presentation of violence in news programmes? The violence of war, the violence of the police against citizens, and the violence of famines, droughts and floods? The violence of poverty? The BBC wallows in the portrayal of emaciated bodies in the Sudan and Somalia.

Individual privacy is rarely respected when it comes to portraying death on television. Frequently, the cameras zoom in on the wan face of the dead person, or the agaonised face of a widow, or a close relative. What is the earthly 'news value' of such representations?

The BBC World Service relishes showing us 'library pictures' of trishul-swinging sadhus in Ayodha over and over again on a day when the whole nation is tense with communal frenzy. Do broadcasters owe it to their profession to 'give the news as it happens without being concerned about the consequences to the community? Further, to portray all post-Ayodha riots in India only in communal terms (despite the obvious economic and political grounds for such flare-ups) is to betray the persistent colonial mentality to the BBC, The BBC, it must be noted, is extremely cautious and spare in its use of provocative visuals when it presents news of IRA-bombings and Ulster rioting.

The satellite channels are beyond the regulation of any Government. Protests of Governments of Asian countries often go unheeded. Advertisements for liquor and tobacco are banned on Doordarshan and most other Asian television networks. But the Hong Kong based satellite channels have begun showing advertisements of different brands of liquors, and of pan masalas. There is little concern for the 'ethics' of advertising, or for that matter with the 'ethics' of broadcasting. The TV viewer has to take it or leave it: advertisement~ interfere every few minutes with his right to information and his right to healthy entertainment, but he does not protest and so continues to be exploited.

Efforts of the Indian Government and the profession to introduce some ethical norms and a sense of social responsibility are seen in *(1)* Guidelines for Advertising on AIR and Doordarshan, *(2)* Doordarshan's Code for Commercial Advertising and *(3)* The Advertising Code of the Advertising Standards Council of India. The Guidelines and the two Codes are reproduced below:

Guidelines for Advertising

a. Advertisement on cigarettes, bidis or tobacco products, pan masala, alcoholic drinks and other intoxicants, gold and silver jewellery, precious stones are not allowed for broadcast.

b. The spots on aerated water (soft drinks) should contain statutory declaration that it contains no fruit juice/fruit pulp and is artificially flavoured and does not contain BVO.

c. Medicinal products should be accompanied by 5 copies of the script (in Hindi or English), 5 copies of the list of ingredients (with percentage) and a sample to get the approval of the Drugs Controller before broadcast.

d. Medicinal spots are always accepted as fixed spots.

e. Ads should not contain any exaggerated, superlative or misleading claim.

All those engaged in advertising are strongly recommended to familiarize themselves with the legislation affecting advertising in this country, particularly the following Acts and the Rules framed under them as amended from time to time:

1. Drugs and Cosmetics Act, 1940

2. Drugs Control Act, 1950.

3. Drugs and Magic Remedies (Objectionable advertisements) Act, 1954.

4. Copyright Act, 1957.

5. Trade and Merchandise Marks Act, 1958.

6. Provision of Food Adulteration Act, 1954.

7. Pharmacy Act, 1948.

8. Prize Competition Act, 1955.

9. Emblems and Names (Prevention of Improper Use) Act, 1950

10. Consumer Production Act, 1990.

11. Indecent Representation of Women (Prohibition) Act, 1986.

12. Code of Ethics for advertising in India issued by the Advertising Council of India.

13. Code of Standards in relation to the advertising of medicines and treatments.

14. Standards of Practice for Advertising Agencies.

15. Code for Commercial Broadcasting, copy of which may be had from the Central States Unit.

f. Advertising shall be so designed as to conform to the Laws of the Country and should not offend against morality, decency, and religious susceptibilities of the people.

g. No advertisement shall be permitted which

    (i) derides any race, caste, colour, creed and nationality;

    (ii) is against any of the directive principles, or any other provision of the Constitution of India;

    (iii) tends to incite people to crime, cause disorder or violence, or breach of law or glories violence or obscenity in any way;

    (iv) presents criminality as desirable;

    (v) adversely affects friendly relation with Foreign States;

    (vi) exploits the national emblem, or any part of the Constitution or the person or personality of a national leader or state dignitary.

Code for Commercial Advertising

This Code was presented to Parliament in mid 1987. It incorporates the Indecent Representation of Women Act and the Consumer Act, both of which were passed by parliament in 1986. It suggests 33 Do's and Don'ts for advertisers. Here are some of them.

Advertisements should conform to laws and should not offend against morality, decency and the religious susceptibilities of people.

The success of advertising depends on public confidence and no practice should be permitted which tends to impair this.

The Director General shall be the sole judge of the Code.

The following advertisements should not be permitted:

1. Ads which deride any race, caste, colour, creed and nationality, or are against the Directive Principles or the Constitution.

2. Ads which tend to incite people to crime or cause order or adversely affect friendly relations with foreign states.

3. Ads which exploit national emblem, any part of the constitution, or the person/personality or national leaders or state dignitaries.

4. No advertisement shall be presented as news.

5. Ads which have any relation to religion, political or industrial dispute.

6. Ads which promote chit funds, money lenders, jewelry fortune letters, foreign goods, and private saving schemes.

7. Guaranteed goods will have to be made available to Director-General of Doordarshan for inspection if necessary.

8. No disparaging or derogatory remarks of other products or comparison with them should be made.

9. Ads which portray women as passive or submissive.

10. Ads which are likely to startle viewers such as gunfire, sirens, bombardments, screams, and raucous laughter.

❏

6

Development of Television in India

Television came to India on September 15, 1959 with experimental transmission from Delhi. It was a modest beginning with a makeshift studio and low power transmitter. The objective was to find out what it can achieve in community development and formal education. The funding of $20,000 and equipment was offered by United States. One hundred and eighty teleclubs were set up within the range of 40 Kilometers of transmitter. Every club was provided with a television set by UNESCO. All India Radio provided the engineering and the programme professionals.

The Akashvani Auditorium was converted into the studio from where the regular programmes of Indian TV were put on the air although the first experimental programmes were telecast from a makeshift studio in Akashvani Bhavan. The service itself was also known as a Pilot project, aided by UNESCO, because the programmes, put out on mere two days a week, was intended to be experimental in nature to test the efficacy of television medium in carrying relevant and useful messages of social education to the power section of society.

In 1961 television programmes for teachers were started. A daily one hour service with a news bulletin was started in 1965 including entertainment programmes. In 1967 rural programmes and Krishi Darshan were started, for farmers in 80 village teleclubs in Delhi and Haryana.

In 1972 TV services were extended to a second city Mumbai. By 1975 Calcutta, Chennai, Srinagar, Amritsar and Lucknow also had TV stations. In 1975-76 the satellite Instructional Television Experiment brought TV to 2,400 villages in the most in accessible and the least developed areas for one year. From 1976, television was separated from All India Radio and constituted a new body under a new banner called as Doordarshan. At present, Doordarshan is one of the media units of the Ministry of Information and Broadcasting, Government of India. In 1982, a regular satellite link between Delhi and other transmitters, was established to facilitate the introduction of the National Programme. With this the era of fast expansion of TV services through low power transmitters was also heralded. The following are some other land marks in the history of Doordarshan:

1976	Jan. 1	Commercials on TV
1976	April 1	Doordarshan separated from All India Radio and given a separate banner-Doordarshan
1982	Aug. 15	Colour TV introduced
1984	July 15	First Mass Appeal Programme - Humlog
1984	Nov. 19	Second channel at Delhi
1986	Aug.9	First Regional network.
1993	April 1	The Metro entertainment channel.
1993	Aug. 15	Five DD Satellite channels
1994	Aug. 15	Major restructure - DD-l to DD-13. Relay station service from state capitals.
1995	March 14	DD-India-International channel
1995	Nov.14	DD-3-Infotainment channel.

At present, Doordarshan telecasts programmes on nineteen channels. These channels supplement and complement each other. DD-l is the primary channel, the flag-ship of Doordarshan. The Programmes are addressed to the entire country. There are three components in these programmes - National, Regional and Local. The National and Higher Education TV programmes are relayed by all territorial DD-l transmitters. The regional component is separate for each state and is mainly in the language of that state. The metro entertainment channel targets at urban viewers, particularly younger age groups. These programmes are relayed in 46 cities. DD 3 is a composite service and telecasts three feature films each day, covers sports in the evenings and puts out a composite programme of culture, current affairs and business news in prime time.

DD-4 to DD-13 channels are ten Regional language channels. Each channel telecasts two types of programmes. The Regional service and additional entertainment programmes, DD-14 to DD-17 telecast the programmes for four Hindi speaking states. DD India has 18 hours of programmes. It is accessible in more than half the world. DD-CNNI is a channel of news and current affairs.

Commercial advertisements were introduced on Doordarshan in January 1976 and sponsorships of programmes was allowed in 1984. The popular programmes of Doordarshan created for the first time a national market for consumer goods which could be reached by manufacturers with limited resources. Doordarshan continues to be the most effective medium for advertising at minimum cost.

The major coverages of Doordarshan (1997) include world cup cricket matches, exit poll telecast, the confidence vote, union and state budgets, Olympics-96, Miss Universe Pageant, Rathyatra, natural calamities of airplane crash in Haryana, cyclones in Andhra Pradesh, fire accident in Orissa and so on.

Salient features of reports and recommendations of working group committees and projects.

1966 Chanda Committee	—	Separate Corporations for Akashwani and Doordarshan.
	—	Liberation of AIR from the rigid financial and administrative procedures of the government.
1977 Verghese Committee	—	Establishment of an autonomous National Broadcast Trust under which Akashvani and Doordarshan would function.
	—	Radio and TV should work for the public purpose and within the framework of a broad perspective of national communication policy.
	—	The autonomy of the authority and independence from control of the government should be guaranteed by the constitution.
1985 Joshi Working Group	—	Urgent reforms in structure and management styles for support to creativity.
	—	Creation of an institutional arrangement which provided co-ordination and interaction among political, administrative and communication spheres for policy guidelines and evaluation of software.
	—	Establishment of a National Doordarshan Council to render advice to the Minister on the

broad social objectives and the modes of TV programming.

1991 Vardan Committee   —   Electronic Media should cease to be the exclusive state preserve.

                                —   Prasar Bharati Act be entrusted with the functions of licensing, monitoring of programmes and quality rating.

Social Objectives of Doordarshan

* To act as a catalyst for change

* To promote National integration

* To stimulate a scientific temper in the minds of the people.

* To disseminate the message of family planning as a means of population control and family welfare.

* To highlight the need for social welfare measures including welfare of women, children and the less privileged.

* To promote interest in games and sports.

* To provide essential information and knowledge in order to stimulate greater agricultural production

* To promote and help preserve environment and ecological balance.

* To create values of appraisal of art and cultural heritage.

Television as Mass Medium

Amongst all the mass media today, television attracts the largest number of viewers. Its audience is greater in size than any of the other media audiences. This is because television is able to attract the audiences of all age groups, literate and illiterate and of all the strata of the society.

In India, from the beginning *i.e.* 1989, television has been used more for education and information purposes than for entertainment. It has performed different functions as compared to the television in west. Even today, though commercials have entered Indian television in a big way, it's basic purpose has not changed. It continues to perform it's function of national integration and development.

Dr. Rajendra Prasad. while inaugurating India's Television Service on September 15, 1959, hoped that television would go a long way in broadening the popular outlook in line with scientific thinking.

There is no doubt about the fact that the technology has given us a major tool in television. It is a very powerful persuasive mass communication medium. How and why we make use of this tool will determine the effectiveness of this tool to enhance the development process.

In India uptil now, television is government owned medium. Therefore, it has to further the cause of development and spread the message of people's participation in development programmes launched by the government. The Indian model of television programmes is unique as it is expected to pass on the culture from one generation to other and persuasion.

Doordarshan, India's national network, has 41 major Kendras (stations) with studios, production facilities and regular programmes originating from the stations and 921 transmitters. Today, Doordarshan is competing with all cable TV networks in meeting the entertainment needs of the people.

Television in India, through it's programmes presents a composite national picture and perspective of India's rich cultural heritage and diverse thinking. They represent various religions and cultural expressions and activities of people, belonging to different parts of India, thus it reflects the Indian society. Television has been able to influence the people living in a remote areas of our country as its outreach has covered the remotest villages and tribal pockets. It is ushering information explosion.

The growth in television both in technology and reach in the last three decades has been phenomenal. It was basically conceived as a mass medium and a mass educator for its large population scattered in remote and culturally diverse areas. It is supposed to disseminate the message of development and modernization to create awareness for generating public participation. It is expected to support government plans and programmes for bringing about social and economic change and to protect national secutity as well as advance the cause of national integration.

Television, being an audio-visual medium, brings us into contact with events in an exciting and clarifying way. For example, a live telecast of a national event such as celebration of golden jubilee year of independence, or launching of a satellite, offers meaning to the events that no amount of reading or still pictures or even films could match. However, this incomparable quality of reality and immediacy is not found in all television programmes, especially those programmes which are prepared specifically for education purposes. Television is considered as a mirror of a national's personality. It can recall the past, dwell upon the present and peep into the future of a society. This role of television is all the more relevant to a country like India, having continental dimensions and innumerable diversities. It has the capability to reach simultaneously millions and millions of our people. Since it can transmit not only words but pictures as well, the significance of television as a medium of mass communication has universally been realised and recognised.

In a country like India where population and illiteracy are the burning problems, electronic media provides tremendous reach for disseminating audio-visual information even in remote areas. India has diverse cultures, religions and traditions. Therefore, medium like television can play a very important role in developing common understanding among the people and bringing them closer. It opens up the prospects of educating villagers in the remotest areas, in the affairs of the nation and associating them in the task of development, along with creating wider vision of the world.

Television provides masses a common experience at the same time, in a verifying degree. A telecast can use combination of various audio-visual materials and methods, such as, objects, models discussion, demonstrations, plays, exhibits, chalkboard and so on. This helps in clarifying the messages to audience varying in their comprehension level. Thus, it makes mass communication more effective and appeals to the groups of varied nature. Television, like radio, is also primarily a one way channel of communication.

There have been developments in television medium so as to make two way communication possible, but in India this technique is used occassionally only. For example, at the time of elections we are able to watch communicator and receiver communicating on TV from a distance. Normally the communicator on a television screen can not enjoy the rapport with his audience which makes difference between a one-sided performance and a true interaction of communicator and receiver.

Like film, television also stimulates and reinforces ideas, beliefs and tendencies already possessed by the viewer. For example, television repeats and thereby reinforces the messages on family planning, importance of girls education, marriage age, environment protection, energy conservation etc. Thus, it serves persuasive function.

Television has more flexibility and mobility in its coverage due to audio-visual presentation. This is the reason why it has become a family medium. Family members receive messages in their own environment. It can show what happened and how it happened. It can show landing of a man on mars, functioning of heart or division of cell through animation. Above all, it can provide entertainment also. Thus, television as a mass medium informs, educates, inspires and motivates.

As far as educational messages to the masses are concerned, television can be the most powerful educational medium because it combines speaking, writing and showing. You not only talk to the masses at one time but you show them what you mean. Thus, TV presents mass demonstration to thousands of viewers at the same time.

Discussing the importance of television as mass media. Saxena says, "Television in India has acquired today newer dimensions, greater popularity and a much wider reach. The moving images of television fascinate people, demand attention and eventually influence their thoughts and behaviour. The small screen has indeed turned out to be large enough to compress, within itself, India's tremendous cultural diversity over a rather broad social spectrum. Television has become part of our popular culture-part of our life itself".

Satellite Instructional Television Experiment (SITE)

The one year long Satellite instructional television experiment (SITE) which commenced on 1st August 1975 and concluded on 31st July 1976, marked the beginning of a series of innovative and constructive educational television programmes for national development and for educating the Indian masses living in remote rural areas. The SITE educational programmes were also aimed at making the children sensitive to, and learn, community living and improve their basic concepts and skills in the areas of numeracy, language and Science. The programmes were directed at creating a positive attitude to formal education and making education interesting, creative, purposive and stimulating. The educational programmes were so designed as to familiarise children with facts and matters normally beyond their observation and experience.

The Satellite for this experiment, A TS-6 was provided by the National Aeronautics and Space Administration (NASA) of USA and the ground segment was prepared by the Indian Space Research Organisation (ISRO) working in collaboration with All India Radio/Doordarshan. The educational and developmental programmes were beamed up to the satellite from earth stations set UP. in Ahmedabad and Delhi and were broadcast towards India using the high power transmitter and the large antenna aboard A TS-6. These programmes were received in about 2400 villages in six different states of India.

One of the purposes of the experiment was to provide a system test of direct broadcast technology in relation to a large developing country. It also aimed at demonstrating that a developing country like India could fabricate, manufacture and maintain the required earth stations, rebroadcast transmitters and community receiving sets in far off villages with adequate efficiency and reliability.

The experiment was also considered as a learning experience to design, produce and telecast relevant educational and developmental programmes to widely spread areas with different problems and languages using, on a time sharing mode, a single broadcast channel. One and a half hours of broadcast in the morning was denoted to school children while 2.5 hours in the evening were meant for general audiences in the villages. The evening programmes included half an hour of common programmes in Hindi which originated in Delhi.

The evaluation of the experiment provided a great deal of information and insight into how things worked and what can be done in the areas of technology, management, programme making and programme support to turn this new broadcasting innovation into a powerful aid to education and development for hitherto neglected rural areas.

The Experiment: SITE covered 2330 villages spanning in 20 districts of six states (clusters) namely Andhra Pradesh, Bihar, Karnataka, Madhya Pradesh, Orissa and Rajasthan. Instructional TV programmes for adult viewers were telecast in the evening for about two and a half an hours which included half-hour national Hindi programmes in Hindi, Kannada, Oriya and Telugu.

(a) The study explored:

      (i) The extent to which a climate for development was created by SITE.

    (ii) The extent to which SITE accelerated the process of development.

    (iii) The extent to which the attitudinal and behavioural changes took place as a result of SITE.

(b) Results of the experiment were:

1. As a System test of satellite broadcast technology in a country like India, the experiment was singular success. The research and development capability generated during setting up of this experiment was an invaluable spin-off.

2. It was more effective than all other media in attracting the female audience.

3. The continuous feedback through everyday interviews showed that the audience favoured instructional programmes as compared to sociocultural programmes.

4. In the area of agriculture, large number of innovations triggered by the television programmes. Farmers adopted only those new practices which did not demand additional expense on infrastructure.

5. A large longitudinal survey showed large gains in information, awareness and knowledge in areas such as health and hygiene, political consciousness, overall modernity, and family planning. It was also found that the gains were greater for under privileged sections of the rural society such as females and illiterates. The gains increased with the degree of television viewing.

6. A survey of children showed positive gains in the area of language development and in the attitude of seeking knowledge and information from sources other than conventional classroom teaching. They learnt new.

stories and songs and activities such as making of models and toys became popular in most of the schools.

7. In both attitudinal, as well as, in behavioural information, the overall modernity increased as a result of TV viewing. It was higher among female frequent viewers as compared to male frequent viewers.

Doordarshan Programme Services

Doordarshan offers three tier programme services: National, Regional and Local.

National Programmes. These programmes originate from Delhi and are relayed by all Kendras and transmitters. These programmes are in Hindi and English. This is considered a weak point by many media and development experts. It includes news bulletins, serials, TV documentaries, classical dance and music programmes, quiz shows, panel discussions, telecast of major events and so on. These programmes have national character. National programme can technically reach over 87 percent of the population through 868 transmitters. The programmes are for about 15 hours each day.

Local Programmes. Local programmes are very important from local people's participation point of view. Local talent gets chance for exposure through television. These programmes are produced in regional language and local dialect. This contributes to making television popular and effective as a mass medium. Local programmes are telecast for about one hour, within the time allotted for the regional programmes.

Regional Programmes. These programmes are produced in regional language in each state capital, which is linked with all the relay transmitters in that particular state. This offers opportunity to project the state's culture, issues, problems etc. on television, which may not be possible through national programmes. There are 12 regional Kendras in addition to the regional programmes produced by the metro channels and one composite zone centre for North East.

Thus, regional programmes are telecast ftom 16 states for about four hours a day. Regional programmes help people to identify themselves with them.

Types of Doordarshan Programmes

A. Information

1. *News and Current Affairs.* This includes news bulletins, direct coverage of parliament and State Assembly proceedings, direct coverage of National events, news magazines; programmes on issues and personalities in the news.

2. Sports

3. General information- Human rights, consumer affairs legal issues, gender equality, science and technology, economy and business, tourism.

B. Education

1. *ETV:* This covers Higher education TV, school TV and Enrichment programmes.

2. *Social Education:* Health, fitness and hygiene, agriculture and rural development, women, children and youth and social service messages are included in this category of programme.

3. *Culture:* It includes programmes related to language, literature, arts, theatre, classical music and dance heritage.

C. Entertainment

1. *Drama:* It covers plays, serials, situational commedies (Sit COolS), daily soaps.

2. *Film Based:* Feature films, songs and dance sequences and film magazine programmes come under this category.

3. Light and popular music and folk music programmes.

4. *Others:* Game shows, quiz, talkshows, and pro-gramme promotion are included in this category.

FORMATS OF TELEVISION PROGRAMMES

Various formats are used for the delivery of messages on television. The format should be selected keeping in mind the target group and the content of the message. For example, children may find it boring to watch a documentary on ecological imbalance but they may find animation film interesting. Moreover, the preferences of the audience also should be considered while selecting the format.

The commonly used formats are:

Actuality. In this type of format, the audience sees and hears people in the undertaking being discussed. The programme may be introduced by a host, but trom then on, rather than interviewing people the programme cuts directly to the people involved. For example, child labourers working in a fireworks' factory.

Animation. Here a series of still drawings or individual shots are combined to give the illusion of movement. 25 separate pictures can make one picture showing full animation per second. Making animation is time consuming and expensive also as each frame of the film has to be shot separately.

Demonstration. Demonstration of recipies, other articles or working of an equipment or any other machines often form the part of television programmes. These could be studio or on the field demonstrations.

Documentary. Documentaries feature any subject of interest or give detailed information on real situations, people, news. For example, documentary on vermiculture, puppetry, environment, political situations, regional handicrafts, achievements of Indian railways or a government and so on. According to Rayudu, "they create interest, enlightenment, or entertainment. Television documentary takes the form of a direct presentation of the substance of a problem or an experience or a situation".

Illustrated talk. In this format an expert or a host presents a talk or information using the illustrations related to his talk. These illustrations may be the examples that the presenter has in the studio or in the field. The programmes may cut away from the presenter to show examples of what is being talked about. The illustration could be diagrams, figures, graphics, designs, sketches, photographs or a shot of real situation. Illustrations make the talk more explanatory and interesting.

Graphics. Graphics means pictures. The camera moves across the series of painted pictures, which are created on a particular topic. they are divided in to several sections or 'episodes' to make the message explanatory. These pictures are drawn horizontally with soft edges to fit the TV screen so that the picture fades out to the edges of the paper, rather than stopping abruptly.

Interview. This is face-to-face conversation between a host and the interviewee or an invitee. These are one of the most difficult programmes to do well. It could be an interview of renowned person, or outstanding personality, literary person, group and so on. Sometimes interviews are made interesting by shots showing the interviewee engaged in whatever is being discussed.

Drama. Dramas have been very effective in involving the viewers in television programme since they represent the life realistically. A drama is a play which presents a true-to-life story in a dramatized form with actors playing the parts of the story's characters. The story develops through what the characters do and say. Dramas on television have provided a cheaper substitute for theatre plays which are beyond the reach of the middle class man.

Panel Show. These programmes have a group of experts and a moderator who introduces the experts, explains the theme, anchors the discussion and concludes. Mostly this format is used for discussion of current events or affairs where the audience is interested in learning various opinions on an issue.

Puppets. Puppet shows are used especially for children's programmes because they add novelty. They are cheaper also as they require short period for rehearsal and much less payment to those who play puppet as compared to actors of a play. Many times, puppet is used in the role of the comperer.

Talk Shows. Talk shows are conducted by a host or a guest expert, where the host introduces the topic and invites views or opinions or experiences of the participants on the same. This requires, quick thinking and responding. Resolution of problem is not a goal of this kind of activity. However, helpful information can be provided, professional thinking can be shared, suggestions for possible action can be offered for consideration, and sources of additional help can be identified, for example, sources of legal counseling or marriage counseling. This interchange is witnessed by other viewers, and they are also encouraged to consider the situation of the participants and the host.

Television as an Educational Medium

Television was introduced in the country with the main objective of using it for educational purposes. The first experimental television service in India was inaugurated in Delhi in 1959. During 1960-61, a series of social education programmes were telecast and curriculum based, school television programmes were launched in Delhi on an experimental basis. Television was introduced in the schools with the major aim of providing experiences and facilities that the school could not afford to provide, to fill in gaps in the curricula, to maximize the learning opportunities and to improve the teaching-learning processes. Educational Television (ETV) was found to be very effective in improving the academic performance of students, increasing their interest in science and improving the standard of teaching. Regular TV service was launched in Delhi in 1965. However, the expansion of ETV service took place only from 1972 onwards, when an educational technology programme was initiated, which was directed at utilising communication technologies for bringing about qualitative improvement in education, widening access to education, and reducing existing educational disparities between different sections of the population. The scheme was formulated in the context of expansion of television facilities and the use of a satellite being made available for educational purposes. It was intended to stimulate the use of television as well as other instructional media like radio and film to bring about qualitative improvement in education. Under this scheme several facilities were expanded and new infrastructure created for software development in radio and television. The availability of satellite and plans for expansion of satellite technology for TV and radio network opened up new avenues for the large scale use of the mass media in education. School TV programmes are part of regional service. The school programmes are Doordarshan production with active involvement of the state educational administrators and teachers. These are curriculum based programmes.

Barriers of ETV

Television as a medium has certain barriers. It has the element of anonymity inherent in its operation. It is strictly a one way communication. There is too wide gap between the 'sender' and 'receiver' and there is no physical identification. It offers one way communication leaving no scope for personal contact. There is no room of repetition, clarification or collaboration.

Higher Educational Television (HETV)

The University Grants Commission (UGC) has taken the initiative to utilize the time slot available for higher education to telecast programmes in higher education titled countrywide classroom, through which higher education is spread to remote and backward areas of the country. The commission is at present supporting seven educational media research centres (EMRCs) and ten audio visual research centres (AVRCs) for training of personnel and production of software. The consortium for Educational Communication (CEC) provides the institutional framework to sustain and enhance the ongoing media activity of the EMRCs and AVRCs and explore new technological advances in the field. It has also started making monthly programmes and producing educational programmes for transmission through the enrichment channel of Doordarshan. The CEC has also taken steps to produce programmes on contemporary issues such as environmental awareness, safe drinking water and the prevention of AIDs. Doordarshan has been telecasting the programmes of Indira Gandhi National Open University since May 1991.

It is regrettable that UGC countrywide classroom has not been able to meet the higher education needs of the rural undergraduate students, as the programmes do not reflect their culture and fulfill their needs so as to be appropriate to them. Moreover, they are not able to make use of the programmes meant for them as they do not understand English. These programmes are produced in English. Very few programmes cater to the undergraduate students of all disciplines which is expected by enrichment programme.

INSAT for Education

With the success of SITE in educating people in rural and remote areas, the government of India developed a plan of operation for the utilization of television and other facilities under the INSAT series and with the installation of high power and low power transmitters (HPTs and LPTs) in the country. The INSAT for education project began in October 1983 with the transmission of educational television programmes for children in the age group 5-11 years. This coverage was initially meant for clusters of villages in six states: Andhra Pradesh, Bihar, Uttar Pradesh, which came to be known as the INSAT states. In 1986 and 1987, the transmission was increased to cover the entire six states and all the Hindi speaking states of the country with the help of INSAT-1B, HPTs and LPTs. At present ETV programmes are telecast in several languages including Hindi, Gujarati, Marathi, Oriya and Telugu. These ETV programmes are relayed by all HPTs and LPTs in the six INSAT states and other Hindi speaking states. These programmes reach more than 500 million people of our population.

The UGC countrywide classroom offers enrichment programmes which are not based or restricted to the syllabus. Instead, it seeks to provide new insights, to bring in new findings and to take students on vicarious tours of places and laboratories that are not within their reach. Inter-relatedness of various disciplines and of development problems are stressed. It attempts to overcome the obsolescence of the syllabus and presents the latest advances in all field, especially the newly emerging ones. The programmes include applied science and social science, Indian culture, general knowledge and career guidance. Thus, enrichment programme is meant to link academic education to the real world.

TELEVISION AND DEVELOPMENT

Television aimed at disseminating development information and foster the process of modernization and encourage public participation and support in developmental programmes, protecting national security and advancing the cause of national integration.

"Perhaps we have ascribed inappropriate expectations to the medium, or perhaps the medium has its own limitations."

The primary purpose of television in India is development through education, information and enlightenment, to improve the quality of life of the largest masses of the people, to bring communities and societies, regions and the states together as one nation through mutual awareness and sympathy while preserving their cultures, customs and traditions. The secondary purpose is entertainment.

Ever since the first five year plan was launched in 1951, the role of communication for development support has been stressed in every five year plan. Funds allocation especially for television also increased in the sixth plan. Massive expansion of Indian television took place during this period. Seventh plan aimed at television reaching the remotest part of the country.

The only example of using television exclusively for development communication was the Kheda Communication Project (KCP), which not only aimed developing and demonstrating a new approach to the use of television for development and education but also to try out a more meaningful direction for Indian Television, KCP succeeded in demonstrating effectively that TV could be used for development and social change. It received world-wide recognition and it was awarded a UNESCO prize for rural communication effectiveness. (Bhatia and Kamic,1989). After commissioning of Ahmedabad transmitter and with the increase of individually owned television, there was the pressure to close down PIJ transmitter and had no transmission between August 1985-May 1988. Community Television sets were left unused. Programme quality also deteriorated after it's restart in May, 1988. There was commercial pressure on professionals, more government guidelines to be followed for programme making. Finally, by October, 1991, Ministry of Information and Broadcasting, decided to stop it's transmission.

According to Sinha, "The premature death of this development communication experiment leaves many unanswered questions. Those who believe that television can play a meaningful role in developing the community at large must carry out a postmortum on the successes, the failures, and the lessons to be learned from the demise of this model of development communication".

SITE and KCP evaluation studies have rendered that development depends on many factors. Television can disseminate information supportive of development, but unless a development project has strong support from powerful groups and proper infrastructure to match the demands generated by that information, such information soon becomes superfluous. Thus, the Indian Television's dilemma is—should it continue with it's original objectives and commitments to development or join race of entertainment with other channels?

The commitment of Indian television is to support the formal and non-formal education systems. However, the impact of television transmission for primary school students, for higher education, and for distance education is being questioned by society at large and by educational policy makers. indian Television stands at a crossroads in the role it has to play in improving the quality of life. However, the increasing dependence on sponsored commercials a source of revenue required for its functioning and growth and the competition it faces from other open channels attracting audiences with entertainment programmes have presented considerable threats to Indian television. In the beginning it was successful in its role of development communication to the deprived masses, but slowly the nature of its role as an agent of change seems to have disappeared.

While describing television an agent of social change, Saxena (1996) expressed that the process of change in a developing society has generally been slow. All the more, in a highly tradition bound country like India. Our people generally resist change. So, mass media strategies have first to create in them a general awareness of what all is going on elsewhere. There to motivate them to 'accept' and 'achieve' some thing new. And eventually, to let them decide how best and fast could that be done. At different stages of this transition, television, being visual, played a more dynamic role. Take, for instance, Doordarshan's very first major project, a citizenship through Television, introduced by Delhi TV. A number of teleclubs were established in and around Delhi to let the viewers take advantage of the social messages, beamed through TV. The UNESCO in a report also commended this project.

At the time of introduction of television, the official policy stressed that TV was to be used as a medium of social education as well as an instrument to support programmes specifically it was stated that TV would be used as a weapon against illiteracy and ignorance. It would bring about awareness among the people of sociological problems and make them conscious of national goals; it would create a sense of participation in India's efforts to usher in a new social order; it would play a vital role in cultivating civic consciousness and respect for law and order, public morality and so forth and, in the field of entertainment, it would mould public taste to higher aesthetic levels.

In reality, TV has turned out to be a family entertainment medium. Doordarshan audience research has also shown that the development programmes do not have large viewership. However, the programmes on health, nutrition, environment protection, energy conservation, pollution, adult education, consumer education, agriculture, animal husbandry, and family planning are being telecast by Doordarshan. Rural programmes are one of the most important target specific programmes of Indian television. Nearly 80 percent of Indian population lives in villages, and India is an agrarian country. The basic objectives of rural programmes of television in India are:

(a) To familiarise rural viewers with the latest technical and scientific know-how about farming, agriculture implements, fertilizers, good quality seeds, cottage industries, rural development, weather forecasts etc.

(b) To provide healthy entertainment (Folk music/plays/puppet shows).

(c) To acquaint the audience with the importance of education, personal hygiene, health and family welfare.

The rural programmes have been criticized for not reflecting the ruralness in their approach and content. Development practitioners have attributed it to the following factors.

1. All production centers are located. in the urban areas and programmes are being developed and produced by the urban professionals who do not have rural orientation or experience of rural problems. Thus, rural problems, needs and aspirations do not get reflected in the rural programmes of television.

2. Compared to urban viewers, rural viewers are less in numbers. Therefore, the impact of programmes on the expected size of rural population is not seen.

3. Many rural families are still not able to afford a television set.

An Audience Research Unit of Doordarshan conducted a study in 1993, covering 420 villages from 15 states. The study revealed that the development oriented programmes do not have large viewership because of:

— lack of local specificity

— unavailability of regional programmes

— variations in TV ownership patterns

— viewing by many viewers perset.

The telecast of Krishi Darshan - a programme on Agriculture and Rural Development (ARD) was started in Delhi in 1967 and now all the 41 Doordarshan Kendras telecast similar programmes. When the reach of television was limited, Doordarshan had made special efforts to reach the rural audience. It was through SITE experiment, Kheda communication project, and INSAT scheme of Area specific programmes from 1982, which included ETV programmes, programmes from all production centres.

The Joshi working group on software for Doordarshan also observed : The trouble with many development programmes, like Krishi Darshan is that they are produced within the studio often with urban men in rural garb. It is often an urban view of rural programmes, or a view of problems of urbanised villages. Considering the immensity of the task of fighting poverty, we recommend that more than half the time of Doordarshan must be related to the development.

Findings of several studies confirm that rural development programmes on TV need to be given sharpness, and thrust so as to make them more useful and relevant. According to Doordarshan study there are many schemes of providing community TV sets to rural areas - some centrally sponsored, some by state governments and some by local community organisations.

There is a need to evolve extension departments, agricultural universities, departments of agriculture and other allied institutions in producing effective and appealing television programmes for rural development.

It requires development of scientific attitude, inculcation of values for modernization and support from the leaders of the groups, communities and society to foster the multi-faceted process of development through television. No one agency or medium can do this. It requires the support of the society as a whole.

Thus Indian television is at a cross roads as far as its role in the development of a nation is concerned. Sinha, analysing the role of television in development today, pointed out, "It is unfortunate that despite the best intentions, development communication projects with a participatory approach rarely get beyond an experimental status because of social, political and economic constraints. Development communication cannot be treated 'normal' television and probably requires separate training for those who produce rural media and separate standards for judging its quality and success. The social use of development communication in India is not only lopsided in terms of distribution between the rural and the urban, but is also grossly inadequate to meet even the needs that exist in the metropolitan sector."

Nowadays television is concentrating more on earning revenue through sponsorships and advertisements. This has pushed aside the purpose of developmental communication and encouraged consumerism. This has resulted in to domination of entertainment programmes on Television. The dilemma before Indian television today is who will take care of development communication. Sinha suggests that Doordarshan, can have seperate television for achieving developmental objectives. Thus, high cost entertainment TV could earn its revenue while low cost development communication could be the state's responsibility.

Diffusion of Television In India

TV audiences have expanded tremendously in India during last ten years. It is estimated that 57.7 million house holds in India have TV sets. The number of people who can watch TV programmes in their own homes is 296 millions.

Such a large number of TV viewers provide tremendous potential for development. But television is not being utilized generally for the purpose of promoting literacy, improving nutrition or limiting family size. We all know that TV content is dominated by entertainment programmes.

There are three main reasons for the diffusion of television in India. Firstly, with the launching of satellites, increased number of transmitters, availability of TV sets on installments have increased the access to television broadcasting. Secondly, as a result of competition among the channels to do business and become popular among the audiences, every channel including Doordarshan are producing soap operas and entertainment programmes. This provides a very wise selection of programmes to the viewers. Such programmes motivate people to buy television because they feel satisfied having entertainment at home and at cheaper rate. The income from advertising has also contributed to the diffusion of television in India. More and more advertisers are attracted to sponsor interesting entertainment programmes. This has encouraged the producers to produce variety of television programmes which ultimately attract people and motivate them to own television.

Singhal, Doshi, Rogers and Rahman have summarized the Pros and cons of the Growth of Television in India as follows.

Pros and Cons of the Growth of Television in India

Pros	Cons
1	*2*
1. Political will to expand television services.	1. Use of television as a propaganda apparatus.
2. The government intention to use TV for educational development.	2a. Lack of local infrastructure to support TV messages.
	2b. Entertainment programmes get higher viewer ratings than educational shows.

Contd.

1	*2*
	2c. TV encourages socio economic inequality.
3. High advertising incomes for ˙Doordarshan.	3. Propagation of consumerism especially among socially disadvantaged viewers.
4. Satellite television can reach remote rural areas	4a. Most TV sets are located in urban areas.
	4b. Centralizing influence of TV, which disregards regional socia-cultural norms.
	4c. The use of Hindi and English on Indian TV network alienates speakers of other languages.
5. High government expenditure for TV broadcasting.	5. Opportunity costs to education for health and other development programmes.

CABLE TELEVISION IN INDIA

Cable networks are a recent phenomenon in India when compared to video and Television. It started in India in 1984, patronized first by tourist hotels. Cable television offers its subscribers a large number of special-interest channels as well as signals of local area, and super station channels, with special-interest and "Super station channels imparted by satellite. The cable channels are linked to a centrally located VCP through cables. Cable networks with dish antennae became widely prevalent after July, 1991.

Cable TV is different from television as it is capable of greater decentralized programming thereby offering greater scope for narrowcasting or programming for a well-defined, within a boundary audience. In cable TV, programmes are 'piped' to viewers sets from an ideally placed common antennae, instead of each viewer individually .

receiving signals from his/her private antennae. It has the advantage of improved reception from local transmitters and offers the possibility of relaying services from distant and foreign transmitters beyond the reach of domestic antennae. Thus, it provides the subscriber with access to multiple channels.

Cable networks fall under the purview of the Indian Telegraph Act 1985, which lays down no restrictions except for requiring a licence when cables are to be laid across public property.

Now a days, many housing societies or multi-storeyed buildings are connected with a central control room from where video players transmit taped programmes.

Though, it does not present as wide and personal a selection of programme content as video, it does offer similar programming at less cost.

Cable TV operators do originate some programmes of their own related to local events, such as celebration of festivals. They also carry local advertisements.

Cable TV brings variety of national and international channels to the cable linked households. The survey concluded by Audience Research Unit of Doordarshan in May 1992, covering 10 big cities of the country such as star TV and BBC are yet to build up their audience becuse these programmes are in English and their accent is not easily followed by even English knowing people. Due to the quick growth of cable TV, Doordarshan's advertising revenue affected advertisers as turned to satellite channels as their rates were lower. As a result, Doordarshan launched metro and other regional language channels which are available all over the country through satellite. This again attracted the advertisers.

With the phenomenal growth of satellite and cable television in India, the cable Television Network (Regulations) Bill was introduced in 1993 so as to regulate the operation of cable television networks in the country. The number of cable operators and the households having cable connection has been steadily increasing along with the number of channels and types of programmes. This resulted in to educated masses, feeling concerned about the impact of cable TV on familial, social and cultural life of the people.

Vardan Committee was appointed by the Government of India in 1991 to study the relevance of cable TV invasion. The committee observed some disturbing implications of this development.

The committee pointed out that no country can sit back passively and let some foreign agency decide what kind of programmes should be broadcast to the people of the country. At the same time, it is neither desirable nor feasible to stop these transmissions or ban their reception.

The committee also recommended arrangements to be made under which the programmes put out by the licences are continuously monitored to ensure that prescribed guidelines are not violated. It suggested that a single statutory/autonomous body known as the broadcasting council of India envisaged under the Prasar Bharati Bill be assigned the task of laying down guidelines and monitoring the quality of programmes, find out warnings and suggest punitive action in cases of violation of the guidelines, etc. The Government of India subsequently introduced a legislation in the parliament in August, 1993. The Bill provides for a registering authority, takes resources to the programme code and the advertisement code, to be framed under the Act. It has also been made mandatory for the cable operator to transmit at least one Doordarshan channel of his choice through the cable serial. However, it has been felt that the thrust of the proposed legislation is towards making it a tool for regulation rather than providing an approach to develop cable television as a social and economic resource.

In India the victim of instant communication has been Doordarshan. Satellite transmission not only made communication easy and instant but also brought in competition. Now a days, DD is making strenuous efforts to improve image.

❏

7

Educational Television

HISTORICAL DEVELOPMENT OF EDUCATION TELEVISION

Television entered India three decades ago on September, 15, 1959 (Audience Research Unit, 1991) as a pilot project funded by the Ford Foundation. It started with 20 TV receivers in an around Delhi, and transmitted one hour educational and development programme twice a week. Over the years, the coverage of television remained static. In other words, the emphasis was on consolidation rather than expansion. The coverage of Delhi transmitter and the duration of telecast, however, increased. Thirteen years latter the second television centre came into existence at Bombay on October 2, 1972. Between 1972 and 1975, four more Doordarshan Kendras (Television Centres). Srinagar (January 26, 1973) Calcutta (August 9, 1975), Madras (August 15, 1975) and Lucknow (November 27, 1975) were commissioned.

A significant landmark in the history of television in India was the one year Satellite Instructional Television Experiment (SITE) launched on August 1, 1975 involving 2330 villages of the economically backward stares. An American satellite was extensively used to telecast message to promote the socio-economic development of rural viewers, through intensive communication. The available resources-human and machine were fully mobilised to make the experiment a success. However, the enthusiasm created by the SITE could not be sustained in the subsequent post. SITE part of the project. However, in the mean time television went colour in India on August 1982.

Educational Television Programmes

The following educational television programmes have been introduced in India:

(1) Secondary School Television Project (STV),

(2) Delhi Agriculture Television (DATV) Project (Krishi Darshan),

(3) Satellite Instructional Television Experiment (SITE),

(4) Post-SITE Project,

(5) Indian National Satellite (INSAT), and

(6) Higher Educational Television Project (HETV) of UGC.

The brief description of these projects have been given in the following pragraphs.

(1) Secondary School Television Project (STV)

The school television programmes were started in Delhi on experimental basis in October 24, 1961 with three lessons per week in Physics and Chemistry and one lesson each in English and Hindi for Class XI. These programmes were syllabus-based and were telecast in school hours as a part and parcel of school activities. The aim of introducing television service in school system was to improve the standard of teaching in view of shortage of laboratories, space, equipment and dearth of qualified science teachers. The service was an experiment to find out what could possible be accomplished to minimise the specific difficulties of higher secondary schools in Delhi, especially in teaching science.

Commencing on the school television project, *Paul Neurath* (1968) stated that 'by and large, the televisions schools did some what better in the test than did the non-television schools.'

The main objectives of STV are two fold:

(a) To teach science subjects and thus, improve the quality of instruction in science, and

(b) To overcome the dearth of adequately qualified secondary school teachers.

(2) Satellite Instructional Television Experiment (SITE)

SITE, one of the largest techno-social experiments conducted in human communication, was started on August 1, 1975 for a period of one year. It is landmark in the use of sophisticated advanced technology for instructional purposes. The main objectives of this experiment conducted in 2330 village of six states, were to study the process of existing rural communication, the role of television as a new medium of education, and the process of change brought about by the community television in the rural structure. SITE has shown that it was possible with the new technology to reach a number of people in the remotest areas. Two types of programmes were telecast:

(i) Developmental education-programmes in the area of agriculture and allied subjects, health, family planning and social education were telecast in the evening for community viewing, and

(ii) The school programmes of 21½ minutes duration each in Hindi, Kannada, Oriya and Telugu were telecast on each school day for rural primary school children of 5-12 years age group.

(3) Delhi Agriculture Television (DATV) Project: Krishi Darshan

Encouraged by the success of school telecast, an experimental TV programme, Krishi Darshan, was initiated on January 26, 1966 for communicating agricultural information to the farmers. Community viewing facilities were provided in 80 villages in the union territory of Delhi. The research on 'Krishi Darshan' reported that the experiment was successful and that there was substantial gain in the information agricultural practices.

(4) Post-SITE Project

A new SITE continuity project was initiated in March, 1977 when a terrestrial transmitter was commissioned at Jaipur. Developmental programmes were telecast by this project. The main objective of SITE continuity project were to:

-   (i) Familiarise the rural masses with the improved and scientific know how about farming, the use of fertilisers and the maintenance of health and hygiene;

-   (ii) Bring about national and emotional integration, and

-   (iii) Make rural children aware of the importance of education and healthy environment.

(5) Indian National Satellite (INSAT)

Instructional television has further strengthened through the use of satellite technology. INSAT-1A, an indigenous multipurpose satellite, launched on Aprill 10, 1982 was declared unusable on September 6, 1982. Later on INSAT-1B, launched on August 30, 1983 became fully operational on October 15, 1983. Six states namely Andhara Pradesh, Bihar, Gujarat Maharashtra, Orissa and U.P. are covered under INSAT service. In each state, a cluster of 3-4 districts has been selected on the basis of backwardness of the area, availability of suitable developmental infrastructure and utilisation of existing production facilities.

The prime objective of the INSAT service is to bring the rural and backward areas into the national main stream, by quickening the development activities in these areas with mass media support. Therefore, the service is aimed at making rural masses aware of the latest developments in the area of agricultural productivity, health and hygiene.

Besides development programmes for community viewing, educational programmes (ETV) for two different age groups of school children (5-8 years and 9-11 years) are telecast daily. A capsule of 45 minutes duration consisting of two separate programmes—one for the lower age group and the other for the upper age group-are telecast regularly. Each programme runs for a duration of 20 minutes with five minutes change over time from one lesson to another.

(6) Higher Education Television Project (HETV) of UGC

The UGC-INSAT education television project also known as 'country wide classroom' was inaugurated on August 15, 1984. The planning and production of the programmes are actively managed— by the University Grants Commission (UGC). Under this programme, a one hour programme in English is on mise subjects presented on with the objective of general enrichment for undergraduates, educated public and the teachers as well. These programmes are aimed at improving the quality of higher education to create a dynamic classroom situation.

In order to give impetus to this scheme, a Mass Communication cell has been set up in the UGC and six Audio-visual Media/Mass Communication Research Centres have been set up at different institutions of the country. Besides producing programmes at these centres, some programmes are imported from other countries and are edited to suit the requirements of the Indian students. Presently, a one hour programme is telecast daily between 12.45 p.m. and 1.34 p.m. barring holidays and Sundays.

These programmes are produced in English by Mass Communi-cation Research Centres set up by the UGC at various universities such as Jamia Millia Islamia, New Delhi: Gujarat Vidyapeeth, Ahmedabad; Rookee University, Roorkee etc. The programme produced by various production institutions are pooled by the UGC for reviewing their quality and handling them over to doordarshan for telecast.

Indira Gandhi National Open University (IGNOU): Besides the printed text and occasional face-to-face contact sessions, IGNOU course-materials include audio and video cassettes, which are available for use at study centres and also on sale for home so for optimum utilisation of these audio-video components, IGNOU telecasts its video programmes for half an hour, thrice a week, from 6.30 a.m. to 7.00 a.m. on Mondays, Wednesdays and Fridays for the IGNOU students who would otherwise not have an opportunity to take advantage of these programmes.

Most of the IGNOU programmes supplement the printed texts-the master medium of learning-and cater,to a specific group of learners. Of course the general public also view these IGNOU programmes, and they do so with great interest.

Teacher's Programmes. In order to make the primary teachers aware of the innovations in teaching-learning processes, management of televised instruction, child psychology etc., the Central Institute of Educational Technology (CIET) produces programmes for teachers, known as 'Hints for Teachers'. Each programme of 45 minutes is telecast on every Saturday during school in their respective language of instruction. Doordarshan Kendra, Bombay also telecasts a 20 minutes programme for teachers every week.

SOME RECENT DEVELOPMENT IN TELEVISION

There are certain advanced electronic devices which are utilised by developed countries in their systems of teaching and learning. Though, many of these are not in frequent use in India, you, as a student of distance education, should have some basic about a few of these gadgets.

(1) Satellite Based Communication

The recent development in 'educational broadcasting in India is the emergence of the satellite based communication. It opened the doors for a new era in audio-visual communication. The first educational experiment to exploit the potential of satellites in disseminating information was undertaken in 1975. The experiment, popularly known as SITE, established that the remotest rural masses can also be approached through satellite based television programme.

Thereafter, INSAT-1A and INSAT-1B have provided us with the means to strengthen distance education systems in India. With the satellite technology available to us, India is able to beam television signals throughout the country making the benefits of the technology available at every doorstep. But not every home in our country has a TV set to receive the signals and thereby conceiving the benefits. The day when every home will have a set is till far off. The INSAT telecast could help break the feeling of isolation among widely scattered communities. India is quite advanced in having her own satellite technology and it has helped educators make comprehensive plans for education and development.

Some of the main advantages of satellite based communication systems can be summarised as follows:

(i) *Geographical Coverage.* In India where geographical and other factors add to the difficulties in establishing a nation wide network, satellite communication has proved more relevant and effective. It has the capacity to beam TV signals over a large distance and even in mountain areas where terrestrial system cannot serve.

(ii) *Impetus for Modernisation.* The technology of satellite communication is very helpful in promoting faster social change/development in a country like India. By bringing the world to the village through television, the communication system has opened the window for innovation and change and thereby quickened the process of modernisation.

(iii) *Immediacy in Implementation.* The satellite communication system being a centralised system the planning and implementation of educational innovations require a minimum amount of time. It can reduce the implementation time of any educational scheme.

(iv) *Cost Effectiveness.* Satellite technology provides a cost effective alternative educational system, the characteristics of the satellite to cover large masses spread over a vast distance makes it more cost effective than the terrestrial system. Since the cost of providing signals is not related to distance, remote communities can be served as cheap as communities in more central locations without incurring extra costs for cables, station building etc. Besides television broadcasts, INSAT-1B is being utilised. for various other purpose such as radio, telephone disaster warning and meteorology. It has provided the facility of two transponders (transponders are components of a satellite that retransmit signals to the earth) simultaneously available for the television network.

(2) Telephone Clubbed with Television

To make the television programmes a two-way communication, telephone facility can be clubbed with television broadcasts. The learners can raise their doubts/queries and ask for clarification. Due to lack of efficient telephonic services in 'India, it may take us more time to make use of this device for educational purposes.

(3) Video Tapes

Video-tape is an effective and useful medium for distance education. The video-tape technology, a comparatively new device in education, provides all the advantages of television, while eliminating its crucial disadvantage of imposing a rigid time schedule on its users. The video-tape, besides, may serve as an effective medium for illiterate learner who depends on spoken words and on visual images for communication.

Education video-tapes can be stored for future and can be used in wide range of teaching-learning situations, as and when required. Video-tape provides flexible learning situations as the students-user can exercise control over the presentation of the medium. Students can monitor the replay of the learning material with their individual pace of learning. That is, the video-tape technology allows learners to stop, interrupt and discuss the material as often and for as long as they wish.

(4) Multi-Media Package

The possible use of television programmes as a multi-media package is shown in figure:

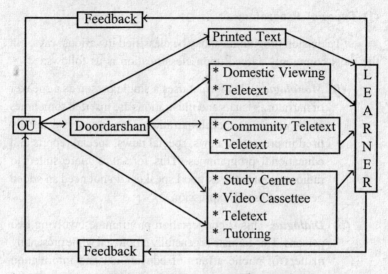

Fig. Use of TV in Multi-Media Package

A third scheme for the distribution of audio-visual component of a multimedia study package is the video cassette technology which is not so popular in the education sector in India because of the high cost of video cassette recorders/players (VCRs/VCPs) and the non-availability of educational programmes on cassettes. Only about four percent of the households, mainly in major cities in India possess VCRs. IGNOU is the first educational institution in the country to make use of video cassettes for teaching-learning purpose of its learners. VCR facility is made available at study centres where VCR facility has been provided by the university. Therefore, even for IGNOU the video cassette is of limited utility today.

Production of Educational Television Programme

The production of television programmes is a complex process and is performed in a team-mode. Before we discuss the process of the production of educational television programmes, we would like to discuss the type of television programmes which affect the programme production decision.

(1) Types of Programmes

Television programmes may be classified in various ways, but the most commonly agreed upon classification is as follows:

(i) *Monologue.* This format uses a single person as a speaker or narrator. Visuals and illustrations are inserted sometimes in the course of speech/narration. This format is generally used in presenting news, special news, special reports and educational programmes. This format is more suited to radio programmes, as good speakers do not need an added gesture of facial expression.

(ii) *Dialogue.* This is conversation programme involving two persons. This formate is generally empfoyed while presenting matters of public affairs of educational and information programmes. They are accompanied by appropriate visual support.

(iii) *Interview.* This formate is very effective when personal appeal of a well-known personality is expected to have an impact of its own. There are two parties in an interview based programmes. An interviewer, as a host of shown raises consecutive will prepared questions concerning a given subject. The guest-expert answers the questions with detailed explanations and illustrations where necessary. Renowned personalities and foreign dignitaries can be brought close to the viewers through interview. This formate is suitable for themes in the area of social studies.

(iv) *Panel of Forum.* In this formate a panel of experts discuss the subject matter which involves an element of controversy, or a subject which lends room for different opinions. The participants selected for a panel may also have different points of view. No script is necessary for such format but the narrator should be an experienced and expert communicator. This formate is very productive and may stimulate thinking among learners.

(v) Quiz. This formate requires the presence of two parties: *(a)* a quiz master (sometimes with a few assistants) and *(b)* a few participants. The quiz master puts a few questions to the participants and they compete to give the right answers. The vital part of these programmes is 'audience participation', an audience-member may have a chance to appear as a constant in the programme or, he may take part sometimes by sending his answer by post.

A television quiz differs from a radio quiz in more than one way. In a television quiz the questions are presented visually. The questions may include drawing of charts of maps of filling up of blank sections. Some experiments, some renowned personalities or some historic events can be shown and questions can be asked on them. The quiz format needs considerable thought, planing and efforts for its presentation.

(vi) Drama. This format is popular with the radio and with the television. Presenting a drama on television is difficult. The participant has to memories the whole content in contrast to the radio situation. This formal can effectively deal with the question of presenting simple problems and resolving them. It is difficult to depict the complex learning concepts through dramatisation. Furthermore, it is extremely complicated and expensive to produce a television drama. To produce a drama programme, one has to make careful production preparations and ensure effective production management.

(vii) Simulated Classroom. A simulated classroom is created and teaching activities are performed. This formate is very easy and economical. It needs completely scripted rehearsals before it is produced.

(viii) **Actualities.** The learners can be shown the actual happening of the events or educational activities. This format helps longer retention of what is learnt. It has emotional appeal and can hold learner's attention for a longer time. One has to be very prompt and efficient when one attempts to over actual/real event. It is also very expensive to pick up events from remote areas. We need to take care that time is not wasted and that the event being described has educational value.

(2) Script-Writing for Television

The preparation of the script is the final stage of television programme planning. The script contains information on characters, sources, content and sound and visual components. Thus, a script is a pre-visualisation of the type of programme to be produced. There are five main types of scripts. We describe them below:

(i) **Complete or Detailed Script.** A detailed script contains all relevant information for audio plus visual tracks. The speech and the visuals are clearly specified in order of their occurrence in the proposed presentation.

(ii) **Semi-Complete Script.** A semi-complete script lists topics and gives content-guidelines. Thus, it gives some (but not the whole) information about the characteristics, sources, content and types of eash segment of the sound and the scene planed to be presented. It is, usually, the subject experts who present a television programme based on a semi-complete script. This is the most popular type of script for educational programmes.

(iii) **Rundown of Fact Sheet.** The type of script list the topics, themes or items that are to be shown on camera. It also gives very broad indications of what should be said in the sound track. No special guidelines are given on production details of the visuals. This type of script is written for commercials usually.

(iv) **Open Script.** An open script does not give the entire sequence of wards for the mediator or the subject expert to use. Only outlines of topics and sub-topics are given. This may be referred to as an outline also. It is not much different from an action/time segmenting script.

(v) Action/Time Segmenting Script. This type of script lists the shown segments and sets in the order of sequences, beside their corresponding running and segment times. This format is more suitable to routine shown events, such as the news, panel discussions etc.

Steps in Script Writing

Script for television begins with a statement of the objectives. The questions about the script type does not arise at the initial stage. What is more important is the effect we want to create for/on the learner. We have to take pedagogical principles into account while preparing a script.

A script-write plays a key-role in a television programme production. He works in the 'language of the television.' He translates the ideas/content of the subject of presentation into the language of the TV *i.e.*, the language of pictures, words, sounds and electronic effects.

In writing script for television, there are certain steps for a writer to follow:

(1) Definition of objectives in behavioural terms, *i.e.*, defining what a learner is expected to accomplish after viewing a programme.

(2) Analysis of content and specification of themes and sub-themes based on research. (The content is arranged in a sequential manner and converted into appropriate visual terms at this stage.)

(3) Layout of programme, identifying shots and list of segments and sub-themes.

(4) Selection of most suitable format for presentation.

(5) Specification of programme length depending on the content and the characteristics of target audience.

(6) Preparation of the draft script.

(7) Pretesting, modification, rewriting and finalising the script.

Characteristics of a Good Script Writing. The following are the main features of goods script writing.

(1) It should be simple and clear.

(2) It should developed logically.

(3) It should be maintain the educational value of the programme.

(4) It should take care of individual differences among learners.

(5) It should be based on empirical findings of research studies.

(6) It should be attractive and must reinforce learner's interest.

(7) It should not be too long and heavily loaded with the content.

Procedure for Programme Production

Television programme production is a collective art. It includes personnel from software (academicians, producers, communication research, artists etc.) and hardware (cameraman, technicians. engineers etc.) All these people work in a team for the common cause of producing effective television programmes.

The process of production of instructional television programmes can broadly be discussed under four stages:

(1) Planning Stage

Three acts are performed:

*(i) **Defining Goals.*** This is the first step where the tangible objectives are fixed in behavioural terms. The objectives

are decided on the basis of what we want the learner to accomplish after viewing the programme. The target audience is identified for without identifying the target audience you cannot fix goals for your programme.

(ii) ***Preparation of Programme Brief.*** The programme briefs are prepared on the basis of need assessment (*i.e.*, the priority areas where television support is needed). The programme brief includes statements about objective, the take-off point the skills (s) assumed to have already been mastered by the learners, the scope of content to be included in the programme and the communication strategy, *i.e.*, the kind of treatment to be given to the content.

(iii) ***Script-Writing.*** On the basis of the predetermined objectives and the content outline, the script is written by the professionals. The format, the length, the content load etc. defined in the programme brief are followed while writing the script.

(2) Preproduction Preparation Stage

The stage include the following two steps:

(i) ***Preparation of Necessary Support.*** Preparation of personnel, collection of production facilities, arrangement of sets, sound and light and related activities are undertaken at this stage.

(ii) ***Rehearsal.*** This step is very important. It is here that the graphics slides, etc., to be used are adjusted, The presentation, the content, the length of the programme. the suitability by artists etc., are also judged during rehearsals.

(4) Evaluation Stage

The evaluation of educational television programme must be done continuously from the planning stage till the programme is used. Such evaluation is undertaken at two stages and two types of evaluation.

(i) **Formative Evaluation.** This is purposive evaluation to ensure the quality of the media product. The necessary improvements/changes are incorporated based on research findings. It is undertaken during the development of the programme, before something is 'formed'. It starts from the preparation of an audience profile and includes assessment of informational needs, preparation of writer's; briefs, script and prototype programme testing. Formative research is generally done by in-house researchers who work in close collaboration with the programme producers and the subject experts. This type of evaluation has flexibility in methodology to suit the objectives requirements of the problem.

(ii) **Summative Evaluation.** Summative evaluation is taken up after a programme is produced. The purpose of summative evaluation is to measure the overall impact of the programme which can help in framing long-range plans. It includes feedback collection, surveys and especially mounted field studies. Summative evaluation strictly follows the methodology of the fundamental research.

Advantages of Educational Television

From this theoretical perspective, we can state that, in favourable conditions, students learn efficiently from educational television. While television can be a powerful educational tool, its value is totally dependent on the quality of materials we transmit and the skill with which it is used.

The conclusions of research projects on educational television have shown that television is an effective tool in the hand of educators, if it is utilised imaginatively. It has proved its effectiveness/ supremacy in teaching certain subjects such as agriculture, science, geography, oceanography etc. Here we discuss the major prospects of educational television:

(i) **Social Equality of Education.** Television promotes the goal of social equality in education catering to the masses of rural background and those living in slums of urban areas. Television increases the effectiveness of instruction and cuts down dropout rates.

(ii) **Reduce Dependency on Teacher.** The students learn from television with their own efforts. They need minimum help from the teacher in case television is introduced into service.

(iii) **Higher Quality of Instruction.** Television programmes are well planned/organized and better presented than the usual classroom instruction.

(iv) **Flexibility.** Rapid and Continuing change in curricula and instructional methods are made possible through educational television. Courses can be constantly modified not only to update them but to incorporate the constantly changing needs of the society and the expansion of knowledge. This is not possible with some of the advanced electronic media like the video-disc.

(v) **Cost Effectiveness.** If television is utilised on a large scale, it proves cost effective. It can provide education throughout the country at a minimum cost without lowering the quality of instruction. The initial expenditure, of course, will be high.

(vi) **Use of the Best Available Teacher.** Education television makes educational opportunities equal throughout the country. The students in rural and deprived areas of the country, where educational resources are not available, get the same quality of education as the counterparts in the urban centres. The best teacher is equally available for very student. Thus, television bridges the gap between the poor and the rich, the privileged and the under privileged the rural and the urban.

(vii) **In-service.** Educational television can be used for in service training of educators in non-school hours. NCERT is telecasting a programme per week for teacher to improve their teaching methods and skills.

(viii) **Stimulation.** Through educational television, we can control the stimulation (the audio and the visual) to get desired response (learning).

(ix) **Mass Education.** Educational television can cater to the explosive increase in student numbers.

(x) **Logically Simple.** In operating an effective distance education system, educational television is logically very simple. The problems of planning, implementing and operating distance learning can be overcome to some extent by teaching through television.

(xi) **Combination of Audio and Vuleo Components.** Television has the advantage of the audio as well as the video. That is why it has a greater appeal than the radio and the print-media.

Limitations or Educational Television

As we have already mentioned the potential of television depends on how effectively it is being utilised for educational purposes.

In spite of the numerous advantage listed above, television has its limitations as a medium of education, some of the disadvantage are as follows:

(i) **Limitations of One-way-Communication.** Television is essentially a one-way-communication medium and as such it did not provide for interaction/discussion and hence does not provide for immediate feedback on learners' reactions, queries and doubts. It is a 'passive medium' as some educators who call it, as it turns learners, into mere (passive) receivers of information. The absence of active participation and lack of provision for feedback are likely to fail to sustain the interest and enthusiasm of learners.

(ii) ***Problem of Pacing Learning.*** The student may learn at his own speed through television broadcasts. He has to be attentive to grasp the content. The tele-teacher teaches at a speed which he assumes to be fairly suitable to an average learner of his target audience. He cannot cater to the individual differences in study-pace.

(iii) ***Costly Affair.*** Teaching through television is, a costly affair. The high sophisticated electronic gadgets demand huge amounts to be spent on the production/telecasting.

(iv) ***Insufficient Viewing Conditions.*** There are no adequate arrangements for viewjng the programmes in colleges/ schools.

(v) ***Poor Accessibility.*** Television is still beyond the purchasing capacity of a common man. It, therefore, cannot become a medium of the masses.

(vi) ***Difficulty to Integrate.*** There are difficulties in building television as a part and parcel of on-going activities of a classroom/school. The difficulties are due to absence of uniform syllabus, absence of teachers with similar training and calibre etc.

(vii) ***Visuals Becoming a Distraction.*** Sometimes the visuals themselves create distraction and interference in learning.

Scope of Educational Television

The extent and the pace of expansion of television that India has witnessed during the past three years has no precedent anywhere in the world including the developed countries. Beginning in July, 1984, the climax reached in the second half of 1985 when installation of a transmitter-a-day programme went uninterrupted till the end of the year. As a result, now Indian television has a network of 200 transmitters covering 70 percent of the total population of the country. By any standards, it should be considered a miracle and a real achievement.

The expansion of television network in India has strengthened the possibility of disseminating education to a wide area. In the following years, Indian educators and media planners will be getting increasingly involved in distance education (with the establishment of more and more state open universities) producing a considerably greater quality of course-wise and programmes. The programmes may be produced for both telecast and video cassettes in order to get the maximum benefit from this visual medium.

Institutions such as IGNOU and the state open universities will play a crucial role in the development of educational technology. The visual medium will improve the quality and influence of self-instructional materials. This will force the college to have more electronic gadgets for pedagogical activities, and training institutions will be required to incorporate the instructional technology in their curriculum.

Suggestions for Educational Television

The following suggestions in this connection are being placed here for educational television:

(1) To see that formative evaluation is effectively used in producing quality programmes, we should develop a training module for all those who are involved in planning, producing and evaluating programmes. The producer, being the overall in-charge of programme production, should be thoroughly trained in utilising research findings and thereby producing research supported programmes.

(2) Unfortunately, there is no training programme/institution for formative evaluation. Open universities engaged in the production of audio-visual programmes can come forward to formulate suitable training strategies. IGNOU being a

premier institution and the large consumer of educational media, can set the example for the rest of the institutions including Doordarshan and All India Radio (AIR). IGNOU has expertise in both research and production, and is equipped to undertake training courses of various durations and types.

(3) Research should be adequately exposed, not only to research methodology, but to the process of producing programme for education and development, *i.e.*, they should have expertise in researching, planning scripting, producing and editing programmes.

(4) The research should be good not only in drafting a report, but also in putting research findings in such a way that the producer concerned can make use of research inputs to improve the quality of programmes.

(5) Television is a potential medium of imparting training if it is properly planned and implemented. Training, refresher and orientation courses for various functionaries of an open university-course writers, counsellors, faculty etc., can be conducted through multi-media packages including television as an important component. The experience of NCERT (National Council of Education Research and Training) in conducting training programmes for primary school teachers should prove valuable for higher education as well. Regular/continuous and/or periodic training courses also can be organised using TV as a major medium.

(6) To encourage communication between a producer and a researcher, they should be allowed to inter-change other's positions. A researcher should be able to work as a producer and vice vesa.

□

8
Impact of Television on the Society

Television has profound impact on our society. It has changed the life styles of the people and has become a major influence in our culture. Unlike printing, which took hundreds of years to influence the culture, TV's impact was almost instantaneous.

Television has occupied an important position in homes and therefore, it is bound to make an impact on the individuals and the society Television, as a technology has changed the complexion and manner of conveying ideas to people and therefore, there is a need to examine the individual's relationship with the television.

Explaining the importance of television, Joseph aptly mentions, "Having earned a niche for itself in ways that are inimitable and unprecedented, TV has worked its way as an indispensable member of hundreds of millions of families across the world. To say that it merely educates, informs and entertains is an understatement. For in the seven decades since its invention by John Baird, the fascinating minutiae of how the medium works and influences has put it in a class of its own. From an apparently innocuous box it has metamorphosed into the protagonist, altering the very character of human transactions and shaping the way human beings think and behave. This has opened a Pandora's box and fulled a stormy debate on the role of television in human society".

In view of the fact that television in India is fast developing as a major source of mass enlightenment, leisure and pleasure, it is essential that it's impact in various areas is analysed. This can go a long way in providing guidelines for future developmental programmes of television in India. In terms of critics, comments and reviews no other medium, print, radio, cinema, caught the fancy of the analysts as television has.

Deodhar strongly feels that television has made contributions to the lives of people of India. Traditional media people consistently underestimate television's culture changing effects, mainly because they overlook certain characteristics that are so obvious that one takes them for granted. The most important feature of television is it's ability to deliver simultaneously into the intimate environment of millions of homes, touching lines of the entire household, ideas mingled with powerful drama.

Television has brought a revolutionary change in the way people receive information and understand the world by shifting them from direct experience of life and environment to the second hand or contrived experiences, which make people feel that they are directly experiencing the events or different places.

Research studies have pointed out that perceptions of the television messages, images and ideas shape the entire social system. The present out reach of television has created awareness and appreciation of the socio-cultural ethos of our different regions. Television has contributed to breaking the social barriers and inculcation of the scientific temper in our masses. Studies have shown that exposure to media leads to the appreciation of social and cultural ethos. For any social change to take place flow of information is of prime importance. It increases the understanding of the people regarding the issue and develops common feeling for the need for social change. Information bridges the gap of understanding between the people and helps them to unite for the cause. Television has done this job by contributing to the information explosion. Saxena also points out "Today's information explosion has opened the" floodgates of knowledge and curiosity. This is being attributed to the vast television exposure. A majority of our people live in remote villages, cut off from, what is Known as, modernity. Till late, they led a life submerged in age old conservatism. But now they are able to see and appreciate what is going around, adding to their information gain".

In United States of America television created a great impact on homogenization of a heterogeneous society. It played an important role in providing a common denominator to multi-lingual, multi racial American society which led to certain uniformity in societal reaction to situations or events, in developing common response in personal and social communication, in better appreciation of people with diverse beliefs and life styles. Nationwide television thus, could provide a platform for cultural meeting.

Television has made far reaching impact on various groups of people as well as in certain areas of our life, which are discussed here.

Children. Extensive communication research on the use of Indian Television for development purposes, has been conducted under SITE and KCP, but in-depth studies on impact of television on family life are few. However, television's impact on children has been the area of interest for social scientists.

The effect of television on home and family and particularly on children has become a matter of concern for behavioural science researchers.

Looking at the 'influence, it seems television has become like a member of the family. Studies have shown that it has upset the tone, tenor and stability of household activity and atmosphere, drew children away from their assigned and imperative tasks and discipline in growing up. It has strongly affected their attitudes and emotions. Thus it holds dangerous potential for damage of children's personalities.

Children watch the programmes with undue sex, violence and adult themes and glorified affluent lifestyles. This raises undue expectations among children and thereby pressures on the family. There are no programmes left on television schedule which could be exclusively called children's programmes, except channels like cartoon's, which again take children in to fantasy world.

Children and even housewives sit glued to TV regardless of time.

Various studies have been conducted regarding the impact of television on children. The observations of these studies have been:

1. Television provides children with thrill. The thrill syndrome results in behaviour abnormalities.

2. Television viewing has led children to under exposure to print.

A study by Media Advocacy Group (1980) observed that across all income and sex groups, parents have a problem with unrestricted viewing by children. They felt helpless in controlling the TV viewing by children. Inspite of its entertaining nature, television violence develops among viewers the sense of fear, victimization, mistrust, insecurity and dependence. The study suggested that the violence terror scenario may have several consequences which include the cultivation of aggressive tendencies, the accommodation to violence, the personalisation and isolation of offenders, the sporadic triggering of violent acts, and the levels of vulnerability and dependence felt by different groups living with the images of a mean and dangerous world.

Trivedi (1991) investigated the impact of TV on children. The study revealed that:

(1) Their activities of play outside home had decreased, they had given up playing indigenous games and their interests in cricket and other costly games had increased.

(2) Mischievous nature of children had calmed down after the introduction of TV in the house. Children had stopped wondering outside the house during TV programmes.

(3) TV advertisements created an adverse impact on the demands among children for new goods and items to be purchased for them and household. The demand for items of the daily use, such as fancy soap, etc. normally not used

by the members of the households, have increased more. These tendencies were more in middle class and posh class.

(4) The overall impact of TV on education of children was not reported to be adverse.

Television takes away children's play time which causes negative effects on children' s development. Thus, their physical and cognitive development get adversely affected. Watching television for extended period of time impacts upon the availability of time for their other activities such as playing, reading, visiting friends or relatives. It limits the time for homework and other forms of learning and thus contributes to lower academic performance.

Research has also indicated that children do not distinguish between programmes and advertisements. Children under 8 cannot appreciate commercial's 'selling' intent and they do not have the defenses against commercial appeals that adults have.

There are also positive effects of television on children. It fosters prosocial behaviour in children, for example, interaction with family members and friends, mannerisms, ways of greeting people and so on. TV viewing enhanced children's selection of materials used in spontaneous play.

There is growing sense of unease at what has been happening in the world of television and the manner in which ideas conveyed by television.

The television explosion has been experienced by western countries, which has drawn people's attention to the fact that:

* the more TV a child watches, the greater the influence it has on the child.

* Television promotes violation and/or aggressive behaviour.

* watching TV for long hours adversely affects reading and writing skills.

* Television as a passive activity takes children away from other, more direct, experiences.

* Television may encourage and influence early sexual activity, drug and alcohol abuse.

* The passivity induced by watching too much TV can lead to obesity.

Maniar (1994) studied the influence of television viewing on adolescents, which threw light on the positive side of television. The findings revealed high influence on development of civic competence and moderate influence on other development tasks such as body image, sex roles, independence, future roles, preparation for family life and preparation for career. Adolescents reported that the programme related to health such as Gharelu Nuskhe, Yoga, Head over Heels, Aerobics, Das Kadam etc. made them curious of health and body and helped them to adopt good health practices and made them figure conscious. Television viewing facilitated their discussions on sex matters and understanding of the changes occurring in their body.

Television made adolescents aware of social issues like dowry and adoption of child. They became informed about various career opportunities through the serials like Aur Bhi Hai Rahen. They also reported that their civic competence increased and feeling of patriotism developed in them after viewing programmes and documentaries or conservation of resources, environmental degradation, political discussions and analysis, and serials like Saudaa, Bharat Ke Shahid, Mashaal etc. They also became aware of consumer rights and laws, women and law, through programmes like Rajni, Apake Adhikar, Nari Tu Narayani and so on. They also learnt about the cultures of various states of India as well as other countries.

Nathani (1986) found that television viewing motivated adolescents to participate in sports, drama, music and adventurous activities. Mahajan (1988) found that television helped people in increasing their familiarity with different religions.

It is evident that television has both positive and negative impact on children. The world as TV represents it is not always true to reality but children who grow up with such representations tend to believe and know the world as picturised on TV. This is mainly due to the reason that children specific programmes are hardly telecast by Doordarshan. Thus, children are left with no alternative but to watch whatever is offered. Parents have to decide the kinds of controls they will exercise to limit the time and content of their children's television viewing.

Family. Apart from children as a specific group, family as a whole has also been under the profound impact of television.

The rich and middle class families rushed to purchase television sets shortly after the medium entered the popular culture. Many lower class people went into debt to own this luxury item which gradually has become the necessity. Many family activities, which were cherished earlier, such as after dinner conversations among family members, parents, reading bedtime stories to the children, praying or reading religious books at night were replaced by TV watching.

Television has been reported to be giving a feeling of importance and relaxation from closed environment and monotonous living conditions. male members of the family have started spending more time at home. People have shown increase in the knowledge of political, social and economic issues of the country through the programmes such as talks and discussions.

It has been reported that there was marginal saving on account of TV in comparison to earlier expenditure on entertainment. It did not show any impact on the aged and old in the family except that they found it easy to spend their time. In case of entertainment, many viewers of TV have expressed that they get more entertainment and great satisfaction of its utility by watching sports and games on TV rather than sitting in the stadium or viewing film in a theatre. They enjoy watching film or sports programmes in relaxed, cosy and comfortable way. This affected the film industry and it did face serious challenge in eighties due to decrease in revenue. It is trying to face the challenge competently by excelling in technical aspect and its music and sound system.

Advertisements on TV have helped people to make their choice and selection of goods of household use. It has boosted consumerism among the people and raised aspirations of the people and their standard of living. It has resulted into westernized life style and widened the gap between information rich and the information poor.

Socially, it has been observed and reported that the frequency of visits to relatives and friends which helped in maintaining affectionate and intimate social relationships have been considerably reduced after the television invasion of homes.

A study by Trivedi (1991) showed that religious activities of the families were disturbed due to TV. Religious serials and programmes on TV were looked upon by people as adding sanctity to their house.

Politics. Television has contributed to political education of the masses. It gives extensive visual coverage to the political events of the country because of which people have become familiar with the day to day political programmes of TV and have become familiar with the national and international political figures. It has made many people interested in politics who found it a boring subject in non-TV days.

Indian Television has been criticized for over highlighting the activities of the ruling party and programmes taken up by it, which often raises doubts about the reliability of such broadcasts. It is observed that television has been effective in creating some kind of political awareness even among children and illiterates. Such as names of the prime minister., chief minister, importance of voting, how to vote, which party has won in the election, etc. To some extent, TV has familiarized rural masses with international political personalities also.

A study was conducted in ten villages of Ranga Reddy District of Andhra Pradesh to assess the impact of television on rural folk and to see how far the present political programmes on television are useful to the masses in creating political consciousness among them. The study revealed that television created interest in knowing further about politics, parties, increased knowledge about the prevailing situation in the society, and value of voting. Persons watching news in only Telugu 'were politically less aware as compared to those watching in Hindi and English in addition to Telugu. There was small increase in the political awareness of the people watching for longer hours.

IMPACT OF CABLE TV

Cable TV has proliferated all over the country. A variety of channels are available to the viewers and viewers have favoured them. As a result, the viewership for channels like BBC and STAR TV is increasing gradually. Various types of programmes are being telecast by these channels such as, news, serials, sports, film based programmes and music programmes. This has affected adversely the cinema houses in many cities as the percentage of people who prefer to watch movies in theatre has gone down by 25 to 40 per cent. Video libraries which had mushroomed in eighties are also closing down. There are differences of opinion regarding the impact of foreign programmes on Indian culture. Studies have shown that the expansion of cable and satellite TV will have profound effect on children, *i.e.* on their studies, work habits, play activities, sleeping pattern, their relationships with others, etc.

The expansion of TV viewers through satellite, cable TV or Doordarshan has enormously increased the scope for advertising.

Eashver (1994) studied the impact of cable TV on women in terms of activities, time management and interactions with family members and the outside world. Findings of the study revealed that cable TV did have a profound effect on the activities of women. It increases considerably the isolation of women by restricting her interactions with the husband, children, other members of the family, friends, and neighbours. This happens both due to her own involvement with the TV, as well as the involvement of the other members of the family, in watching the cable TV and regular TV programmes.

The second major effect of cable TV emerged was that it restricts the exposure of the housewife to the other media including regular TV, press, radio, books etc. They watched two feature films a day, thus having exposure to all kinds of feature films.

The advent of cable TV has more than anything else awakened people to the threat posed by the electronic media to the printed word. Their apprehensions are quite understandable. With the advent of Cable TV, viewers are exposed to a variety of programmes generally more interesting, entertaining and informative than anything seen on Doordarshan before. Viewers of all ages sit glued to the television. With the coming of satellite television in India, children spend upto four hours everyday watching TV programmes. It provides them thrill and entertainment which does not add to their knowledge or creativity. According to several school principals, in New Delhi, children were showing behavioural abnormalities. They were reading and writing much less and generally suffering from under exposure to printed material.

Consumerism. Television expanded the consumer culture and made it a mass culture by providing new outlet for selling the products. It became a major medium of advertising. The commercialisation of Indian television intensified the nation wide policy debate about television's role. Those favouring commercialisation claim that it provides funds for improving production of TV programmes, while the detractors of the policy argue that such TV programme quality comes at a high price.

It encourages competition among advertisers for larger audiences. Moreover advertiser cater to urban masses and the needs of poor are neglected. Teleshopping networks have developed all over the country. It is another method of selling consumer goods. It is designed to stimulate instant sales. This has further boosted the consumerism.

A study conducted by ORG revealed that majority of the viewers under the study purchased ommercial products after seeing them advertised in television. Younger viewers, heavy viewers and those with higher levels of mass media exposure showed higher levels of consumerism.

Education. The educational network of Doordarshan kept on expanding as the Television Service developed, adding newer areas and dimensions. Today, most of the programme originating Kendras of Doordarshan run regular programmes, bearing on education whether formal or informal or both. Television programmes are now regularly available from primary classes to university level.

Besides Doordarshan, organisations like IGNOU, UGC, NCERT and Education Department of State Governments are fully involved today in the use of television as a medium of education.

Recently, IGNOU conducted a two-way-audio and one way video experiment by linking up the experts in Delhi TV studio and the audience in the studios in the far off cities. Here audience could ask questions and get instantaneous replies from the experts on television. This provides the opportunity for audience to participate and give feed back in the communication process.

Doordarshan puts out programmes for various age groups. Some of its centres telecast programmes on 'Adult Education'. Bombay Doordarshan's programme entitled 'Gyandeep' was the most successful one by Doordarshan in the area of Adult Education. It was considered very effective in educating the adult audience, in whose life the gap was created due to illiteracy or failure to continue schooling. The similar programme by Delhi Doordarshan did not gain the popularity.

Television has imparted non formal education to people and made them better informed, aware and educated in the areas like consumer education, vocational education, education to industrial workers, civic education, safety, health, legal education, and so on. Such efforts are sporadic and therefore do not create boosting impact. Most of them lack messages of general interest.

Vedantam, an education correspondent of the 'Deccan Herald' felt that at present 10 percent of TV time set aside for education is not enough, if we want the next generation to become something good. Doordarshan has failed to create an entertainment channel which educates at the same time. UGC programmes on TV are highly academicised in nature, catering to those, who already have access to that kind of education. She felt that Doordarshan has not been able to deliver the goods. Perhaps, it is unable to cope with its multifarious responsibilities. It has lack of direction especially in its educational thrust. So, if this area of responsibility at least is shifted to another organisation, where specialists in the field could devote their complete attention, we may be able to look forward to a more constructive, balanced and really useful TV education. Something on the lines of the BBC open university programmes.

Very few studies on impact of these programmes have been carried out so as to draw any conclusions or generalisations.

Non Formal Education. With the launching of National Literacy Mission, the emphasis was laid on the utilisation of television for adult education and the programmes of general interest and social awareness were broadcasted. The impact studies of these programmes revealed that adults watching television had become better sources of information, males discussed television programmes more and females gained more knowledge in the areas of health and nutrition innovations, family planning and social problems. Television helped adult in developing favourable opinion regarding adults education.

Cherian (1986) studied the impact of the selected Health and hygiene, nutrition and family planning programmes of PIJ Television (Under Kheda Communication Project) on the rural people of the Kheda District. The findings revealed that there was significant gain in knowledge in the experimental groups about the importance of green leafy vegetables, polio vaccination and laproscopy.

Many studies have highlighted the fact that the deprived sections remained unreached by the television medium.

The broad content of rural programmes included areas like agriculture, animal husbandary, employment schemes, agricultural institutions, interviews with progressive farmers, documentaries on villages, cooperation and marketing, social education, healthcare and cultural programmes.

A study to examine the status and role performance of television *vis-a-vis* other media in villages threw light on the following points.

* About 30 percent of the villagers remained completely unexposed to television. The non-participation among females was to the extent of 53 percent, while it was about 23 percent among the males.

* Illiteracy had been found to be an important barrier to television exposure and this was contrary to the general presumption that TV can effectively communicate with the illiterate audience.

* These having exposure to other media like print, radio, etc. maintained greater interaction with Television.

* The community TV sets exist only in better-off villages.

* The interior villages mostly depended upon traditional channels like the weekly market, kin groups, mends, local leaders and to a fairly large extent the radio.

To summarise, television has had some influence and undoubtedly on the social, cultural, political environment of the urban and rural masses. In-depth studies need to be taken up to find out the impact of television in various age groups. Although television has contributed to development of a nation, it's potential for development has not been fully tapped.

However, the major satellite and cable television companies in the world view India as one of the top five TV markets in the 21st century. And now with the supreme court judgement on freeing airwaves from government monopoly, and private broadcasters, TV programme is poised to break new grounds in a big way as never before.

Originally television was a novelty, but now it has become medium. It is diffusing rapidly in India and intensifying the debate about it's socio-culture impact on Indian society.

Advantages of Television

Television has the intimacy of radio and the believability of personal participation. It has intimate approach due to which it becomes more appealing and attracts the attention and interest of the people. As it combines all the elements, namely, sight, sound and motion it becomes possible to show variety of indoor and outdoor situations, scenes and places effectively. Thus, it is very effective in stimulating and inspiring new insights, discoveries and inventions.

Television breaks the barrier of illiteracy, as due to its combination of sight, sound and motion, understanding of the message becomes easier, whereas, with the print media like newspapers and magazines, readers have to put a lot of efforts on reading and understanding the message which may not be possible for illiterates. It provides entertainment, informs, educates and persuades and thus performs all functions of mass media.

It makes news releases and features action oriented and colorful for greater impact. The visual experience of watching TV is more dynamic and meaningful due to the movement and sound associated with it. Thus it becomes most exciting and efficient means of mass communication.

Television can bring the live programmes right into the living room of the audiences. This provides the vicarious experience of participating in the event.

Limitations of Television

Television requires a fully developed Television network and electrical supply for broadcasting the programmes. Therefore, inspite of 85 percent of area covered by television network in India, people in remote as well as rural areas are not able to take advantage of television due to lack or absence of electrical supply.

Television is an expensive mass medium compared to other mass media, because not only the television sets are expensive but both production of television programmes and their utilisation are expensive unless they are used extensively. Moreover, TV programme production requires trained personnels.

There is a need to learn about the beneficial and harmful effects of television, exploit it's positive potential and prevent the damage it can do to the various groups of people.

TELECASTING

Television extends the senses of vision and hearing beyond their natural limits. It involves electrical transmission and reception of pictures in motion and accompanying sounds. Like motion pictures, television consists of series of successive images which are registered on the brain as a continuous picture because of the persistence of vision. Human vision employees many hundreds of thousands of separate electrical circuits in the retina to the brain, to convey simultaneously in "lwo dimensions the whole content of the scene on which the eye is focused, in electrical communication, however, it is feasible to employ only one such circuit (the broadcast channel) to connect the transmitter and the receiver.

This fundamental disparity is overcome in television by a process of image analysis and synthesis. The scene to be televised is first translated into an electrical image, and then broken up into an orderly sequence of electrical impulses that are sent over the channel one after the other. At the receiver end, the impulses and translated back into a corresponding sequence of lights and shadows and these are reassembled in their correct position on the viewing screen. This sequential reproduction of visual images is feasible only because the visual sense displays persistence; that is, the brain retains the impression of illumination for about 0.1 second after the source of light is removed from the eye. IF the process of image synthesis occurs within less than 0.1 second, the eye is unaware that the picture is being reassembled piecemeal and it appears as if the whole surface of the viewing screen was continuously illuminated. It is then possible to recreate more than 10 complete pictures per second and thereby simulate the motion of the scene so that it appears to be continuous. To depict rapid motion smoothly 25 to 30 complete pictures are transmitted per second, and to provide detail sufficient to accommodate a wide range of subject matter, each picture is analysed into 300,000 or more elementary details. This analysis implies that the rate at which these details are transmitted over the television system exceeds 4,000,000 per second.

This dream of extending human vision, as the telegraph and the telephone had extended communication by means of signals for words, began to be realised in 1883 when a German scientist Paul Nipkow, invented a scanning device that could breakdown an image into a sequence of tiny pictorical elements. Based on the photoconductive properties of selenium, the fact that its electrical conduction varies with the amount of illumination, Nipkow's device was a spirally perforated rotating disk with a photoelectric cell that converted light into electrical impulses. Until the advent of electronic scanning, all workable television systems depended on some form or variation (*e.g.* minor lensed disks etc.) of the mechanical sequential scanning method exemplified by the Nipkow disk.

Response of selenium to changes in light was slow. However, in 1913 research in Germany resulted in a potassium hydride-coated cell with improved sensitivity and the ability to follow rapid changes of light. This made possible for the first time a practical working system.

K.F. Braun of Germany had introduced a cathode ray with fluorescent screen, that produced visible light when struck by a beam of electrons. In 1907, Russian scientist Boris Rosing suggested its use in the receiver of a television system that, at the camera end, made use of mirror-drum scanning. He succeeded in transmitting and reproducing some crude geometrical patterns. However, before this in 1904 the British physicist J.A. Fleming had invented the two-electrode valve and American Lee De Forest had added the grid in 1906 and made amplification possible, which was another essential step towards practical television.

In 1908 the Scottish electrical engineer A.A. Camphel Swinton outlined a method, that is the basis of modern television. He proposed the use of cathode-ray tubes magnetically deflected, at both camera and receiver, the former being a mosaic screen of photoelectric elements, the image of the scene to be transmitted was focused into this screen, the back of which was then discharged by a cathode-ray beam tracing out a line-by-line scanning sequence. In 1917 the U.S. inventor D.M. Moore produced the neon gas discharge lamp and made it possible to vary the light intensity at the receiver by varying the electrical input to the neon lamp, thus in effect producing modulated light. This was adopted by J.L. Baird in England and C.F. Jenkins in the U.S. Both of them began experimenting in 1923 with mechanical methods using the Nipkow principle. Baird gave the first demonstration of true television in 1926 by electrically transmitting moving pictures in half tones. These pictures were formed on only 30 lines repeating about 10 times per second. The result were crude but with this television became practical technology and further research was stimulated. It also formed the basis for some experimental broadcasting in England between 1929 and 1935.

In the USA, Ernest P.W. Alexanderson of General Electric laboratories began daily TV tests on the experimental station W2XAD in 1928. On September 11, 1928, General Electric presented the first dramatic production on television, 'The Queen's Messenger'. Sound of this programme was carried on radio station WGY. Three motionless cameras were used and the image for the viewer was seen on a 3-by-4 inch screen. In 1931 the Radio Corporation of America (RCA) made experimental tests over station 2XBS in New York.

Mechanical scanning had its drawbacks. It could not provide sharpness of detail. Further advances were possible only after the development of electronic scanning, the roots of which go back to experiments by Heinrich Hertz and Wilhelm Hallwachs (in the 1800's) to Einstein's publication of theory of photoelectric effect (1905) and to Karl Braun's discovery that he could change the course of electrons in a cathode-ray tube by subjecting them to a magnetic field (1906).

Vladimir K. Zworykin, a student of Rosing went to America after the World War I and developed a crude, but workable, partly electronic TV system in 1923. He evolved the principles of the iconoscope the basic tube of the television system, that was demonstrated at the New York World Fair in 1939. In 1930, Philo T. Farnsworth had, also developed a new electronic scanning system that made TV pictures suitable for the home.

In Britain the Electric and Musical Industries (EMI) set up in 1931 a television research group under Sir Isaac Shoenberg, which evolved a complete and practical system based on *(1)* a camera tube known as the Emitron—an advanced version of the iconoscope-and *(2)* an improved height-vacuum cathode-ray tube for the receiver. Shoenberg proposed the use of 405 line with 50 frames per second, and interlaced scanning to give 25 pictures per second without flicker. The British Government authorised the British Broadcasting Corporation to adopt these standards as well as the complete EMI system, from the outset of the world's first public high-definition service which was launched in London in 1936. Until 1964 they formed the sole basis of the British service, later being gradually superseded by the international 625-line standard.

In the USA, the National Broadcasting Company (NBC) a subsidiary of RCA, then presided over by David Sarnoff began experimental broadcasts from the Empire State Building in 1932. On November 6, 1935, E.H. Armstrong announced his development of frequency modulation (FM) broadcasting which was adopted for the transmission of sound for television in 1941. By the mid-1950s electronic television was fast advancing in all respects and questions of basic standards (number of lines and frames per second) were discussed. The USA soon adopted a picture repetition rate of 30 per second while in Europe it became 25 per second. These two standards have been perpetuated and all the countries in the world use one or the other, though technical advances have now obliterated the original need for disparity. The arguments in relation to the number of lines was based on the need for an effective compromise between adequate picture definition and, a frequency bandwidth that could be technically and economically acceptable. World standardisation has never been achieved, though for new television services all countries are adopting one of only two standards, namely 525 lines per picture at 30 picture per second—the U.S. standard-and 625 lines at 25 picture per second, usually known as the European standard. Converters are used-when programmes are transmitted between countries with different standard. Regular television broadcasting began in the United States in 1941 but most other countries apart from Great Britain were not ready to begin services until 1950, when television was widely introduced throughout the world. Technical advances have been continuous since 1945 onwards particularly the great improvements in camera tubes, the image orthicon and the vidicon, the latter of which was able to effectively exploit the photoconductivity principle. By the early 1950s television had become so widely established, that the time was ripe to tackle the problem of creating television images in natural colours.

A German patent of 1904 contained perhaps the earliest proposal of colour television. In 1925 Zworykin filed a patent for an all-electronic colour television system. However, the first practical demonstration of television in colour was given by Baird in 1928. He used mechanical scanning with a Nipkow disk having three spirals of 30 apertures, one spiral for each primary colour in sequence.

A team led by H.E. Ives at Bell Telephone Laboratories in 1929 transmitted 50-line colour television images between New York City and Washington, D.C. In the same year Frank Gray of Bell Laboratories applied for a patent that described a method of transmitting two or more signals over a single channel, thus introducing new principles that were the foundation of modern (compatible) colour television as it was developed about 20 years later. It soon become clear that two basic approaches to colour television were possible *(i)* Frame-by-frame sequential transmission of signals corresponding to each of the three primary colours, *(ii)* Signals representing the three primary colours were transmitted simultaneously. The first method was relatively simple but involved a increased rate of scanning in order to avoid colour flicker, with resulting transmission difficulties both from the higher bandwidth and the inability to use existing black and white receivers to reproduce any pictures originated in colour. This system was called non-compatible. In the second system, which appeared daunting at first, any pictures originated in colour could still be receivable in black and white on a black and white receiver.

In 1938 George Valensi or France patented a method that enabled the output from a single transmitter to be received by special (colour) television receivers and the ordinary (black and white) receivers.

In the late 1980s experimental work on colour television was taken up in Britain and the U.S. Peter Goldmark of the CBC in United States and Baird in UK demonstrated sequential systems using rotating colour filters on the cameras and the receivers. The CBS method was used for some experimental broadcasts before World War II and later Federal Communications Commission authorised it as a service in 1951. However, only a few months later this was abandoned.

The National Television Systems Committee (NTSC) of the U.S. gave serious attention of this work and in 1953 a system capable of operating within the current black and white standards was developed and was accepted by the FCC. The basic principle of this NTSC system is the combination of two image transmissions. One carrying informations about brightness including the finest details of a television scene to which black and white receivers respond; the other of coarser structure carrying colour information. In the USA public broadcasting using the NTSC system began in 1954. The same system was adopted by Japan in 1960. Other countries favoured modifications of this system. One such system was devised by W. Bruch of the German Telefunken Company, known as PAL (phase alternation line). The other SECAM (System electronique couleur avec memorie) deffering rather more radically was developed by Heneri de France in Paris. Both the alternatives PAL and SECAM aimed at reducing the sensitivity of the colour system to certain forms of distortion encountered in transmission and broadcasting and has special application to European conditions. Countries were divided in their preferences. In 1967 Britain and West Germany began colour broadcasting using the PAL system while in the same year France and the USSR introduced colour using SECAM system. One or the other of these three systems was adopted by all countries later.

Short History

In August 1921, The Times of India in collaboration with the Posts and Telegraphs Department broadcast from its Bombay office a special programme of music 'at the request' of the then Governor Sir George Lloyd who tuned in at Poona. This was perhaps the first experimental transmission rather demonstration transmission in India.

In 1922, F.E. Kosher, Managing Director of the Indian States and Estern Agency Limited approached the Governor for the establishment of broadcasting services in the country. A few months later, after a broadcasting conference held in Delhi, sanction for broadcasting was given to the Calcutta station which operated in conjunction with the Radio Club of Bengal. Its first programme was in November 1923. Later a similar service was started by Bombay Radio Club in June 1924. Both the stations operated on small transmitters loaned by the Marconi company. Similar stations were also set up in Madras, Karachi and Rangoon. The Hindu has reported the formation of the Madras Presidency Radio Club on May 16, 1924 with Viscount Goshen, Governor of Madras, as its patron. The report referred to representative of the Marconi company who addressed the meeting "on the working and progress of Radio Clubs in England and some of these recently organised in Bombay and Calcutta". The resolution said, A club to be called the Madras Presidency Radio Club be formed in Madras whose primary object will be to stimulate interest in and further, the study of Radio communication and allied arts," and was moved by C.V. Krishnaswamy Chetty who had brought components of a tiny 40 Watt transmitter from England. Formal inauguration of this service took place on July 31, 1924. Later a 200 watt transmitter was used to broadcast a two-and-half hour programme of music and talks every evening with a special morning transmission on Sundays and holidays. The Club was located in Holloways Gardens, Egmore (now occupied by the play fields on Don Bosco school). This Club was on the air until 1927 when financial difficulties led to its closure. The transmitter, was donated to the Madras Corporation which resumed a regular service on April 1, 1930 and continued it until 1938 when the station was absorbed by all India Radio. With the publication of Indian Radio Times on July 15, 1927, the Indian Broadcasting Company announced the imminent opening of its Bombay station. It was inaugurated by the then Viceroy Lord Irwin on July 23, 1927. Five weeks later the Calcutta station of the company was opened by the Bengal Governor Sir Stanley Jackson. Both the stations had a 1.5 KW transmitter with an effective medium wave transmission range of approximately 48 Kms.

The inauguration of IBC's Bombay station and the London-Bombay "Beam Wireless Service" was reported by the Times of India in a banner headline reading, "Viceroy Inaugurates a Wireless Era For India." Messages of greetings were received from Sir John Reith, newly appointed Director General of the BBC and from the Union Internationale Radiophonie, Geneva. In his welcome address to the gathering at the "Radio House", at Apollo Bunder in Bombay, the IBC Chairman, Sir Ibrahim Rahimtoola said that the Bombay station "is only the first in a chain of stations which we hope will one day cover the whole of India." The Statesman of August 27, 1927, quoted a Rangoon message to the effect that "Every item of the programme in connection with the opening of the broadcasting station at Calcutta, was distinctly heard in the buildings facing the High Court, But subsequently moved to No.1, Garstin Place when formal broadcasting commenced." C.C. Wallick from the BBC was appointed the Station Director and Nripendra Nath Majumdar, a musician of repute to assist him. A programme journal 'Betar Jagat' was also started in 1929. Both the stations had a strong cultural orientation and attracted some of the best talent. The Calcutta station initiated a "Ladies Hour" programme and a Radife Drama Club. A music lesson programme was started in 1930 under the direction of the famous K.C. Dey. This was followed by lessons in Rabindra Sangeet by Pankaj Mullick.

The IBC went into liquidation after a short life of three years, having accumulated a loss of Rs. 2 lakhs only. But because of public insistence the service was continued by the liquidator of the company at the expense of the Government of India.

TECHNICAL FEASIBILITY OF DECENTRALISED TV AND RADIO

As you are aware, there has been a phenomenal growth in television coverage in recent years. In fact, television in the true sense was born in India in 1984. We had a modicum of television operating in the country till that time, but no one could have imagined in 1982, that in just 8 years from then we would be in the state that we now find ourselves in. This has had its positive as well as negative aspects, but we could discuss that a little later. Today the Doordarshan network consists of something like 479 transmitters the bulk of which are low power transmitters (LPT), meaning those with power outputs of 100 watts or less. Out of these 479 transmitters, the high power ones are only 55 which will increase to 84 after the completion of on-going schemes. In terms of coverage, we today claim to provide signal to something like 76 per cent of the country's population which is contained in only 54.5 per cent of the area of the country. In other words, half the country in a physical sense is still not covered. And we might add that when we say 76 per cent of the population is served by television, we are telling only a half truth. This number includes the population in the fringe areas where people must use very tall antennas and in several cases, also boosters to be able to obtain satisfactory reception.

Upon completion 'of the on-going schemes, which will mean setting up of another 30 odd high power transmitters which are in various stages of implementation, (we will probably complete the programme in the next year or year-and-a-half), the population coverage will increase to 84 per cent and the area coverage to 69.6 per cent. But if we apply the more stringent international standards which determine the usefulness of a service, then the actual population coverage will be no more than about 60 per cent. This is startling, as it is generally believed that TV is now available throughout the country.

The present network of transmitters is supported by 18 programme production centres which have been in operation for quite a while now. The number next year is likely to rise to 48 after the on-going projects are completed. Several of these remaining 30 programme production centres have been completed, but we have not commissioned them basically because we have an acute shortage of staff, particularly in the cadres of producers and production assistants. We also have a very large fleet of field production facilities (Outside Broadcast Vans and EFP Vans-roughly 23 of them which have given us a great deal of mobility).

We have a vast network of TVRO terminals which work with the INSAT satellites for the purpose of receiving satellite delivered programmes for rebroadcast purposes. We also operate a full-fledged teletext service, presently only in Delhi but hopefully, we will be able to extend it to Bombay shortly and Madras and Calcutta a little later.

The backbone of the system at the present time is this very large network of low power transmitters (LPTs). We chose this model very appropriately in the early '80s because this met three basic requirements which had been set for the expansion programme at that time. The first was that we must be able to implement the expansion programme in the quickest possible time. It was also laid down that equipment must be obtained from indigenous sources and most importantly, we had to be able to locate these transmitters in areas of high population density so that we could have maximum yield by way of population coverage in the quickest possible time. This model served us very well because at that point of time, investing Rs. 30-35 lakhs in an LPT enabled us to cover a city, let us say as large as Aligarh with a population of over 5 lakhs. Today this model of expansion has become inapplicable and unremunerative for the simple reason that we have covered all towns with a population in excess of 50,000. Every new LPT that we set up now will not serve a very large population. The big problem with this LPT model of expansion has been that we have consumed our frequencies very rapidly and we already have pad to move over to the Ultra High Frequency (UHF) band. The VHF bands I and III have been more or less exhausted. So this approach has been inefficient from the frequency utilisation point of view.

This LPT model of expansion has led to the creation of a network which is Delhi-centric. We have a national programme which is satellited and received at various locations and rediffused using terrestrial transmitters. There is no local programme injection except at the 18 programme production centres which I mentioned previously. But this has been only the very first step forward in our movement towards the ultimate objective, which has been declared as a 3-tier broadcasting structure with distinct elements of national, regional and local services. Parallel with this development of a national service, we have now also introduced regional services. We have satellite-based regional services operating in 3 states-Anhbra Pradesh, Maharashtra and Tamil Nadu-where the programmes produced at the capital centres are uplinked to the satellite, received back at all the transmitting centres in the states concerned and re-broadcast.

We have also established similar regional services in 3 other states, *i.e.,* West Bengal, Kerala and Punjab but in these states, we use the terrestrial microwave network, not the satellite.

Our emphasis on expansion of the national service has been viewed adversely by some media critics. In fact, in the morning, Dr. Rao made a forceful plea that if we cannot link up the LPTs with local or state programme production centres, these might just as well be closed down. He asked whether there was a way by which this could be done. Well, the easiest way, of course, is to send a team of people with sledge hammers to break them!

We were going in the right direction, but somewhere along the way, the national service came to be confused with a Delhi originated service. This was not the concept. The national service was expected to be composed of programme contributions from the regional centres. It was basically an assembly function that was to take place at Delhi. This was certainly not conceived as a Delhi-based service. But one tends to take soft options. Because of various constraints, both in terms of the manpower, financial resources and so on, that concept could not be realised. We must admit that in today's context. the national service does tend to be an extension of the Doordarshan Kendra at Delhi. However, we have wilfully moved on to the development of the regional services (the second tier of the eventual structure), and these already operate in 5 states.

Hopefully, when adequate satellite capacities become available (we have had major setbacks in the INSAT system), we should be able to extend this regional services to all other states. Then the worry we all have about LPT's carrying programme services that are irrelevant need not to exist. We think that kind of a situation will develop in the course of the next few years. If our own satellite programme does not move forward as planned, we will still have the lease option and we should be able to obtain additional capacities.

This is where we stand at present. The question specifically posed to me is about the second channel. We see the second channel as the third level of the proposed 3-tiered structure, which is the local service. As you are aware, we have a second channel already operating in the 4 metropolitan cities-Delhi, Bombay, Calcutta and Madras. We have proposed the establishment of the second channel in 16 other places, all state capitals except the smallest ones.

Is it possible to establish a second channel purely from the point of view of technology? The answer, quite clearly, is yes, but let us see how that can be done. The simplest way, of course, is to develop additional networks of transmitters. We have a network of transmitters servicing the first channel We need, more or less, a similar number of transmitters to service the second channel. We did a rough exercise, again a-year-and-a-half ago, and we came to the conclusion that if we have to build a second channel providing an aggregate of 95 per cent coverage of the country, then we will need to establish something like 220 high power transmitters and 129 LPTs and transposers.

Money is not the only problem. An even bigger problem is the limitation of available space in the radio frequency spectrum. As we said earlier, we have consumed Band I in the VHF range, and more or less consumed Band III as well. We have moved on to the UHF range of frequencies. We met with some resistance initially because this meant that people had to buy different antennas, and in certain cases, additional tuners to be fitted to the old black and white sets which had only single channel capability. But now, by and large, viewers have got used to the change, channel converters are now inexpensive, and UHF antennas are available. So, UHF is being accepted by the general public.

Frequencies are allocated by the International Telecommunications Union (ITU) through a process of Administrative Radio Conferences. There is enough room in the frequency allocations made by the ITU for several television channels, in every country. But it is not obligatory on the part of the administrations to follow the table of frequency allocations laid down by the ITU. They can make changes subject to the condition that these do not adversely affect the operation of radio communication systems in other countries.

When the Indian administration, which is represented in the ITU by the Wireless Planning and Coordination wing of the Ministry of Communications, looked at the totality of requirements projected by various radio communication users in the country, they developed what is called a National Frequency Allocation Plan. In this Plan, we find that the number of channels, the total spectrum space available to television broadcasting, is considerably less than the space allocated to this service in the table of frequency allocations laid down by ITU, If one were to restrict the use of frequencies to what has been allocated in the National Frequency Allocation Plan, we are afraid there is not enough room to support even a second channel, leave alone a third.

There is a very strong case for opening up more and more frequency channels to television broadcasting. We have initiated some action in this direction. This again has to go through an inter-departmental consultation process and we are hoping that over a period of time, we will be able to get access to the entire spectrum that the ITU has allocated to Broadcasting service. If that happens, there will be enough frequencies available in the allocated spectrum to support 3 channels of television.

We submitted our requirements to the ITU projecting that we would need to set up a satellite facility that would provide 4 TV channels in the Ku band. Incidentally, in the Ku band, beams coming out from the satellite are very narrow and one cannot cover an area very much larger than, say, a state or perhaps, two adjoining states. That, in my opinion, is a very attractive feature of this particular band, because you can tailor programming to the area served. We said we would eventually have to aim at something like 4 TV channels in each state, or a combination of two states. In order to cover the whole of India, we sought frequency allocations in orbital positions for 12 beams emanating from a satellite or a set of satellites, each beam supporting 4 TV channels. So that made 48 TV channels in all,

4 of them in each of the 12 beams. We managed to get the orbital slots and also the frequencies, but then we were not able to implement the proposed system because, at that time, the value of satellite-backed TV services had not become evident to the policy makers.

Following the Satellite Instructional Television Experiment (SITE) which was conducted in India in 1975-76 and subsequently, the STEP experiment which was carried out with the help of a Franco-German satellite, the Department of Space had begun to look at the possibilities of launching a series of satellites and came up with the concept of a multiple-purpose satellite network catering to the requirements of broadcasting, telecommunications as well as weather prediction. Today it seems surprising that at that point of time, when the report offered by the DOS was examined by the Cabinet, investment on the space segment was approved, but that on the TV ground segment was not approved.

The government did not see the relevance of a satellite system to TV at that time (today the TV component happens to be the core of the INSAT system). The need had not become evident then, so one could not suggest a massive investment in broadcasting satellites. However, eventually the INSAT system was approved in totality and it is common knowledge that this radically transformed the TV situation in the country.

We know, of course, that it may be the right way to go for certain kinds of services, such as value added services not addressed to the common man, services for which some people are willing to pay (one might perhaps use scrambling to ensure access only to those who subscribe). Some of the value-added services one could consider are High Definition Television (HDTV) and some of the international services, which could be re-broadcast from these satellites, such as Murdoch's Sky channel. For such services, DBS is, in my opinion, a better alternative, because it is less expensive than a parallel network of terrestrial transmitters and provides a one shot service instantly, but developing a terrestrial network of transmitters is a tardy process requiring years to accomplish. The negative aspect of course, is the higher cost of consumption. We are hoping for the day when the cost of DBS receivers comes down to within the reach of the common man. We do not think that the day is far off. We might add that when S Band direct reception sets produced by companies like Shyam Antenna, were first introduced in the market for INSAT reception, one talked of a price level of seventeen to eighteen thousand rupees for a suitable add-on to a colour TV cost. The same equipment now costs around eight thousand rupees. Thus, inflation notwithstanding, the prices have come down to half. We are hoping that there will be a breakthrough in technology and it will be possible to market these receivers even more cheaply. This is the reason why we are personally not very enthusiastic about investing our capital money in establishing a terrestrial network of transmitters for the second channel, apart from the 16 that we mentioned previously. Our belief being that in another 4-5 years the whole scenario is likely to change and the satellite option will become far more viable.

The third possibility is cable TV. We might say that cable TV is now more real in India than most of us imagine. Networks have begun to proliferate and we know of some which have more than 2,000-3,000 subscribers. The only reason why they have not grown even further is that there is a certain degree of ambiguity in the perception of the related law. One doesn't know whether this activity is legal or illegal; we might add, even the government does not seem to know. There are provisions in the Indian Telegraph Act that some people claim are violated, but others do not agree. The government has woken up to this uncertainty and an inter-departmental group has been set up to look into the whole matter. Hopefully, in the next few months, this group will make an appropriate recommendation to the government. But it is important to recognise that cable TV has already become a reality in this country and it is serving a very large number of people.

What does it take to establish a cable TV network? I have done a few calculations for some typical scenarios. Assume, for instance, that one were to establish a network in a metropolitan city like Delhi with a subscriber density of something like 5,000 in a cell of 1 km x 1 km. If we take into account the cost of the trunk line, the distribution amplifiers, splitters, and everything else that is needed, it turns out that the investment per subscriber is only about Rs. 1,000, which we do not believe is very expensive, considering that a good TV antenna today costs Rs. 300-400.

If one considered a village or a small town situation, one would not expect more than 100 subscribers in this typical cell of 1 km x 1 km. The investment here would be of the order of Rs. 2,500 per subscriber. Again, not a large sum of money, especially in an area where the DDI network does not yet reach.

This is the initial capital investment. The recurring expenditure will depend on the cable operator, and the software offered by the cable network. In Thailand, people pay something like 100 US dollars for an initial connection, and a monthly charge of about 25 US dollars.

If the cable operator decides to put into the network a public service television channel (a DDI programme), the VCR playback of a bought out programme and an international satellite channel (for example, CNN), his investment will not be very large. But, on the other hand, if he produces programmes specially for the cable network, his investment will have to be very large and the amount of subscription that people will have to pay will increase correspondingly. This is why we are am not considering a typical scenario in relation to recurring costs.

Despite relatively insignificant costs, many people think that cable TV is relevant to the Western societies, but not to India. We do not claim to have an understanding as to whether or not cable TV is the right thing in our country. Social scientists know better. But, may we point out that you may take a view on cable TV, decide it is offensive to public interest and as a consequence take appropriate regulatory measures, but what can you do about signals coming from across the borders, especially through satellites? Soon American programmes will begin to be seen in India. Right now you can pick up CNN being transmitted 24 hours a day through a hired transponder on one of the Russian satellites. Chinese signals are being received in India. We know of several Intelsat signals which are receivable in India carrying different programmes from time to time (Intelsat is a commercial system).

Something even more startling has happened recently. A satellite retrieved from space after a mislaunch has been acquired by a Hong Kong based company (a consortium that includes Chinese and British investors) and successfully launched. It was a copy book launch, absolutely flawless, and the satellite (called Asiasat) will be operationalised in a month's time. We are ourselves negotiating a lease arrangement with Asiasat for a few transponders. Nineteen of the 24 transponders have already been sold out. What is not widely known is that a few of these transponders have been bought by a private production company which obviously has a cable TV as well as a DBS interest in this part of the world.

So, sooner or later we are going to have access to programmes, perhaps tailor-made for sub-continental audiences, transmitted by external sources which will be available throughout India.

❐

9
Satellite and Cable TV Invasion

Satellite broadcasting has been with us for about two decades and cable TV systems for far longer. Yet, it is only in the last few years that trans-national satellite broadcasting (TNSB) has come of age and made a real impact. It was only at the end of the 1980's that TNSB truly came into its own.

The cataclysmic and rapidly-moving events in Eastern Europe provided the ideal "content" for TNSB. Even more dramatic footage was provided by the Gulf War, and it was the "live" coverage of this by CNN in 1991 that marked the real beginning of TNSB in India. Though its reach was extremely limited, CNN provided a ring-side view of the Gulf War to hundreds of thousands of Indians. "Dish antennas," first seen in India in 1975 with the advent of the Satellite Instructional TV Experiment, reappeared on larger scale. However, the popularity of CNN proved to be short-lived: the end of the Gulf War saw a waning of its popularity, with the US-oriented news being of little interest to most. But the lull was short-lived. The advent of SATELLITE TELEVISION ASIAN REGION (STAR) in mid 1991, with its four English channels broadcast through ASIASAT, gave a fillip to TNSB. This was the first satellite based service broadcasting to such a large region, from East Asia to the Middle East, and covering almost 40 countries. The channels, up-linked to the satellite from Hong Kong, consist of a music channel (MTV), a current affairs channel (BBC), an entertainment channel (STAR Plus) and a sports channel (Prime Sports). In addition, the satellite carries a Chinese channel and has leased out transponders for other specific channels (*e.g.*, to Pakistan T.V).

Other new TNSB channels, covering India, have also come up, and more are planned. Amongst the existing channels are ATN which is uplinked from Moscow and uses a Russian satellite and Zee TV uplinked from Hong Kong, and using ASIASAT, both begun in late 1992. Other new channels include ASIANET and SUN-TV, both aimed specifically at the Indian audience.

Cable has become the major means for receiving and distributing satellite broadcasts, as well as other programmes. In India, therefore, there is a direct relationship between the advent of TNSB and the growth of cable systems. Each has led to the growth of the other, and the "Positive feedback cycle" has resulted in phenomenal growth especially in the last 2-3 years of both satellite reception dishes and cable systems. This has posed a variety of issues and challenges, while simultaneously throwing open many opportunities.

Viewership and Access

In examining the impact of TNSB and cable TV, it is obviously necessary to look at the depth of impact as also the extent of that impact. The number of TV sets in the country—indicative of the extent of impact—has necessarily to be only an estimate, since the requirement of a licence was abolished in 1984. The decade since then has witnessed phenomenal growth: the number of TV transmitters has increased from 46 to 540 during March 1984 to December 92 (on 31 December 1992). Meanwhile, in the same period the number of TV sets has also increased equally dramatically—from 3.6 million to an estimated 34.86 million. This would mean a possible peak audience of over 200 million persons.

The cable TV and TNSB too have seen phenomenal growth in percentage terms, the absolute numbers are yet small. One survey indicated total TV viewership in urban areas as 125 million, cable viewership as only 12.9 million and satellite TV at just 1.65 million at the end of 1991. Another estimate indicates the extent of penetration of STAR TV in September 1992 at 3.7 per cent of total households on all-India basis, 5 per cent in urban areas and 10 to 20 per cent in major cities. According to these estimates. While the urban TV viewership jncreased from 125 million to 135 million between December 1991 and September 1992, the same period saw cable viewership increase from 12.9 to 15 million and satellite viewership jumped dramatically from 1.65 million to 6.5 million. It is likely that the growing popularity of TNSB, and especially of the Hindi channel, ZEE TV, has ensured continuing growth at the same or higher levels, so that there may be some 15 million viewers of TNSB in urban areas of the country today. While there are no reliable estimates about cable and TNSB reception in semi-urban and rural areas, the growth in viewership there has—by all accounts—been even more rapid.

The changing pattern of viewership is best exemplified by the precipitious drop in popularity of Doordarshan's primary channel. There was a time when viewership of some of Doordarshan's popular programmes was estimated as over 80 percent, with one MAHABHARAT even crossing 90 percent as indicated by the "Television Rating Points" or TRP. Now, the rating of the most popular programme the Hindi feature film is down to 49 per cent, and that of the most popular serial JUNGLE BOOK to 36 per cent. As many as four of the top ten spots are taken up by the Hindi news bulletin, with TRPs of 17 to 21 per cent.

One reason for the plunge in Doordarshan ratings is the availability of competing channels and their popularity. A recent survey done in Bombay and Ahmedabad indicates that while Doordarshan remains the predominant channel with viewership of 76 and 83 per cent in Bombay and Ahmedabad respectively, the viewership for the VCR channel on cable is also high *i.e.* 64 and 58 percent in the two cities, and the TNSB channel of Zee TV is equally popular with viewership of 56 per cent in Bombay and 68 per cent in Ahmedabad. The English language channels have much smaller viewership, ranging from just 2 per cent MTV in Ahmedabad to 14 per cent STAR plus in Bombay.

However, the drop in proportion of viewership does not necessarily mean a decrease in absolute viewership. Studies have indicated that, following the introduction of cable TV and TNSB, total viewing hours increase considerably, so that even with a big decrease in viewership, the viewing hours for the earlier channels may show only a slight reduction.

The addition from August 15, 1993 of four more Doordarshan channels plus the expansion of the Metro channel to be delivered country-wide by satellite, has added a new dimension to satellite broadcasting. The viewer now has a plethora of channels available-four channels from STAR TV, ZEE TV, five national channels from Doordarshan, a number of regional channels of Doordarshan, CNN, ATN, plus other channels intended for China, Pakistan. ASIANET, the first regional language private satellite channel, began its broadcasts from August 30, 1993, using a high-power Russian satellite. The introduction often new satellite-networked regional channels from October 2, 1993 by Doordarshan, will add further variety.

With this phenomenal growth in the number of channels, it is important to stress that actual availability to the individual viewer and household is dependent on the cable operator. The proposed regulatory mechanism for cable systems seeks to bring some order and to organise this nascent industry on sound lines.

Legal Dimension

In the 1970's, there was much debate in international fora about national sovereignty and trans-border broadcasts especially in the context of direct broadcasting satellites. A New World Information and Communication Order was proposed, and had much support from the developing countries as also from communist countries. The thinking in these debates-primarily in UNESCO-was reflected in concerns expressed in the United Nations, and more concretely in the International Telecommunications Union. This resulted in allocations of frequencies and orbit slots to interested countries for direct broadcasting aimed specifically at their own country. These techno-legal restrictions were, however, overtaken by both political events and technological advances. Further, the marriage of satellite broadcasting and cable systems has made it possible for home viewers to receive even a low-power satellite signal: through the cable system, which can easily afford to install the large antenna that may be required. Thus, TNSB itself is probably not violating any laws or international regulations; however, in India, the cable system, which is the primary means of disseminating the signal, almost certainly is. Till the new laws governing cable systems become operative, most cable system are presently illegal in one way or another. With regard to the content of the programmes too, there are legal problems. One example is the advertising of alcoholic drinks and tobacco products over TV: while this is banned in many countries, it is carried on TNSB. At the moment, there is no means of redress for this, or for progress that violate any other laws or nonos of the receiving nation. There is also the issue of intellectual property rights in relation to the definition of the extent of coverage by the satellite signal. Thus, there are a number of techno-legal and politico-legal issues that are yet a grey area. The fact is that technology and its usage is way ahead of the law in this field.

Social Impact

Large-scale cable networks and TNSB are both too new for any discernable impact to be visible or measurable. Therefore, the effects have to be deduced on the basis of trends, observations and perceived impact. A survey conducted in Delhi in January, 1992, indicated some perceptions with regard to TNSB and cable: These are:

(i) While 84 percent of the respondents found the MTV programmes entertaining, 60 percent felt that they would have a socio-cultural effect on the younger generation. The reactions included the view that the younger generation will adopt the western life style, that MTV will hamper their studies and they will be more inclined to migrate to the West. However, some respondents felt that the younger genertion will become smarter and more aware because of this exposure.

(ii) With regard to BBC, while 58 percent of the respondents felt that it has' 'wide, in-depth and balanced coverage", surprisingly 42 percent felt that "stories about India sometimes reflect bias and distortion of facts".

(iii)   About 80 percent of the respondents felt that foreign serials were entertaining. An equal percentage opined that "STAR serials are more imaginative and creative". Yet, 35 percent felt that foreign serials are "not relevant to our culture, history, region and society"; and 42 percent said that the foreign serials "are always glorifying Western society and their culture, which will adversely affect our children and youth."

(iv)   With regard to films shown on the "VCR Channel" of cable systems, the audience was almost exactly divided between those felt that "the number of films shown...is too many" and those who stated that "their number was just right". As many as 70 percent felt that the moral and ethical values of our society will be affected by the onslaught of films. While there was concern about the depiction of sex and violence, some felt that there is already so much exposure to this that cable TV will not make much difference.

(v)   A substantial proportion of respondents between 45 and 62 percent were worried about the negative effects of cable TV on children. A majority *i.e.* 57 percent felt that "children will be adversely affected". The sports activities of children will be curtailed, felt 62 percent, while 51 percent felt that reading and other creative activities will be adversely affected.

While there is clearly great concern about the effect on children and youth, many feel that adults themselves often contribute to indirect negative effects. A school Principal reports that parents who watch late-night shows or movies on cable or TNSB, get up too late to make and pack lunch for their children. They are therefore given some unwholesome "readymade" food or are given money to eat out. Parental attention to children's school work and extra-curricular activities is also declining.

Clothing, speech and behaviour too is widely reported to be strongly influenced by foreign programmes coming through TNSB and cable. Morality and values also seem to be changing, though it is debatable whether TV is the only or primary cause. Life-style changes are probably more easily attributable to TV programmes.

It is important to note that the social impact caused by TNSB and cable is not limited only to the small percentage of the population who have access to these programmes. This is because there are two other factors at work:

(i) The emulation or "Sanskritisation" effect, due to which those who are "lower" in the social and/or economic hierarchy aspire to climb "up" and hence adopt the practices, behaviour etc. of those who are "higher" in the hierarchy. Thus, even those with no access to TV are indirectly affected because they emulate, to the extent possible, the behaviour patterns of the better off who, as viewers of TNSB or cable, are directly influenced by them.

(ii) The' 'cloning effect," because of which programmes-irrespective of source-begin to look so alike as to be indistinguishable, but for the artistes or the language. This happens because policy makers assume that the only way of being as popular as the competitor is to imitate him or her. Thus, competing with popular foreign serials means making serials just like theirs, and competing with the "VCR Channel" means broadcasting two or three films a day, as they do. The result is that the domestic channels begin to look the same as the trans-national channels, with similar story lines, formats, editing style and approach. Consequently, there may be little to distinguish, in terms of effect, between a domestic channel and TNSB. Thus, through this "cloning effect," TNSB affects even those who only view domestic channels.

The commercial orientation of the VCR channel and of the TNSB channels ensures a high proportion of advertising. These advertisements made at great cost and carefully tested to ensure maximum effectiveness-sell not only products, but also life-styles and role-models. Obviously, they would create an effect on the viewer. This effect is considerably enhanced by the mutually-reinforcing relationship between advertisements and programmes: both, in direct or indirect ways, promote or glorify a certain life-style with associated behaviour patterns and value.

Economic Implications

The economic effects of cable and TNSB may be ana lysed at three different levels: individual, organisational, and societal or national. There is, at the moment, little or no specific data on this: therefore, what follows is necessarily somewhat speculative.

At the level of the individual, the combination of TNSB and the new economic policy has contributed to the creation of a strongly materialistic ambience with pressures on the individual to consume more. The widening of wants, created by both programmes and advertising, has been supported by building of brands. This has created unprecedented levels of demand for all kinds of products including soft drinks. The pressure to consume is further increased by creating wants amongst children, who then influence parents to buy. Apart from the direct effect of advertising, there is also the indirect promotion—through the TV programmes—of a consumerist life-style. The impact on individual and household budgets has been substantial in terms of both-an increase in absolute spending and a change of priorities. The hedonistic "me first" and "here and now" generation is here, and is largely a creation of television.

For organisations, the consumerism promoted by TNSB is welcome to the extent it could generate more sales and bigger profits. However, the globalisation inherent in TNSB, coupled with liberalisation of the economy, has brought international brands to the country. This means competition, and often lower market shares and profits.

For organisations directly connected with media, there is the potential of more business. Avertising agencies can hope to get some share of the larger market for sales promotion etc; the print medium is already benefiting from more of advertising for both products as also for programmes or channels; and production houses and freelancers can hope to get production contracts, for programmes or advertisements. However, globalisation may create the opposite effect here too: instead of local media organisations getting more work, they may lose even some existing work, as common, foreign-made advertisements and programmes make their way into local channels. Doordarsh an also has lost some of the advertising revenue it may have gained, with advertising going to competing TNSB channels. Of course, as in all such cases, the total market too has grown. At the same time, liberalisation and opening up of the economy to foreign products could, in the long run, bring more advertising revenue to Doordarshan—especially with the growing rural market and Doordarshan's strong presence in rural areas.

Conclusions regarding the economic implications at the macro, societal level have to be even more tentative, and somewhat hypothetical. However, some trends are already visible and can be attributed substantially to the heightened media exposure due to TNSB. Primary amongst these is the spurt in demand for' 'branded" products and especially for foreign branded products. This will lead to increased outflow of foreign exchange, and will have its own effect on domestic manufacturers. One such effect is the collaboration or tie-up, in which even a well established Indian firm is forced to be the junior partner. Thus, when a major U.S. soft drink firm entered the Indian market some time ago, the biggest Indian producer took an adversary or competing position. However, the same Indian company now intends to collaborate with another US company to introduce its products in India. Other such examples are already known, and certainly many more will follow.

With this presumption, it is probable that there will be increasing globalisation of production technologies, designs and brand names, even while actual production operations shift to countries that provide the lowest costs and most conducive ambience. While this will help to provide employment in developing countries, the biggest proportion of costs will be in technology, design, marketing and in brand names- all of which will be funnelled back mainly to developed countries.

Life-style changes will be as critical as direct and visible economic impact. For, it is these that will create changes in the consumption pattern and generate demands for certain specific brands, goods or services.

Some Features

The proliferation of satellite-delivered channels, the expansion of the cable systems, increasing privatisation and commercialisation of television channels: these are foreseeable features of the immediate future, "Niche channels", serving specific audience segments, are likely. As in radio, all-purpose music channels will be replaced by separate channels for Western classical or Hindustani or folk music; a sports channel will be replaced by separate cricket or athletics channels; etc. This narrowing of audiences will greatly facilitate tailor-made marketing strategies and advertisements targeted at these specific groups. At the same time, larger audiences will be required to ensure economic viability. This can be achieved only by widening the geographical coverage. TNSB—with its ability to cover vast areas and large populations—does this best. In the process, it is the answer to every marketeers dream: delivering large, but similar-specific-characteristics audiences representing 30-35 years age group, with Ph.D's, and a deep interest in dogs.

New technologies will make it possible for a single spacecraft to carry a large number of transponders, each capable of carrying multiple channels, resulting in lower costs. Advances in satellite and reception technologies, and the use of higher frequency bands will reduce the size and also cost of satellite direct reception equipment, making it easily affordable. Easy access to satellite uplinks anywhere in the world, and no restrictions about uplinking or coverage area, will make TV truly transnational. Software too will tend to be electric and from varied sources.

In the days to come TNSB undoubtedly makes for a more informed, more aware person with, possibly, a much more non-parochial outlook. To the extent it promotes a certain unity, it may be contributing to the emergence of the "global citizen" of tomorrow.

Cable, on the other-hand, could ideally provide the decentralised, community-centered communication that could prevent alienation, and promote positive community-feeling. There is, thus, the potential of great good in TNSB and cable TV. Will the future see a society of clones, each greedy, selfish and uncaring, or will it see a plural, diverse and humane community? Only time will tell, but how we use the powerful media of cable and satellite TV will certainly influence the outcome.

T.V. AS AN EDUCATIONAL MEDIUM

That the organisers of the seminar on "Autonomy and After: Government Media" have shown their concern about educational TV by inviting an academic to participate in the deliberations is a gesture of immense satisfaction to me personally. This is so essentially because educational TV is still almost a non-ooncern for the Government media in this country. We are aware of the UGC Programmes being telecast by Doordarshan and also various Science Quiz Programmes that have been appreciated by the masses all over the country. Besides, there are many programmes in the form of serials and those in the area of agriculture etc., which impart education of one or the other type to people who may show their interest in them. But we need to make a distinction between educative TV and educational TV. Depending on who the receiver is, almost any programme will show a few features of educative TV, for example, by watching serials on wild life, we learn about animal behaviour, environment and ecology, and similarly, from serials like Mahabharat, we learn about human nature, socio-political conflicts, different values, history, etc. All this is educative TV, and the media in India provides a reasonable amount of such TV. But educational TV, as I said above, is still a thing of the future in our country. While saying so, what is in my mind is something like Channel No.8 of Houston TV in Texas (USA). All the programmes on this channel have clear-cut educational objectives and the production and presentation are all geared to achieve those educational objectives. We have very little of this type of educational TV available in this country today.

While talking about 'autonomy' with respect to education one is inclined to think of two types: *(i)* autonomy of the institution, and *(ii)* autonomy of the clientele.

In all probability, and we are certain about it, most of the participants of the seminar will remain concerned with the former, *i.e.*, the institutional autonomy-matters pertaining to the organisational structure of Doordarshan, role of producers, handling of current affairs and entertainment programmes, technical feasibility and cost effectiveness of multi-channel transmission vis-a-vis the autonomy proposed in Prasar Bharati Bill.

As for the latter, *i.e.*, autonomy of the clientele, very little will be said and much less discussed as the notion is relatively new. For educational TV, the clientele consists of the students who use TV as an educational medium; by the autonomy of the student we mean that stage of educational affairs in which students can decide on the objectives of the education which they are looking for, decide on the pedagogical methods and materials they would like to use to achieve those objectives and also decide on the type of evaluation to establish whether the educational objectives they set before themselves have been achieved or not.

We are bringing in this notion of 'learner autonomy' partly because my concern is open and distance education, the ultimate objective of which is 'learner autonomy', and partly because we hope that autonomous Doordarshan will be not only 'sensitive' to the educational needs of the people of this country, but also be aware of its own potential as a significant educatior. Thus, besides generating sufficient will to fulfil its responsibilities as an educator of immense strength, it will play a key role in building a society of 'autonomous learners' .

This is, seemingly, an unattainable objective. Autonomous Doordarshan cannot even reflect on this objective unless it becomes aware of both the rudimentary and the complex problems involved in planning, developing, producing and implementing/presenting educational programmes. Our media lack this awareness at present, as has already been pointed out.

It is with this view-point that we think it advisable to talk about some of our experiences with media, especially when used for educational purposes.

1. We (at Indira Gandhi National Open University) have learnt that an otherwise experienced and technically sound producer cannot necessarily be a good educational TV producer. Initially when we started preparing our video and audio programmes it was felt that if the topic was given to the producer, he/she would produce the relevant video/audio on his/her own. It was before long that this practice had to be given up in favour of giving an academic brief to the producer to work on. 'Academic brief is a page (or so) long note saying who the programme is addressed to, what its theme is, what is its length, how it may begin, what discussion points may it touch upon, what its focus may be, etc. Sometime later it was felt that in addition to the academic brief an elaboration to the academic brief known as an 'academic note' also was needed-this note it was suggested could be 8-10 pages long, making suggestions about visuals besides incorporating the essential text expected to be presented. Still later, it was realised that constant discussion, interaction and exchange of ideas between the academic and producer was not only desirable but also essential in order to produce a pedagogically effective media unit. The conflict was something like this:

(a) the producer thought that he/she was the right person to produce the audio/video and he/she was qualified to do so. On the other hand, the academic thought that he/she was the right person to do so, for he/she was the master of the discipline being presented through the audio/video programme. It is obvious that to produce an effective educational programme the producer has to be an academic also, or, the other way round, the academic has to be the producer too. It is, therefore, not without reason that the BBC/UKOU (British Broadcasting Corporation/United Kingdom Open University) usually appoint as producers the academics trained in audio/video production.

(b) secondly, it has been observed that an average producer pays greater attention to the 'frame' and how the spaces in the 'frame' are filled properly and adequately, besides being inclined to give an 'entertaining' slant to the programme. The academic on the other hand, remains concerned with the 'content', *i.e.*, the message he wants to convey to the student. It may be for similar reasons that a producer remains concerned with !he presentability of the presenter and other faces and their voices while the academic would like to get the message conveyed by a person who can talk about and/or present the themes with understanding and authority.

A simple lesson from this experience is that we have yet to make a beginning in the area of educational TV. The case of producer-academic conflict is a mere example; the point to be made is that educational TV has yet to address itself to the very basic issues it should be concerned with. It is obvious that we need training of a different sort, a training that effects a merger of the academic and the producer, as we need, in this case, neither the pure academic nor the pure producer but an academic-producer or a producer-academic. What kind of training will it be? Who will give it? And who will be the clientele? These are the questions which need to be answered to take the very first steps towards making educational TV a reality.

2. It is believed that Doordarshan is already giving a lot of telecast time to educational programmes prepared at Educational Media Research Centres (EMRCs), arranged through UGC and other agencies, centrally as well as from the States.

In this connection, some commonplace observations are in order here:

Very many schools have been given TV sets, presumably to be used for students. However, invariably these sets adorn the rooms of the principals and in many cases they are out of order and cannot be used.

Most of these programmes are telecast twice a day, when all the learners concerned are at school/college/university.

One wonders whether the programmes are really for the learners. Or are they for the general public, the masses!

Besides, these programmes are mostly in English and therefore, they may not be serving even as educative TV.

Obviously, the problem is that of TV time. The prime time is allotted to news, current affairs, entertainment or popular serials-educational programmes have no place there. In such a situation, there is a strong case for a separate educational channel on which the entire time will be that of the learner. Will autonomous Doordarsban have the institutional will and also the necessary funding available to create such a channel? If the funds are not available, will Doordarshan ignore this need!

3. Coming to the nature of educational TV, there is a major controversy regarding the programme—ordinary TV or fancy TV.

Ordinary TV may be the label given to any educational TV programmes used as mere extensions of the classroom. Perhaps a very good example of this kind of educational TV is available at Ramkhamhaeng University, Thailand, where one teacher/lecturer is projected through TV to hundreds of students seated in big halls. Such TV programmes are also used to bring an outstanding teacher, a well-known academic and the like alive to students thousands of miles away from the teacher/academic. Such educational TV saves time and money and yet provides enlightening educational exposure to learners.

Fancy TV, on the other hand, tries to be highly selective in each and every respect. The basic philosophy being that the educational potential rather than the extended reach of TV should be the basis for providing educational experiences through TV. In such programmes; television technology itself becomes the medium of instruction. For example, a learner can observe in great detail the life and activities of sub-marine plants and animal with the help of TV technology. Such exposure is not possible even in the best of classrooms otherwise. TV programmes of this type would obviously take a lot of time and money to produce, but they undoubtedly cover all the three domains that education is concerned with—Cognitive, Psycho-motor, and Affective.

Autonomous Doordarshan will have to take a stand in the controversy that rages between the two schools of thought-the one for ordinary TV and the other for fancy TV. It may be that the educational TV of autonomous Doordarshan works on a range between the ordinary and the fancy TV (for both have their strengths); and choose either, or a mix thereof depending on the needs of learners. The obvious implication is that for going into educational TV, autonomous Doordarshan will have to be concerned with not only the technicalities of their production, but also their theoretical bases.

4. As far as the clientele groups are concerned, educational TV will have to cater to the needs of age-groups 5-14, 14-20/21 and above. In other words, care has to be taken not only of pedagogy but also that of andragogy. Looked at differently, the clientele groups consist of women, people living in remote areas, poor sections of the society, institutional labour and others. The obvious implication is that not only the academic relevance of the programmes but also the social relevance will have to be taken care of. In terms of the former, the issues involved are that of curriculum, themes and sub-themes within the curriculum, presentation of programmes, evaluation of programmes and the subsequent modifications of programmes. As for the issues of social relevance, a strong suggestion emerges that there also need to be programmes of a general nature. As of today none of these concerns forms the agenda for Doordarshan; autonomous Doordarshan will have to have an agenda of the type suggested above. Though Doordarshan has units responsible for education, in all probability they do not have the required level of professional know-how so essential to meet the demands outlined in the above paragraphs.

5. Lastly, we come to the issue of 'sharing the responsibility'. The present scenario is that in our country private sector has not shown any interest in educational TV so far and is not likely to do

so for quite some time in the future as educational enterprise does not promise adequate returns-neither politically nor economically.

As far as the public sector is concerned, it is mainly the Central Government that has initiated activities like EMRCs, etc., to promote educational television. The problem which the public sector faces is partly born of its dependence on state directives (however convert they might be), and partly because of the absence of appropriate professionalism for educational TV. In the area of production, a major concern of the public sector seems to be the technical aspects of a programme. In order to produce a technically standard programme the public sector is inclined to depend on technicians more than academics. Secondly, the TV enterprise in the country being relatively new and also second hand technology (in the sense, we lag behind the Western World and whatever innovations we bring in are passed on to us by others), we have had no time in developing that kind of professionalism which synthesises production excellence with academic credibility. It must take us some time before we can claim our authority in this area.

Autonomous Doordarshan will do a great service to the country by working for that synthesis. Such synthesis should help TV become truly educational. A truly educational TV should attract the attention of the private sector too. This, we believe, is not wishful thinking, for there is evidence of such a phenomenon existing in the UK, the USA and Germany.

❏

10

Future of Television

During the last three decades television has radically altered the lives of people throughout the world. Now, rapidly evolving technological developments, such as video cassettes and video discs, are about to free television viewers from the constraints of the broadcast schedule. Satellite transmission and cable television, including over-the-air and cable pay-TV, are transforming important aspects of the industry. And the introduction of holography, fiber optics, and other exciting and useful innovations is close at hand.

Through the electronic magic carpet of television, millions of viewers worldwide were transported to the scene of the Sadat-Begin peace visits in late 1977 and even witnessed the historic on-the-air decisions that preceded these historic missions. As they do each year, millions more watched the 1978 Super Bowl football game with all its pageantry. Witnessing these events and others, such as the Olympics and the World Cup soccer ,matches, the Papal Mass at the Vatican at Christmas and the Muslim Hajj, and the investiture of the Prince of Wales, has become common place. Americans share all types of experiences by television, making them aware of their diversity but also forging a spirit of unity. Through direct-to-home satellite television, the other nations of the world may well achieve a similar understanding. It is likely that future historians will rank television the twentieth century creation of the industrial and technological movements of the past two centuries—as the most revolutionary and democratizing medium of our times.

So rapidly is the state of the art advancing that, in the decades ahead, virtually every home, school, and business in the United States can gain access to a nearly unlimited number of channels for a multiplicity of uses: commercial, public, and community television and radio; two-way communications for banking, shopping, responding to opinion polls, and the like; facsimile reproduction; and a host of services involving the storage, transmission, and retrieval of data— all part of the emerging Information and Entertainment Age.

In this emerging scheme of things commercial over-the-air broadcasting will meet the mass audience requirements for news and entertainment. Public broadcasting will fill the varied needs of specialized audiences by providing greater choice, diversity, and enrichment. Cable will complement commercial and public broadcasting by improving its signal and extending its reach and by offering, through an abundance of channels, greater opportunities for specialized programmes and non-broadcast services. Free, subscription, and direct-payment mechanisms will coexist and compete, just as they do in the print media. This is the prediction of the research and policy committee of the Committee for Economic Development. These national leaders point out that coherent and responsive national policies must be formulated soon to permit the orderly development of such a telecommunications system in the United States.

SCOPE OF TELEVISION

Television sets may be found in 97. of every 100 homes in this country, an apparent saturation level that has changed little in recent years. Three of every 4 homes, however, now have color sets, as compared with only half in 1970. Nearly half of all TV households own more than one set and better than 1 out of 6 homes are tied into cable systems.

Television is considered the most pervasive medium known to modern man. The average American family devotes more time to watching television—about 6 hours daily—than to any other form of leisure activity. Five of every 7 television stations (there are more than 990 in all) broadcast on the long-established very high frequency

(VHF) bands, using channels 2 through 13, and the remainder on ultrahigh frequency (UHF), channels 14 through 83. More than 9 of every 10 homes receive UHF programmes. Residents of more than 135 cities view the programme fare of three or more local stations.

Most commercial television stations are affiliated with one or more of the three major networks—the American Broadcasting Companies, Columbia Broadcasting System, and National Broadcasting Company. Approximately 100 stations operate on an independent basis Well over 100 individuals and companies, including the most networks, own two or more television stations. However, Federal Communications Commission rules limit multiple ownership to seven television stations, of which not more than five may be VHF (and each may own no more than seven AM and seven FM radio stations). Many companies own both newspapers and broadcast stations, although newspaper owners no longer are permitted by the FCC to purchase broadcast properties in the same city.

The television industry in 1976 made a pretax profit of about 24 percent from more than $5.2 billion in total revenues, with some operations making as much as 30 percent in profits. The profit margin of the networks, set at 8.9 percent in 1963 and 13.2 percent in 1973, was projected to reach 17.9 percent in 1979, according to Wall Street analysts. The average 30-second announcement in prime-time network television costs about $50,000. When more than 86 million persons viewed at least part of the 1978 Super Bowl football telecast, one minute of commercial time was priced at $344,000.

Almost 150,000 persons are employed in television. Although small in comparison with other industries, television and radio are responsible for the livelihood of thousands of persons in related businesses. They include talent agents and managers, programme producers and distributors, commercial and jingle producers, business and promotion film distributors, film processing technicians, researchers, consulting engineers, management consultants, brokers, and station representatives, as well as employees of news services, association and professional societies, unions, station finance companies, and public relations, publicity, and promotion firms. A comprehensive summary of television industry statistics may be found in *Broadcasting Yearbook*.

World Television

During the past decade in particular, television has spread to most of the countries of the world. Its impact ranges from heavy use in the more developed nations to reception largely by the rich in the poorest lands. United States citizens possess about half of the world's TV sets. Usage is also high in Japan, the United Kingdom, West Germany, France, Italy, and Canada, in that order, with the emerging nations, such as those in Africa, enjoyjng the least TV viewing.

The United States exports far more films and videotaped programmes than any other country. More than 150 American companies produce and export TV programmes, with the nine companies comprising the Motion Picture Export Association of America accounting for about 80 percent df total sales abroad., America's competitive position has been enhanced by the rapid growth of color TV; the trend toward commercialization of TV channels in other countries, providing more money for buyers of American programmes; the sales potential of satellite telecasts of special events; and the growing availability of and need for educational films produced in the United States. The United Kingdom, France, and the Federal Republic of Germany also export much programming. Mexico produces many programmes for Latin American countries. Countries in the Middle East obtain most of their programmes from Lebanon and Egypt. Programmes produced in socialist countries are used mainly in other socialist countries.

A cultural imbalance is evident? however. According to a survey by Tapio Varis, a Finnish researcher, less than 2 percent of commercial and non-commercial programming viewed in the United States and China is received from foreign sources; in the Soviet Union, 5 percent; in France, 9 percent; and in Japan, 10 percent. By contrast, such countries as Chile, Mexico, Uruguay, Saudi Arabia, Italy, Australia, and Zambia import more than 50 percent of the programmes viewed by their citizens-Saudi Arabia, in fact, imports 100 percent. Feature films, series and serials, and entertainment shows comprise the bulk of these programmes. British productions such as "Civilisation," "Upstairs, Downstairs," and "Search for the Nile" have been well received in the United States. Most of the imported programmes viewed in Great Britain come from this country.

United States investors own stock in stations throughout the world. Most are minority holdings, representinlg from 10 to 20 percent of total investment. The biggest investors have been the three networks and Time-Life Broadcasting International. American advertisers are taking advantage of the world trend toward the commercialization of television. Only in recent years has advertising been permitted in such places as France, Holland, Hong Kong, Indonesia, West Germany, Italy, and Mexico.

Color telecasts via satellite are viewed worldwide. The Communications Satellite Corporation, a private, profit-making company, was established in 1962 by Congress to own and operate the American segment of this telecommunications system. An eighty-member International Telecommunications Sateilite Consortium coordinates the technology and programme exchanges. The first INTELSAT satellite, known as Early Bird, became operational in 1965. Four years later the beams of these satellites, positioned above the Atlantic, Indian, and Pacific oceans, covered the whole world. In addition, the Applications Technology Satellites (ATS) serve individual regions and countries oʜ an experimental basis.

Cable Televison

In order to bring improved television service into geographical areas of the United States with inadequate reception, the first Community Antenna Television (CATV) systems were constructed in 1949 in the hills of eastern Pennsylvania and Oregon. At the end of its first decade, cable television served 550,000 subscribers through 560 systems. By 1969 there were 2260 systems serving about 3.6 million subscribers. By 1977 more than 3800 systems reached 12.5 million subscribers in 17.3 percent of the nation's 72 million households. An estimated 30 percent penetration of U.S. homes by cable is anticipated by the end of 1981.

Only three to five channels were provided originally. Now, however, newer services not only strengthen existing signals but import programmes into areas already served by television and often originate programmes of their own or lease channels to those who do. Using live, film, or videotape formats, more than 2400 systems originate programming in their own studios, the average for 13.5 hours weekly. Most systems offer between six and twelve channels.

Since the capacity of the coaxial cable, unlike that of the broadcast spectrum, has no inherent limits, future systems are expected to offer forty or even eighty channels. In so doing they could provide not only diverse broadcast services with improved signal quality, but also a wide array of non-broadcast entertainment and information services, including two-way communications, facsimile reproduction of newspapers and mail, and business, home, health, educational, and municipal services. For example, channels will be available to private users such as banks and motion picture vendors, and open channels to users such as supermarket chains and department stores.

Approximately three-fourths of the cable firms are owned by individuals and companies that have other media interests as well. Approximately 32 percent of the systems are linked with broadcast interests, almost 20 percent with programme producers, and 13 percent with newspapers. The operators invest from about $25,000 for a small black-and-white operation to $2 million or more for a color studio. As much as $20 million may be required to establish a system in a large city. The costs of laying cable range. from $3,500 per mile in rural areas to $80,000 in metropolitan areas. Users pay an average of $15 to have the system connected to their households and then an average of $6.50 per month for the service.

Advertisers are charged from $5 to $200 per minute on the local origination channels. Total advertising revenues on these channels exceed $3.5 million. Most of a system's revenues, however, are derived from the fees paid by subscribers. The return on investment is slow; it may be ten years or more before an investor realizes a substantial profit. Cable, therefore, is essentially a franchised monopoly in its service area.

Cable television's commercial success was assured in 1972 when, after a five-year dispute among broadcasters, cable operators, and copyright owners, the FCC for the first time permitted cable systems to operate with distant signals in the Top 100 markets. Various restrictions were imposed, however, and cable TV's development also was slowed for several years by lack of venutre capital.

Pay TV—the system of providing programmes for a fee through a "scrambling" device requiring special equipment and entering the home on a cable or over-the-air—offered the largest economic returns. Commercial broadcasters opposed pay cable television on the ground that any siphoning of programmes would result in public deprivation. In 1975 the FCC adopted new regulations placing limits on movies and sports events that could be shown on cable TV. Cablecasters were prohibited, for example, from showing any film between three and ten years old, as well as many major sports events, even those not broadcast by commercial television.

The FCC's so-called antisiphoning rules were overturned, however, when the Supreme Court in 1977 refused to review a landmark decision by the U.S. Court of Appeals for the District of Columbia in Federal Communications Commission v. Home Box Office. The appeals court found unanimously that there was no evidence pay cable TV would adversely affect either the public interest or over-the-air television; that the FCC had no statutory authority to regulate pay cable TV; and that its restrictions violated the medium's First Amendment right of free speech. The decision lifted a cloud of uncertainty that had hovered over the future of cable

TV and held the promise of greater programme diversity for the viewing public.

By 1978 more than 450 pay cable systems served 1.2 million subscribers. By the end of 1981 the number of subscribers was expected to range between 3 and 4 million.

Satellite transmission of programmes was pioneered in 1975 by Time Inc.'s Home Box Office, followed in 1978 by Showtime, the pay TV branch of Viacom International. Home Box Office serves more than one million subscribers, representing about 80 percent of the pay cable industry. The company produces about 20 percent of its programmes in its own multimillion-dollar studio. Showtime buys all its programmes and offers about 75 percent films, 20 percent entertainment specials, and 5 percent sports.

The UPI in 1977 began a 24-hour satellite news service featuring a continuous voice commentary over a changing series of still photos. In the same year the American Satellite Network was formed by Digital Communications, Inc., as a new delivery system for CATV. Other satellite services, including those for religious programmes, also were started. In all, more than 100 earth satellites were in operation.

An experiment dubbed "Qube," described as a "dramatic leap" in cable TV, began in Columbus, Ohio, in 1977. With an investment of $10 million, Warner Cable Corporation offered Columbus homes thirty channel choices combining conventional television, community channels, premium programming on a pay-per-view basis, and the capacity for subscribers, by pushing five response buttons, to participate in local game shows, vote on referendums, take quizzes, purchase products, and predict the plays of a sporting event.

Cable operators were pleased by the creativity evident in the industry, by the relaxation of controls, by the clarification of regulations involving the use of programmes embodied in the new federal copyright law, and by new technological developments on the horizon. The latter include the eventual replacement of conventional cable with optical fibers and the use of laser (light amplification) devices as the signal source for the fibers. Major problems were yet to be overcome, but the cable industry seemed at last to have come into its own.

Trends in Public Broadcasting

Public broadcasting has emerged only recently as a major force in television and radio. In seeking to provide alternative programming for the American public, the non-commercial medium offered "The Great American Dream Machine," "Sesame Street," "The Electric Company," news and public affairs programmes, and other contributions of merit. An integrated system of national direction, programme production and distribution, and local station influence evolved. But its chief problems were how to determine the right mixture of central and federated control, how to determine the appropriate audience, and how to obtain enough no strings-attached funding. Since politics is public broadcasting's marketplace, strong political winds whirled about the system. Only permanent financing, most public broadcasting advocates argued, could substantially insulate the system from the vagaries of political life and ensure its long-range stability.

The Corporation for Public Broadcasting was established by Congress in 1967, acting largely upon a Carnegie Commission report that declared: "A well-financed and well-directed system, substantially larger and far more pervasive and effective than that which now exists in the United States, must be brought into being if the full needs of the American public are to be served." The commission was referring to National Educational Television, which supplied programmes for non-commercial stations licensed almost exclusively to communities, universities, state authorities, and public school systems. Failing to take into account years of notable educational accomplishments, some critics viewed NET educational and public programming as "pedantic, impoverished, noble, and often deadly dull," with negligible audiences.

In 1970 the newly authorized CPB established the Public Broadcasting Service to manage programming production and distribution and station interconnection. Production centers were designated at seven non-commercial TV stations across the country. In addition, the Children's Television Workshop, producer of "Sesame Street" and "The Electric Company," became, in effect, an eighth center, although it was a nonprofit corporation with ties to no one except that it was funded by CPB, the U.S. Office of Education, and the Ford Foundation. National Public Radio, a non-commercial radio interconnection largely exchanging locally produced programmes, was created in 1971.

PBS was unlike any other national broadcasting network. With a board of directors dominated by the chief executive officers of licensing organizations, it was far more federated and far more loosely organized. The programmes it distributed were produced by the major centers and funneled through the network, but final responsibility for clearance and scheduling rested with the local stations, which could screen programmes before airing. NET merged with WNDT-TV, New York, to become WNET, one of the seven production centers.

Public broadcasting gained steadily in favor. Despite the fact that two-thirds of the TV stations broadcast on UHF channels, by 1978 approximately 60 percent of the nation's households viewed public television about three hours each day. And the 203 public radio stations, although reaching fewer than two-thirds of families with radios, attracted millions of listeners.

President Carter submitted to Congress a proposed Public Broadcasting Financing Act of 1978. The bill would authorize $1 billion in matching federal funds over a five-year period beginning in fiscal year 1981 and make drastic organic changes in the system. It would encourage more journalistic independence, including the right of stations to editorialize; seek to resolve organizational conflicts within the system; trim the bureaucratic structure to eliminate waste, enlarge the role of independent producers and the public; strengthen national programming; require the system to raise $2.25 for every $1 received from federal funds; stipulate that stations receiving funds open their meetings and financial records to the public; and increase the participation of minorities and women.

Congressional debate centered on the funding provisions, with a tax on commercial broadcasters suggested as one alternative source. The administration, however, sought to postpone discussion of other sources pending a report of the Carnegie Commission on the Future of Public Broadcasting, expected in January, 1979.

How a Television Station Operates

Unlike the printed media and the commercial motion picture industry, a television station gives its product away. Anyone possessing a television set can watch hour after hour of programmes free of charge. Yet the station, of course, must earn money to cover its high cost of operation and return a profit. It does so through the sale of commercial advertising time.

Examination of the operation of an actual successful TV station of medium size affiliated with one of the three major networks shows how American television functions. In most respects this station is typical of scores in the United States, although it has a considerably larger news operation than many of its size.

The station is headed by a general manager. Answering to the manager are four major department heads—chief engineer, programme director, news director, and sales manager. The head of the production department reports to the programme director. The promotion director is closely linked to the sales department but answers to the general manager.

Although it is on the air eighteen hours a day, the station creates only about three or four hours of programming in its own studios, mostly local news and homemaker offerings. The rest is obtained from the network and from independent suppliers of filmed shows. To do this job, the station has a staff of fifty-five men and women, plus eight to ten part-time employees. Some of the latter are local college students who usually help with live show production. The station offers a full hour of local news, weather, and sports at the dinner hour preceding the evening network news programme, and another 30 minutes of news in late evening. During the week it presents other local background news and discussion programmes. Fourteen men and women of varying degrees of experience comprise the news staff.

The necessary income with which to operate the station is obtained from three primary sources: the network, national spot commercials the station puts on the air during station breaks, and local and regional commercials. One widely held misconception is that an affiliate station pays the network for the national programmes it puts on the air. The reality is just the reverse.

Each of the three major networks has approximately 200 affiliated stations. In addition, the federal government permits each network to own and operate seven stations of its own, five VHF and two UHF. They are known in the trade as O and O's. An affiliate contracts with a network for the exclusive right to broadcast in its coverage area all programmes distributed by the network. It also has the right to refuse to broadcast any network programme. Rejections occur when the station be lieves its audience will find a particular programme objectionable, or when it prefers to use that block of air time to broadcast a programme it originates or obtains from another source. In practice, most affiliates broadcast more than 90 percent of the network programming. When a network plans to present a controversial programme, it transmits the show in advance to the affiliates on a closed circuit; the station executives then decide whether to use it. The network also provides advance summaries of all its scheduled programmes, letting the affiliates know what to expect on the air.

With certain exceptions, the network pays the station to air a network programme; the price is based on the size of the station's market. In our example, the station's average compensation is approximately $700 per hour. The network pays the station 30 percent of its card rate. During an hour-long show, most of the commercials are put on the air by the network, which receives all the income from them. However, station break slots in which the local station inserts its own commercials, either national or local, are left open. It keeps all the revenue from these spots.

Thus it follows that the larger the number of affiliates carrying a show, the larger the network's audience and the greater the amount of money it can charge an advertiser that places a commercial on the show. Television advertising rates are based on the cost of reaching 1000 viewers. That is why the industry became so concerned in 1977 when national ratings services revealed that both daytime and night-time viewing had declined after almost two decades of an almost continuous rise. Changing demographic patterns of the viewing audience were among several factors cited as the possible reasons for the decline.

To supplement network and local programming, stations obtain programmes from other sources as well, under varying financial arrangements. A common form is the syndicated show, such as the Mike Douglas afternoon interview programme. The station purchases the show from a syndication firm for a flat, negotiated fee. All commercial time slots are open for local commercials. If the station's sales staff is effective, it fills those spots with well-paying sales messages. A variation is the barter programme, of which the Lawrence Welk show is an example. The station receives the programme without charge, and the Welk organization does not provide any compensation. Half the spots in the hour-long programme are sold nationally by the Welk organization. It keeps all this income, from which it covers the expense of preparing the show. The other half of the commercial slots are reserved for the local station's own commercials.

Still another variation is the network show provided to an affiliate without the usual compensation from the network. Enough local spots are left open during the programme for the station to come out satisfactorily from a financial standpoint. The "Today" show and Sunday professional football broadcasts are examples of this arrangement. The audiences for these broadcasts are so high that, in these instances, a local station can afford the non-compensation arrangement.

Occasionally, a station will replace a network programme in prime time with a non-network programme that it considers exceptionally important or more lucrative. This action often angers followers of the preempted programme, so is done infrequently. The Billy Graham evangelistic crusade, for example, will purchase consecutive evenings of prime time, for which it pays the station more than the $700 hourly network rate. This is a good financial arrangement for the station because it receives full income for the hour and at the same time appeals to the portion of the viewing population that finds the Graham message inspiring.

MAJOR FUNCTIONS OF THE TELEVISION STATION

The News Function. The area of news and information is an important, aggressive, and prestige-building division of the television-radio programming structure. Many types of programmes are provided. One is the regular newscast, giving 50 to 60-minute or longer summaries of happenings in the community, nation, and world. A second area is the background and interpretation programme. It may be a newscaster's straight presentation of facts, a panel discussion, an interview, or a documentary. CBS's "Sixty Minutes," for example, gives a news magazine approach during prime evening time and provides information to groups with both general and special interests.

Another category for journalists in broadcasting is the extraordinary news event, such as the Soviet-American "handshake" in space or the assassination of a prominent figure in public life. During these times, regular commercial programmes are dispensed with to permit immediate news coverage. Under strong pressure the reporter must give facts and interpretation instantly, with no opportunity for editing.

Hard-nosed investigative reporting is a basic and exciting function at many stations. Often officials have been indicted, new laws passed, and countless irregularities corrected as a result. Consumer reporting is widespread and growing as newspeople regularly take on malpractices ranging from bait-and-switch advertising to price gouging. Both investigative and consumer reporting require the firm support of station management because of the possible reaction of advertisers as well as other members of the viewing audience. An increasing number of stations send reporters to cover regional stories and even to distant cities and foreign countries, often sharing their coverage in news-exchange agreements with other stations. Assigning reporters at state capitals either permanently or during legislative sessions is standard practice. Other types of outlying news bureaus also are maintained by many stations.

Electronic news gathering systems, providing live-action coverage, are in widespread use. Generally two technicians and a reporter travel in a van or panel truck equipped with a top-mounted microwave dish. Through the use of a miniature camera and a portable tape recorder, an account of the news event is beamed back to a prominent landmark in the city, atop which four "horns" have been placed to pick up signals from all points of the compass. At the studio, tapes are edited on machines to transfer selected segments from original to final form. Edited news segments may go directly to the air at that point, or be transferred to two-inch tape "carts" for random insertion into newscasts. All tape elements are bypassed, of course, when the story is presented live.

The three networks as well as independent services provide electronically fed color news reports of an international, national, and regional nature daily to stations throughout the country for incorporation into locally produced newscasts. Television and radio alike spend a great deal of time and money to keep their audiences abreast of the news. Election-year coverage is especially costly. To most broadcasters, however, the expense of covering news events is well justified. Stations and networks discovered quite early that news programmes rank exceptionally high in public interest and render a public service while building a steady audience and steady revenues. Surveys conducted annually by the Roper Organization, Inc., have shown that since 1963, television has been the source of most news for the American people. In addition, the most recent surveys have revealed that television enjoys an almost 2.5 to 1 advantage over newspapers as the "most believable" news medium.

The revolution in communications technology, while improving the quality of news programming, also has put broadcasters in a better financial position in covering news as well as in other operations. The developments include new videotape technology, high-quality magnetic-strip sound on film, satellite communication, instant-replay techniques, portable film and tape equipment, the use of high-speed jet aircraft to transport tape or film, and efficiently packaged, high-capacity switching gear that simplifies the problem of television pickup from almost any major point in the United States or the world.

In recent years national news consultant companies have been engaged by many television stations to increase the viewership of news programmes. Using the techniques of motivational research and sophisticated surveys, these experts have proposed changes in news programme formats. But many news directors and reporters have decried the application of techniques designed to please the most viewers as destroying the integrity of the news programmes. In one director's words, the result often is "slick, breezy news shows, dispensing glib headlines, socko action films and orchestrated 'spontaneity'—newscasts for people who can't stand television news." Another director accused consultants of becoming absentee news czars: "They dictate who should be on the air, and how the news should be presented, and load up the newscast with show biz."

The consultants' advice to humanize the presentation of news has resulted in numerous "happy talk" programmes with newscasters becoming, as one educator termed them, "Charlie Chuckles" and

"Nancy Yuk-yuks." The practice of crowding a large number of items into each newscast has been another consequence, as well as the replacement of some personnel. The principal consultant firms, Frank N. Magid Associates and McHugh and Hoffman, Inc., along with a number of news directors and station programme directors, have defended research into audience reactions and the resulting recommendations as essential management tools designed to improve news programmes and raise competitive ratings.

Local and regional surveys of this type supplement the long-established national rating systems that determine the life and death of all television programming. The A. C. Nielsen Company bases its ratings on a sampling of 1200 electronically metered homes. Although these reports often are disputed ("I've never been called by a ratings service," many viewers complain), the findings are supported by diaries maintained by 800,000 families either for Nielsen or the other major audience-research service, Arbitron, formerly known as ARB. The local and regional surveys often are at variance with the national ratings, but they merely reflect viewing habits of the particular areas involved.

Editorial Function

Although network newscasts have been accused by numerous individuals and groups of being biased in their presentations, such charges rarely have been made of local station news programmes. More than half of the nation's TV stations air editorial viewpoints, either sporadically or regularly, in clearly marked segments of their newscasts. Some stations have introduced a "letters column," in which comments from viewers are read as a part of the newscasts. Others invite viewers to present their views at a certain time each day, arrange panel programmes involving local community leaders, and air minidocumentaries and, although the cost is high, regular documentaries on subjects of prime interest.

Owners of stations that editorialize view the action as part of their obligation to serve the interests of their local communities. They regard editorials as making an important contribution to the public's understanding of issues, and at the same time enhancing their station's prestige and helping to build audiences. Stations that do not editorialize cite lack of time or manpower for the extensive preparation necessary to do an effective job. Some owners believe that editorializing is not an appropriate activity for a broadcast station. Surveys have shown that most viewers welcome editorials, feeling that such an expression of views helps them to think and to make up their minds about important issues.

Special editorial personnel or news staff members often require more than five hours to prepare the average editorial for broadcast. In order to ensure that the .editorial is received as reflecting the viewpoint of management and to maintain a desirabie distinction between news and opinion, the editorial generally is delivered by the station manager himself, usually in two or three minutes of air time. Some stations present editorial cartoons.

Programming and Production

Broadcasting programmes are planned and produced by the programming department. On small stations, only a few persons may be employed to make commercial announcements, read news and sports summaries, select and play recordings, and introduce network programmes. Large stations, however, may employ seventy-five or more persons to handle a variety of specialized jobs.

Programming policy and scheduling for a large station are handled by the programme director. The traffic manager prepares daily schedules of programmes and keeps a record of broadcast time available for advertising. The writing and editing of all scripts are the responsibility of the continuity director. Assisting is the continuity writer, who prepares announcers' books containing the script and commercials for each programme together with their sequence and length.

The director supervises individual programmes, possibly under the supervision of a producer, who handles the selection of scripts, financial matters, and other production problems. At times these functions are combined in the job of producer-director. Programme assistants obtain props, film slides, artwork, and makeup service; assist in timing the programme; and prepare cue cards. Some stations employ education and public affairs directors who supervise non-commercial programmes such as those presented by churches, schools, and civic groups. Many also have community relations directors, who provide liaison with numerous segments of the viewing and listening audience.

Television and radio staff announcers present news and live commercial messages, identify stations, conduct interviews, describe sports events, and act as masters of ceremonies. On small radio stations they may also operate the control board, sell time, and write scripts and news copy. Announcers on small stations often obtain FCC licenses in order that they also may operate transmitters.

Large television and radio stations may employ a librarian to handle the music files, and a musical director to supervise rehearsals and broadcasts. Television stations also have film editors who prepare films and videotape recordings for on-the-air presentation. The station's files of films and tape are maintained by a film librarian.

Television performances that are aired either live or on tape require the services of a studio supervisor, who arranges scenery and other equipment; a floor or stage manager, who directs the movement of actors on the set and relays stage directions, station breaks, and cues; floor personnel who set up props, hold cue cards, and perform other such chores; makeup artists, who prepare personnel for broadcasts; scenic designers, who plan and design settings and backgrounds; and sound effects technicians, who coordinate special sounds. Working with all these programming personnel are the engineers and broadcast technicians, who use their highly specialized knowledge to convert the sounds and pictures into electronic impulses that can be received by the public.

Advertising and Promotion

As has been noted, network national advertising, national "spot" advertising, and local advertising provide the bulk of operating revenue for television and radio stations. Large stations may also receive income from such services as producing programmes for clients and making films and tapes. The advertising staffs of the national networks solicit advertising from companies whose products or services are marketed through out the country. They provide a continuing flow of up-to-date information about the markets served by their affiliates and make contracts both directly with big companies and with the agencies that represent them.

National firms with large staffs of trained solicitors represent individual stations in calling on agencies and companies for business. They sell spot advertising, which may range from a series of brief announcements to full programmes originating in the local studios and from commercials to 15- or 30-minute programmes. These firms, located strategically in the major cities, make sales presentations for any or all the stations on their lists.

This leaves local advertising to be handled by the station itself. The commercial manager must build a staff of account executives, who often have a triple job to do: sell advertising in general, broadcasting in particular, and their own station specifically. This is true because the local merchant may not be fully aware of the advantages of advertising and may have practically no knowledge of what a carefully conceived television or radio advertising campaign may do for business.

The account executive first learns as much as possible about the prospective client's business. In consultation with the local sales manager and station programme director, a suggested plan, involving possibly a regular programme and a series of commercial announcements, is prepared. If the plan is accepted, skilled writers prepare the copy and continuity. After the advertiser is convinced that the campaign is selling goods or services, the salesperson seeks gradually to sell the sponsor additional broadcasting.

An important adjunct to sales is the promotion department. The promotion manager may be a staff member with no other responsibilities or may be the general manager, the commercial manager, a copywriter, or a salesperson. In order to attract both audiences and advertisers, the promotion manager prepares station advertisements and publicity stories for local newspapers, for trade publications read by agency and company advertising people, and for use over the station's own facilities. In addition, the promotion manager develops ideas for posters and other outdoor advertising; engages in such public relations activities as delivering speeches, answering station mail, and handling telephone inquiries; and attracts attention to the station and its individual programmes through such devices as parades, stunts, and personal appearances by star performers.

Opportunities and Salaries

Thousands of job openings occur in all phases of broadcasting each year. During the 1970s, however, as a steadily increasing number of journalism and mass communications college graduates poured onto the market, and as an economic recession took place, great perseverance and marked evidence of talent were essential for young people desiring to break into the business. A willingness to begin work with small stations, to move to where job openings occurred, and often to seize other opportunities for employment while waiting for the desired job frequently were necessary.

When openings develop, station managers generally turn to their files of job applicants, many of whom are already employed on smaller stations. For many jobs the graduates of schools with highly developed programmes in radio, television, and speech are preferred. These persons already have learned production, programming, and/ or news gathering and presentation techniques and thus generally can perform specified chores almost immediately. At times bright graduates of print-oriented schools of journalism, or of straight liberal arts or business programmes, are transformed into broadcast personnel.

One of every nine persons employed in television is a member of a minority group, and the number is increasing each year. In fact, a study of FCC data has shown that three of every four new employees hired since 1971 have been women or minority group representatives. Only 13.7 percent of the women employees, however, serve in the so-called image-maker capacities of owner-managers and professionals, as compared with 37.3 percent in periodicals. So, despite the increasing number of women such as Barbara Walters of ABC who have become national and local celebrities in broadcasting, the movement of women into higher echelon positions still lies ahead.

Stations are constantly in the market for competent advertising solicitors and continuity writers. Writing commercials requires a knowledge of selling, and more often than not such a job is filled by a woman. Salaries in these fields compare favorably with those requiring similar talents in the other media. Good promotion men and women with large stations commonly earn $12,000 or more.

Beginning salaries for television and radio news personnel are comparable to those paid newspaper reporters and editors. These range from $7500 to $8500, depending upon the size of the station, regional competitive factors, and the training of the applicant. After three to five years, salaries for radio newswriters range from $9500 to $13,000, while television newswriters on large stations may earn more than $14,000. Talent fees for those with on-mike and on-camera assignments push these incomes even higher.

Skilled network employees earn much higher salaries. Those who serve as assignment editors and who produce network shows earn additional fees. Newswriters at network originating points and at stations owned and operated by NBC and ABC are represented by the National Association of Broadcast Employees and Technicians. The union's news jurisdiction includes all writing, editing, processing, collecting, and collating of news, including film. The bargaining agent for all CBS writers and for NBC and ABC on-the-air news personnel in New York City is the Writers Guild of America. Those under individual contract with the networks to write and deliver their own news programmes are represented by the American Federation of Television and Radio Artists, the union that covers all on-the-air performers. They earn talent fees for newscasts and other air work plus a guaranteed wage. Barbara Walters' $1 million a year as coanchorperson of the ABC Evening News and producer of "specials" is a record salary for a journalist.

❏

11
Brief History of Indian Cinema

The first important step in the motion picture industry was the invention of kinetoscope by Edison. It was a peephole box through which one person at a time could peep or see. The box contained a spool of pictures. The pictures were photographed on the new flexible film invented by George Eastman. The spool of pictures was revolved and it created the illusion of motion for the person peeping through the hole of the kinetoscope. Such a "magic" was first shown by a phonograph parlour at Broadway, New York, on April 14, 1894.

Lumiere Brothers (Louis and Auguste) in France combined Edison's kinetoscope with a new projection machine. Now there was no need of the peephole. The Frenchmen invaded the U.S. in 1896 with their improved machine. This forced Edison to improve his own kinetoscope. He combined it with a superior projector invented by Armat in U.S.A. It could project a series of photographs of moving pictures to not just one man but to a whole group of people. The machine or device made by Edison was called vitascope. Vitascope was born on April 13, 1896, just two years after the birth of kinetoscope, and, with vitascope started the glittering career of the motion picture industry.

There is no motion in the pictures: they only give the illusion of motion to viewers. The pictures or photographs on the film do not move. They are static. Advantage is taken of the principle of "persistence of vision". The principle is: if a series of pictures is passed before the eye, the image of one picture stays in the eye and seems to merge with the image of the succeeding picture. When pictures are rotated very fast by the film projector, they can give the illusion of continuous motion. That is the magic of the film.

Cinema has become the most influential art form of 20th century from its marginal beginnings. India holds eminent position in film making in the world. It produces highest number of films every year. Whatever may be the quality of the film, they continue to be the popular mass media. Earlier, cinema was a simple means of mechanical recording, preserving and reproducing moving visual images. With the development of film technology, the art of cinema developed a language of its own. Kumar says, that cinema is called 'the seventh art', and its language has developed over the past 70-80 years to a specialised and sophisticated level. Opinion differ, however on whether cinema is a 'pure' art form or a 'bastard' art.

'Cinema' and 'films' are used interchangeably but there is a difference between these two terms. Cinema has specific means to create imaginary time and space, and utilization of these means defines how cinematic a film is Imaginary time can be created through movement by means of montage, camera movements and movement within the frame and through sounds of human voice, music and noise. Space can be created through image with the help of size of shots, camera angle, depth of field, montage and through sound 'off screen'. Films are made of stories dance, music, drama, photography, painting, architecture and many other things that we call cinema. Films mean the particular movies that we see with all the elements they contain and cinema means the sum of the means made possible only by film technology which distinguish cinema from other arts. The greater the number of imaginaries of time arid space, the more cinematic the film will be.

Development of Indian Cinema

India is the leader in film production. Indian cinema has yielded 28,000 feature films and thousands of documentaries so far. The first exposure to motion picture was received by India in 1896, when

Lumiere Brothers' cinematograph unveiled six soundless short films at Watson Hotel, Esplanade Mansion, Bombay on July 7. The first exposing of celluloid in camera by an Indian and its consequent screening took place in 1899, when Harishchandra Bhatwadekar (Save Dada) shot two short films and exhibited them under Edison's projecting kinetoscope.

Hiralal Sen and F.B. Thanawalla were two Indian pioneers engaged in the production of short films in Calcutta and Bombay in 1900. Around 1902, J.F. Madan and Abdullah Esoofally launched their career with Bioscope shows of imported short films. In 1912, N. G. Chitre, and R.G. Torney made silent feature film 'Pundalik' which was released on May 18, and it was half British in its make.

Dhunraj Govind Phalke, more generally known as Dada Saheb Phalke was responsible for the production of India's first fully indigenous silent feature film Raja Harish Chandra which heralded the birth of the Indian Film industry. The film had titles in Hindi and English and was released on May 3, 1913 at the coronation cinema in Bombay. In 1917, Bengal saw the birth of its first feature film, 'Satyabadi Raja Harishchandra' made by Madan's Elphinstone Bioscope Company. In Madras the first feature film of South India 'Keechaka Vadham' was made by Nataraja Mudaliar in 1919.

After stepping in to 1920, the Indian cinema, gradually assumed the shape of a regular industry. The industry also came within the purview of the law.

The first Indian talkie Alam Ara produced by the imperial film company and directed by Ardeshir Irani - released on March 14, 1931 at Majestic cinema in Bombay. The talkie had brought revolutionary changes in the whole set up of the industry. The year 31 marked the beginning of the talkie era in Bengal and South India.

The thirties is recognised as the decade of social protest in the history of Indian cinema. The decade also witnessed the release of first talkie films in regional languages such as Marathi, Gujarati, Kannada, Assamese, Malayalam, etc.

The decade of World War II and Indian independence was a momentous one for cinematography all over India. Some memorable films were produced during the 40s such as V. Shantaram's Dr. 'Kotnis Ki Amar Kahanl', Mehboob's 'Roti', Chetan Anand's 'Neecha Nagar', Abbas's 'Dharti Ke Lal, Raj Kapoor's 'Barsaat' and 'Aag'.

The first International Film Festival of India held in early 1952 at Bombay had great impact on Indian Cinema. The big turning point came in 1955 with the release of Satyajit Ray and his classic 'Pather Panchali'.

In Hindi cinema too, the impact of neorealism was evident in some distinguished films like Bimal Roy's 'Do Bigha Zameen', 'Devdas', 'Madhumati', Raj Kapoor's 'Boot Polish', 'Shri 420' and 'Jagte Raho', Mehboob's 'Mother India' and so on.

In 1953, the first color feature, Jhansi Ki Rani was made. Mother India (1957), Mughal-e-Azam (1960), Ganga Jamuna (1961), Sangam (1964), Bobby (1973), Sholay (1975), have been some of the successful films at the box office and trend setters in the commercial cinema.

In sixties, mediocre films were made mostly to please the distributors and to some extent, meet the demands of the box office, such as, Mughal-E-Azam, Guide, Sahib Bibi Aur Gulam, Aradhana, etc.

Satyajit Ray, Ritwik Ghatak and Mrinal Sen were the founding fathers of the new cinema in India. Roy was fortunate enough to present his films in almost all the leading film festivals of the world. The national and international awards won by Roy are numerous.

In seventies, the trend for new wave cinema started in India with the release of Mrinal Sen's Bhuvan Shome (1969). This boosted the production of small budget films with simple plots but rich in resonance. It was followed by Sara Akash, Rajnigandha, Chhoti Si Baat, Chitchor, Swami, Arth and Gudgudee.

The new wave cinema movement continued with full spirit in seventies and eighties also. Some of the good movies like Manthan, Bhoomika, Junoon, 36-Chowringhee Lane, Mirch Masala, Trishagni were produced during this period.

Regional cinema also developed almost simultaneously in thirties in Gujarat, Maharashtra, Kerala, Bengal, Karnataka, Assam, Tamil Nadu, and Andhra Pradesh.

Nineties saw the revival of the musical love stories in Hindi cinema such as Qayamat Se Qayamat Tak, Chandni, Hum Aapke Hai Kaun, etc.

Milestones in Indian Cinema		*Main Features*
(1)	*(2)*	*(3)*
May, 1920	Cinematograph Act was made a law.	Exhibition of films made subject to prior certification.
Oct. 1927	Indian Cinematograph Committee was formed under the chairmanship of Mr. T.Rangacharian.	Censorship is necessary in India, to prevent the import, production and public exhibition of films which might demoralise the public, hurt relibrious susceptibilities or excite communal or racial animosities.
1952	Cinematograph Act adopted in its preindependence form.	The British tradition of severe censorship of films.
1969	Khosla Commission was appointed to report on the status of the entire film industry.	Autonomous Censor Board, without any official government control—the examination of film as a whole and to allow kissing, nudity and violence, if they were integral to the theme.

Contd.

(1)	*(2)*	*(3)*
1969	K.A. Abbas challenged the censorship of films in general.	The verdict of the Supreme Court in favour of the film censorship.
1978	Working group on National Films Policy was appointed.	Criticised the rigid approach of the film censors against the exposure of corruption in the Police and the government and political leadership as it portrayal of social prevents reality.
June, 1983	Central Board of Film Censors renamed as Central Board of Film Certification.	

The Talkie

By 1928, some countries in the West had developed the sound film. It also came to be called a talkie. The first talkie shown in India was Universal's Melody of Love at Calcutta, in 1928. Exhibitors of Bombay, Sidhwas, also screened brief talkies from England. Each of these contained several brief coverage of events.

In 1930, came the first attempt to make an Indian talkie programme. It contained a Khadi exhibition with Gandhi, C.F. Andrews etc. speaking and a dance by Sulochana. The first talkie feature film came in 1931. It was Ardeshir Irani's Alam Ara with Zubeida, Prithviraj Kapoor and Master Vithal in the cast.

Prabbat Film Co. was founded in 1929 at Kolhapur, Maharashtra. New Theatres was organised at Calcutta by B.N. Sircar in 1930. Both these film companies played a great role in the development of Indian cinema.

In the year in which the first Indian talkie feature film Alam Ara appeared (1931), 22 more films in Hindi (rather Hindustani) were also made. Three films were made in Bengali and one each in Tamil and Telugu. By 1933, seventy five films had been made in Hindi.

The first attempt at producing a film in colour was made in 1932 by Madan Theatres. The company took its film Bilwa Mangal abroad for processing. Prabhat Films also took their film Sairandhri to Germany for colour prints. Both the films were not high-grade success in colour. The first Indian attempt at colour in the country again came from Ardeshir Irani. He made Kisan Kanya in 1937. In the real sense, of course, colour film came only in the fifties with Mehboob's Aan, Sohrab Modi's Jhansi Ki Rani and Shantaram's Jhanak Jhanak Payal Baje.

Besides the films mentioned above, some other outstanding films till the beginning of the second world war were: Typist Girl (1918) of Chandulal shah, Shiraz (1926) and Himanshu Rai's A Throw of Dice (1929) and Karma (1934). He made Devika Rani, the heroine of most of his films, immortal. Ayodhyacha Raja (1932), Sant Tukaram (1936), Amar Jyoti (1936), Duniya Na Mane and Admi, all of Shantaram. Toofan Mail (1932) and Jai Bharat (1936): the first film on Hindu-Muslim unity, of Wadia Brothers. Chandidas (1932), Devdas (1936) and Mukti of New Theatres, Calcutta. Gangavataran (The Descent of Ganges) in 1937 was the last film of Phalke, known as the father of Indian cinema.

Madras United Artists' Corporation in 1938 started making films in Tamil, Telugu and Malayalam, and also in Hindi.

A great film Shakuntala was made by Shantaram in 1943. Pukar and Sikander of Sohrab Modi in early forties were huge successes. Shantaram also made Dr. Kotnis Ki Amar Kahani in 1945. Mehboob's successful films of the forties included Aurat, Roti and Sister, from the south Chandralekha was a super-spectacle in Hindi.

Influence of major Indian studios started decreasing in the forties. Independent productions were increasing. The "star" system began in which heroes and heroines attracted public more than the studio name. Along with it, came "formula" films in which the themes and their treatment were repeated with a fixed dosage of song and dances. For the first time, "black" money too entered the films. These three characteristics can still be found.

Himansu Rai died in 1940 and Phalke in 1944. Dharti Ke Lal of K.A. Abbas, in 1949, became the first feature film to be shown in Moscow. Shakuntala was shown in the U.S.A. in 1947.

In 1943, the showing of newsreels of "Indian News Parade" and documentaries of Information Films of India, was made compulsory in Cinema theatres. This was mainly a measure to promote war effort. After the world war was over, both Indian News Parade and Information Films of India were dissolved in 1946. On the pattern of the latter, the Films Division of the Government of India was established in 1948.

Calcutta Film Society was formed by Satyajit Ray and Chidananda Das Gupta in 1947. That started the Film Society Movement which gradually spread to other parts of the country. In 1949, a Film Enquiry Committee was set up to give its recommendations on the various aspects of Indian cinema.

The Fifties

One of the most important things that happened in the fifties was the appearance of Satyajit Ray on the film scene. He gave us his famous Apu Trilogy (a set of 3 inter-connected films) during this period—Pather Panchali in 1954, Aparajito in 1957 and Apur Sansar in 1959. His Jalsaghar appeared in 1958.

A great director, P.C. Barua, maker of Devdas died in 1951. Bombay Talkies closed in 1952 and Prabhat Film Co. in 1953.

Raj Kapoor's Awara became a great hit in the Soviet Russia in 1954. The same year Bimal Roy's Do Bigha Zamin won awards at the International Film Festivals at Cannes and Karlovy Vary. In 1956 Ray's Pather Panchali won an award at Cannes. In 1957, his Aparajito won an award at Venice. K.A Abbas made Munna that was widely praised at Edinburgh festival in 1955. This was the first Indian film without songs or dances. Kaagaz ke Phool of Guru Dutt marked the start of widescreen production. Films Division's Jaipur won the first award for a documentary at Venice in 1951.

The Film Enquiry Committee's report came in 1951. Its important recommendations were the creation of a Film Finance Corporation, a Film Institute for training and a Film Export Corporation.

The Film Federation of India was formed in 1951. In 1952 was held the first International Film Festival in India. In 1954, National Awards for films were instituted.

Great colour films appeared during the same fifties. Sohrab Modi's Jhansi Ki Rani was the first colour film in 1953. Shantaram's Jhanak Jhanak Payal Baje appeared in 1955 and Mehboob's Mother India in 1957.

Raj Kapoor (Aag, Barsaat, Shri 420), Guru Dutt (Baazi, Pyasa, Kaagaz ke Phool) and Kamal Amrohi (Mahal, Dawa) were the great new names during this period.

The Sixties

In the sixties, K. Asif's Mughal-e-Aazam was a period (historical) film on a grand scale, with spectacular sets (1960). Ganga Jamuna was another great success. Raj Kapoor's Sangam set the trend for shooting abroad.

The Film Finance Corporation was formed in 1960 to finance and encourage new, young and creative film makers. The Film Institute of India was created in 1961 at Poona to train young talented people in different aspects of film. The Indian Motion Pictures Export Corporation was established in 1963. The National Film Archive of India was established at Pune in 1964. In 1966 Dadasaheb Phalke Award was instituted to honour people for their outstanding contribution to Indian cinema. Devika Rani was the first film personality to receive the Phalke award in 1967. Mrinal Sen's Bhuvan Shome, financed by the Film Finance Corporation, won several awards. It was also a commercial success. Phalke's birth centenary was celebrated in 1970.

enties and After

In 1971, India was producing the largest number of films in the world. Calcutta'71 (1971) was an example of the film taking notice of the current politics. This film was made by Mirnal Sen. Garam Hawa of M.S. Sathyu was funded by the Film Fiance Corporation and won several awards. Ankur in 1974 was the first film of Shyam Benegal and was a great success. The new wave cinema (or parallel or alternative or "the other" or art cinema) which started with Bhuvan Shome was carried further by its creator, Mrinal Sen and others like Benegal, Sathyu, Basu Chatterji and others. Rajnigandha of Basu Chatterji was a very successful film of this "wave" in 1974. That very year, the International Film Festival of India became an annual feature.

Raj Kapoor made Bobby in 1973. This film on teenage love became very popular. A great spectacle Sholay (1975) was shot in 70 mm. Amjad Khan, a heartless dangerous dacoit, became a star overnight. The film set a new trend in multi-star films, spectacular locations and scenes and violence. Side by side films with offbeat, uncommon theme and treatment like Mahesh Bhatt's Janma and Daddy were also produced. In the late eighties and the early nineties, a new trend of love between the very young started as in films such as Main Ne Pyar Kiya, Ashiqi and Love Story. New young artists acted as heroes and heroines.

You can see commercial cinema, art cinema and middle cinema existing side by side. Commercial cinema has the lion's share in the number of films. The producers have an eye on profits, so they try to provide entertainment, even when entertainment means an escape from reality. This type of cinema has all sorts of "masala". It has well-known actors, dances, music, fights, melodrama in story and dialogues. Heroes and heroines are all "white", they can do no wrong. Villains are all "black", they can have no virtue. Commercial cinema works on success "formulas". Dharam Veer, Parvarish, Amar Akbar Anthony, Shehanshah etc. belong to this type of cinema.

Art cinema, referred to above, became po
It continued beyond the seventies too but in a
with Bhuvan Shome of Mrinal Sen in 196
Corporation played an important role in giving
Besides Satyajit Ray, whose films always ha
other names in art or new wave cinema are: Mrinal Sen, Satḥyu,
Chatterji, Shyam Benegal, Avtar Kumar, Kumar Shahani, Karanth and
Ritwick Ghatak.

Art cinema films are low-budget and do not have real life. Their
treatment is artistic and away from the formula.

But, generally, the criticism of art or alternative cinema is that
not many people see it. So, it hardly covers its cost. Cinema, the
critics argue, should be a medium of mass communication. It should
entertain the common man the masses.

So, you have "middle" cinema. It is a sort of compromise
between the commercial and the art cinema. It should show taste and
art but be a financial success too. Benegal's Junoon, Govind Nihalani's
Aakrosh (or TV serial on Partition "Tamas"), Saeed Mirza's Albert
Pinto Ko Gussa Kyon Aata Hai, Ketan Mehta's Mirch Masala,
Mahesh Bhatt's Daddy are some examples of middle cinema.

FILM AS MASS MEDIUM

Film is a means of creative expression. It performs the functions
of mass media. Such as information, education, entertainment and
transmission of culture. Films are widely popular and their audio
visual nature provides them a pervasive power for social influence.
Therefore, they have the potential to play an important role as a
medium of entertainment, information and education and as a catalyst
for social change. Films are popular because they entertain. They are
a facet of a mass culture and mass art. They generate mass mediated
culture arising from elite, folk, popular or mass origins.

Almost every person of the society has participated in the
activity of going to cinema hall and enjoying a film. According to
Jovett and Linton, "obviously there is still some thing unique and

rently appealing about going to the movies", and this is clearly different from other mass media experiences".

The social institution of movie going is firmly established in our society and movies have played an important part as one of the factors contributing to the dramatic changes which have taken place in the last 50 years in the way we live and also in how we perceive the world around us. They have provided us not only with entertainment, but also with ideas, and it would be difficult to conceive of our society without them.

The films take as their starting point those aspects of society with which we have become familiar. They create twist plots and use other narrative devices which infuse the story with sufficient new elements to attract an audience.

Films draw heavily from reality, portraying situations that have resemblance to the everyday stresses and aspirations of viewers' lives. The movies recognise the link between their lives and films in both general and specific terms. The ease of comprehension helps the viewer to assume the role of the characters and to identify with them quickly and effectively. Films appeal to their primary emotions and sentiments. Films provide photographic realism, Vivid visual presentation in which the images are already fully established, easily identified and followed.

Melodrama in films draws suppressed fears and desires into a public realm, but suggests personal solutions. The viewers are active participants in the construction of the image that both represents present reality and allows them to escape as future fantasy.

Tudar (1969), pointed out that the darkened theatre, combined with the heightened intensity of the message stimuli, the increased sense of social isolation that it creates, and the relaxed posture of the movie viewer make the message more emotionally potent.

Thus, films leave lasting impression of the message. For example, films like Mother India, Naya Duar, Awara have their message still fresh in the minds of the people.

The films generate popular culture and create culture waves. Such as in fashions styles and mannerisms. Moreover, by revolving the film stories and characters around the traditional ideas and role stereotypes, they foster the role stereotypes in the society in general. Some of the films like 'Bhigi Palkein,' 'Subah', 'Mrutyudand' did try to show breaking role stereotypes and they were successful in conveying the message.

Roberge (1984) feels, "while cinema is acknowledged as a disseminator of popular culture, it is not described as, a "cultivator" but simply a 'disseminator' of culture. The contributory role of the cinema in cultivating and shaping culture is not acknowledged and it is perceived as a mere instrument or channel". This implies that the cultural quality of cinema should be of good standard". The cinema has always done a remarkable job in crating a type of visual public 'consensus'. Mass production and distribution of message systems transform selected private perspectives into broad public perspectives and brings mass public into existence.

Films combine visuals, movement, sound, theatre, music all in one. Therefore, they are able to communicate effectively and create impact which can not be created by any other media. It is due to this characteristic of films, masses from all levels are attracted to go to cinema.

Due to reality element, films have psychological impact on people. The extent of reality that can be presented through films is far greater than television or any other medium. Their language is universal and this helps in breaking any social or cultural barriers. Therefore, media experts and development communicators feel that films can prove to be the most effective mass medium in a country like India where literacy is low and people can not afford other media such as print or television due to economic reasons. Many people from lower economic status do not mind spending for films as it is the popular form of entertainment. Feature films are produced in several Indian languages. They provide a viable alternative to the people in terms of entertainment.

Since it is a powerful audio visual medium, social, cultural, political, communal problems can be projected well before the masses.

Despite the growth of television and availability of other means of entertainment, films have remained the most popular medium of entertainment for the masses which is a basic necessity.

Thus, films can work as a social monitor. Films have been effective in projecting social evils, for example, the film 'Yeh Aag Kub Bujegi' well presented the evil of dowry, corrupt politicians in film like 'Inquilabb' and 'Kissa Kursi Ka' and so on. Films have been exposing under world elements, black marketeers, bureaucrats, unemployment problem and so on.

According to Malhan, "Through characterisation, demonstration and depiction of scenes and situations, it can even directly help to sell the concepts and norms of national or emotional integration dignity of labour, the bare-foot doctor or engineer, an understanding spouse and the pulls of extra-marital relations." They can stimulate values of good life and citizenship as also participatory virtues of developmental activities.

Each genere of film is capable of creating impact on the masses. For example, comedy and hilarious movies entertain people and relax them. Social or tragic movies provide outlet to the emotions of the viewers.

India has a history of hundred years of cinema. Indian films have been recognized nationally and internationally. Films in India have not only remained the medium of entertainment but film making has emerged as a major art form which is a creative expression of the film makers or artists.

Types of Films

When the talk of cinema, there are two major forms, generally known by people.

1. Commercial Cinema. It primarily aims at providing entertainment to the people. It includes the ingredients of popular

cinema-star system, high budget, abundance of m
dance. It mostly resorts to phantasy to provide er
people. For example, films like Vaqt, Sholay, Muqhdda ... Sikkandar,
Hum Apke Hain Kaun, are a few examples of such films.

2. Art Cinema. It is more realistic and relevant to the needs
of the people and society. This form is not very popular. It is also
called 'paraallel cinema' 'alternative cinema' or 'New wave cinema'.
These new trend films are made at low cost, outside the main stream
of commercial cinema. As said by Malhan, "Their dominant
characteristics were their social concern, purposefulness, realism,
narrative style, exclusion of unrelated songs, dances, and fights and
other familiar devices of commercial package. Their acceptance by
the intelligent and cultivated audiences in the country and the high
praise which some of the really good new trend films won abroad
brought a much needed self-confidence to adventurous or innovative
film makers". National Films Development Corporation provided
institutional aid for the production of these films. Satyajit Ray, Shyam
Benegal, Govind Nihalani, Mrinal Sen, are some of the known art
cinema proponents. However, many times this cinema faced difficulties
in getting financier, or distributor. Many of them remain at award
winning level only and never reach the masses due to these difficulties.
With the popularity of television, some of such films are telecast on
television. Chakra, Ankur, Nishant, Ardha Satya, Damul, Paar,
Bhumika, Hazar Chaurashi Ki Maa are some of the examples of art
cinema.

When we talk of films, there are three major types.

1. **Feature Films.** Feature film means fictionalised film
   exceeding 2000 metres in length in 35 mm or corresponding
   length in other gauge or on video. Feature film means a full
   length cinematograph film produced wholly or partly in
   India with a format and a story woven around a number
   of characters where the plot is revealed mainly through
   dialogue and not only through narration, animation, or

cartoon depiction and does not include an advertisement film. Feature films are about a story enacted by a popular cast and usually has ending. The main objective of these films is not so much to convey a moral but firstly to entertain an audience. They continue to be most popular form of entertainment. Feature films could be commercial or art films. These are produced for mass information and entertainment. These films create cultural waves and to certain degree, change the attitude of the viewers, increase information and modify behaviour. These films have the elements like comedy, drama, suspense, science fiction, detective, or horror.

2. **Documentary Films.** Documentary dramatizes an idea or theme. It uses the factual material in order to dramatize its idea, it tells its simple story in terms of human beings and human interests. Sometimes it uses professional actors in some scenes. Of late, documentaries also have acquired a reputation for artistic merit. They last longer than feature films due to their informative and educative nature.

3. **Educational Films.** These films are produced with instructional objectives only. For example, films on details of geography or history, moon, light, atmosphere, non formal education in slums, ideal school and so on. These films can be used as part of a main lesson or supplementary information. Some of the documentaries also can be used as educational films. In India educational films have not been used widely.

4. **Sponsored Films.** Many commercial organisations produce films as part of a broad advertising and public relations programme on their products, achievements, approaches to their production etc. to attract the consumer, financiers, and excellent professionals as well as to compete in fast advancing market system.

DOCUMENTARY FILMS

The documentary or non-fiction film is an elaborate method of recording the lives and activities of real people, but 'constructed' or 'recreated' nevertheless to tell an interesting story. A Committee set up by the Government of India in the sixties under the chairmanship of M.D. Bhat to define the term 'Documentary Film' for the guidance of bodies like the Film Advisory Boards and the Film State Awards Committee, stated that the following definition drafted by the World Union of Documentary Film Makers in 1947 was most appropriate:

'By the documentary film is meant all methods of recording on celluloid any aspect of reality, interpreted either by factual shooting or by sincere or justifiable reconstruction, so as to appeal either to reason or emotion, for the purpose of stimulating the desire for, and the widening of human knowledge and understanding, and of truthfully posing problems and their solutions in the spheres of economic, culture and human relations.'

The documentary had its beginnings in 1922 when Robert Flaherty, an Englishman, took his camera to the Arctic regions to film the life of an Eskimo family. The result was Nanook of the North, a documentary film that pioneered the documentary tradition in cinema and later in television. But it was John Grierson who popularized the term and who turned the documentary into a popular artistic form. He shot his documentary entitled Drifters on location in the North Sea. It provided a glimpse of the fishermen of that region. Some of his other outstanding documentaries are Weather Forecast, Song of Ceylon, Coal Face, and Night Mail.

By the 1930s the documentary film was an established form and came to be patronised and supported by national governments, particularly during the war years. Film-makers and governments were soon convinced that the purpose of a documentary was social— "setting forth public and private crises and victories, to showing us where man has been and what inevitably man would become unless proper action is taken." 'We have to think of communications',

ɔlving our people in building a future. But this
̣̣e is not imported from the top, it is built from the
. that the common people themselves are in the forefront of
. whole exercise of persuasion.'

Documentary Genres

The label 'Cinema verite' or Cinema of Reality sums up the
type of film a documentary aims to be John Grierson defined a film
documentary as 'the creative interpretation of reality.' S. Sukhdev,
the veteran documentary film-maker, however, revised this definition
to the creative interpretation of recreated reality.' Satyajit Ray wondered
if Grierson's definition was not a little misleading since even fictional
films and even fantasies and fairy tales dealt with reality. The
documentary evolved as a reaction to shooting in a studio with a
selected cast, generally chosen from among the urban elite. The
pioneers of the documentary frowned upon the synthetic fabrication
of the studio and insisted on the existence of real men and women,
real things and real issues. They believed in story-material taken from
life in the raw and in spontaneous gestures and unrehearsed speech.
They wanted the cameras and the sound recording equipment to be
taken from the studio to the field and the factory, to the road and the
dockyard.

Several genres of the non-fiction evolved over the years: they
ranged from the 'naturalist' and 'realist', to the 'experimental' and
the 'abstract.' Somewhere in between were 'ethnographic' films,
'training' or educational/instructional films, and 'propaganda' films.
The genres were defined in terms of the methods of filming (and
editing) actual people and events. The video documentary is perhaps
the most recent format, with its beginnings going back to the 1970s.
CENDIT of New Delhi and SEWA of Ahmedabad were the foremost
organisations that promoted the video documentary in India. A Video
Festival is now held every year in Trivandrum, and the Mumbai
International Film Festival for Documentary, Short and Animation
Films, has a Video Vista Section where over a hundred video
documentaries are screened. The video format is inexpensive, flexible

and easily accessible, and therefore is the ideal alternative to the big media.

The Indian Documentary

The Indian documentary was pioneered by three Europe-trained film-makers. The first was P.V. Pathy, who had his training in Paris; the second D.G. Tendulkar, a student of Sergei Eisenstein in the Moscow Film School; and the third K.S. Hirlekar, who studied film making in Germany. These three led the development of the Indian documentary. They introduced editing, a vivid commentary style, effective music and sound effects. Between 1920 and 1940, more than 1500 short films were produced.

In 1947, Paul Zils together with Fali Billimoria, established the Documentary Unit of India. A master editor and producer trained in Germany, Zils made a number of notable films: Hindustan Hamara, Zalzala, The Ripening Seed, The Vanishing Tribe and Kurvdndi Road. Zils got together with Jag Mohan to edit the quarterly periodical, Indian Documentary.

In 1949 and 1950 as many as 32 black-and-white documentaries were made. The films were dubbed in five Indian languages-English, Hindi, Bengali, Tamil and Telugu. (Today, as many as 16 languages are in use in the Indian documentary). In June 1949, the first three documentary films were released: Kashmir Carries On, India Independent, and Immersion of Gandhiji's Ashes.

The first Indian documentary to win an international award in a foreign film festival was Rajasthan Series I-Jaipur. The first feature-length documentary made by the Films Division was released in 1955. This was Mitrata ki Yatra. Other films that won prizes in overseas film festivals were: Symphony of Life in 1955, Wonder of Work in 1957, and The Challenge of Everest, which won four awards. Thus, in the first two decades of the Indian documentary, over 250 documentaries were produced both by the Films Division and 'outside producers.' Some of the award, winning 'outside producers' were:—S. Sukhdev, who made India' 67; Clement P.

Baptista, Handicrafts of Rajasthan, Shyam Benegal, Close to Nature; N.S. Tappa, Song of The Snows; Satyajit Ray, Rabindranath Tagore, and Tapan Sinha, Jagdish Chandra Bose. Other film-makers of note who made a valuable contribution to the development of the Indian documentary were: V. M. Vijayakar, K.T. John, Santi P. Choudhary (first generation); K.S. Chari, Pramod Pati, S.N.S. Sastry, T.A. Abraham and Neil Gokhale (second generation), and Loksen Lalvani (third generation).

Commenting on the development of the Indian documentary film, P. V. Pathy said in 1957, "The rightful claim to credit for having fostered the adolescence of the documentary film goes to our government. Even the future of our documentary seems to be linked with Government sponsorship." In the mid-1990s, that future was uncertain as multi-channel television grabbed audience interest and cinema exhibitors' resentment against obligatory screening of documentaries and newsreels rose to a crescendo.

Indian Newsreel

The short film in India has had a long history, going back to the first decade of the 20th century. Even before the first feature film was produced in 1912, film directors like Dadasaheb Phalke, made many short films both in the 'Silent' and the 'Talkies' Era. The common subjects for such short films (called 'topicals') were political meetings, funerals of national leaders, strikes, burning of foreign cloth, and visits by foreign dignitaries. The 'topicals' produced in India were confined to the installation functions and weddings of the Maharajahs... The Delhi Durbars of 1903 and 1911 were filmed. Dussehra celebrations, fairs and festivals, the day to day life of people in various parts of India, snippets from Parsi theatre plays and even industries came within the camera range of the early newsreel cameramen.

There were numerous such short films made by private companies like Bombay Talkies, Maharashtra Film Company, Kohinoor and many others. The "shorts" were screened along with the company's feature films. The Aurora Film Corporation pioneered a regular newsreel named 'Calcutta Film Gazette.'

During World War II, the Government set up the Film Advisory Board which later became the Information Films of India (IFI), for the production of propaganda films and newsreels. The newsreels were distributed under the banner of 'The Indian News Parade,' In 1946, these organisations ceased to exist, but two years later, when India became independent, the Indian News Review was started as a successor to the Indian News Parade. Thus there was no official organisation to film the historic transfer of power on August 15, 1947.

In the early years of the Indian News Reel, the emphasis was on projecting national leaders and events. However, with greater experience and the necessity of educating the masses, the emphasis shifted from personalities to issues such as family planning, insurance, savings, the Green Revolution, etc. The commentary which played such an important part in the early newsreels was now given little importance, and the tape-recorder was taken to the fields and the factories as also to remote areas of the country where the common people's reactions were recorded on camera.

The Directorate of Field Publicity, which runs over 150 units in the rural and urban nontheatre areas, screens Films Division's newsreels regularly. The Films Division has arrangements for free exchange of newsreel material with 26 international organisations. The widespread expansion of television led to the winding up of the weekly newsreel from April 1,1984, and the reduction in the number of documentaries, from 250 to a mere 52 per year.

Films Division

The Films Division was set up in Bombay at the end of 1948 as a 'media unit' of the Ministry of Information and Broadcasting. It was closely modelled on the Information Films of India, the Indian News Parade and Kinematographic Services, the organisations established by the British to make propaganda films during World

War II. Indeed, during the early years, the Films Division was identified with the Information Films of India, and audiences looked upon its products as government propaganda. That perception has not changed over the past four decades.

The objectives of the Films Division were well chalked out: 'the production and distribution of newsreels and short films required by the Government of India for public information, education, motivation and for instructional and cultural purposes'. Besides, it aimed at mobilising the use of the dynamic medium of film to disseminate information to the broadcast spectrum of Indian and foreign audiences and to focus attention on important aspects of the country's life and to assist the growth and development of documentary films as a medium of education and communication.

During the first year the Films Division concentrated on producing newsreels. The following year documentaries were taken up and 31 were released, one in colour. In the first two decades the Films Division made over 2,700 films, many of them documentaries on India's cultural heritage. Some notable examples were Taj Mahal, Mahabalipuram, Jain Temple, and Hill Temples of Gujarat and Cave Temples of India. A series of films on Indian classical folk dances was also completed. The titles suggest the subjects filmed-Bharat Natyam, Kathak, and Folk Dances of Assam. Short Biographies of national leaders like Gandhi, Nehru, Tagore and Tilak also proved popular. The Indian Documentary Producers Association (IDPA) was established in the early fifties; its journal, Indian Documentary, though published only for a few years, offered a rare record of the documentary movement of the post-Independence years.

By the 1980s, the Films Division had been transformed into a more streamlined organisation making each year over 200 documentaries, training films for the armed forces, instructional films for farmers and factory workers, arid 104 national and regional newsreels. Asiad '82 challenged the Division to record for posterity the excitement of the Asian Games held in New Delhi. However, it continued to be used as an arm of the political party in power, especially during the Emergency years.

Until 1983 the Division was one of the largest film making agencies in the world, including the National Film Board of Canada and the documentary film studios of Moscow. It had full-fledged centres in Bombay, Madras and Calcutta. It used to release as many as 700 prints of one documentary and one newsreel every week. Several of its documentaries were screened on national and international TV channels.

Some States like Gujarat, Maharashtra, UP, Bihar, Andhra and West Bengal ran their own Film Units to make films of regional interest. Thus it was that about a hundred million people are exposed to the documentaries and newsreels week after week. Some departments like Family Welfare, National Savings, the Directorate of State Publicity, the LIC and the Teaboard have mobile units but nearly all of them are in the border areas. A larger number of mobile units would make for more frequent and regular exposure in far-flung villages. Further, a streamlined non-theatrical exhibition circuit needs to be built up to cover factories, educational institutions, hospitals, panchayats, etc. A greater variety of documentaries could thus reach special target groups.

Future of Films Division

In 1989, the Films Division's collection of documentaries, short films, short fiction films, animation films and newsreels, was 7,012 films. Its main source of revenue has always been rentals from cinema theatres. The rate per film per week ranges from Rs. 2.50 to Rs. 400/ -depending on the status, size and collection of theatres. The exhibitors and the distributors share this expense. Under section 122 of the Cinematograph Act of 1952, the Films Division screens its films for upto 20 minutes compulsorily in each theatre. Theatre-owners complain that they lose over Rs. 30 million annually on account of this show time. In 1988-89, the Films Division earned Rs. 77,826,000, a little more than half its expenditure (Rs. 139,028,074) during the same period. It also earns about a million rupees a year from the sale of stock shots from its extensive film library. In 1996-97, the Films Division produced 22 news magazines, 52 documentaries and short feature films, and released 20,131 prints of 42 documentaries and 18 news magazines. The revenue earned during that year was Rs. 16,633,000.

The Films Division can easily break even and become a profit-making body if it adopts a commercial approach to the sale and exhibition of its prints, and archival footage. It needs to charge for the prints it makes available to Doordarshan, the various Central and State Government bodies, and more importantly, sell prints abroad where there is a promising market for short films, particularly among television networks. At present only Indian embassies and Tourist Boards abroad are provided prints. The External Affairs Ministry has set up a cell for sales promotion of documentaries abroad. Already some of the documentary films have found a good market in West Asia, East Asia, and the West. The Films Division now organises an annual international festival for documentary, short and animation films, called MIFF (Mumbai International Film Festival) where over 500 entries are received from the world over every year. It has tied up with the National Film Development Corporation (NFDC) which commissions short films for the Metro Channel, and also helps the Division to market its documentaries, short films and animation films at international film festivals. Doordarshan too has begun to commission the Division to make documentaries for its national and regional networks. The Division has already adapted itself to the video and television formats.

Fifty years after its establishment, the Films Division continues to remain a 'unit' of the Ministry of Information and Broadcasting, and to do its bidding. An autonomous corporation status, which has now been granted to All India Radio and Doordarshan, would perhaps best ensure its future, and its distinct identity. With over a thousand employees, an annual budget of around Rs. 17 crores (Rs. 170 million), an infrastructure (for animation films in particular) in Bombay and Bangalore that is the envy of many media organisations, and a library with over 40 million feet of precious historical material, the Films Division will need to become part of the new competitive multi-channel audiovisual environment if it is to survive as a vibrant and creative organisation.

Independent Documentary Producers

Most of the films produced by the Films Division every year are the work of its own employees. Only a handful of short films are given out to a panel of outside or 'independent' producers, through a tender system, a practice which has put off young and ambitious film makers, particularly those graduating from the Film and Television Institute, Pune. Further, documentaries can be screened in theatres around the country only through the Films Division circuit. Even after the film by the independent producer has been made the threat of censorship at various level remains, as has happened in the case of several controversial films. In the words of Kumar Shahani, director of documentary 'Fire in the Belly' (on the drought in Maharashtra)-'Once a film is made, there are various stages of censorship, first the Films Division approves, then the Board of Censors has to clear it and finally the Film Advisory Board, which is the super Censor Board, has a big voice and even decides what shot should be there, and what should not be there, which amounts to aesthetic censorship.'

B.D. Garga, who has been making documentary films for four decades, and is wellknown for his films on Amrita Sher-Gil, Sarojini Naidu and Ananda Coomaraswamy, comments thus on how the Films Division functions: 'Independent film producers of repute are also having a tough time in getting films. Films Division sometimes invites a film maker to make a film on a negotiated contract. It takes at least ten days to get an application processed via the Indian Documentary Producers Association (IDPA), Raw Film Steering Committee, the NFDC, and ORWO, but almost all of the films are given on the basis of the lowest tender and it's the money which determines whether you get a film or not. The tender system harms the cause of the documentary film movement. In their anxiety to get a film, some film makers under quote to such an extent that they cover only the raw stock and the laboratory charges. As a result the quality is bad and sometimes films remain unfinished'.

The Working Committee on film policy has recommended the abolition of the system and advocated negotiations. Echoing Kumar Shahani's plaint it points out: 'The script has to be approved by the subject specialist-an official in the Ministry-who has very little idea of the media. He is very particular about his points. The freedom is curbed at the conception level and also at the shooting stage where every film maker projects himself. The subject specialist has to approve narration, presentation, etc. With the various checks and guards which the ruling party employs, there is not a ghost of a chance for a film maker to bring in his vision. The only freedom he is to bring in a certain amount of sophistication. The government policy is such that you can make slick films but you can't make thoughtprovoking ones.'

The ruling party's absolute control is evident in the subjects chosen at the start of each financial year, not by Films Division but in consultation with the Ministries of Defence and Agriculture, and with public sector undertakings. As though this was not enough, officers are appointed by these organs of Government to help in the production. It is no surprise, therefore, that the Division's films are simple narratives loaded with government propaganda. It is this credibility gap that makes the public suspect even the worthwhile offerings of the Films Division.

Despite these stringent regulations, the Films Division has been turning out a good number of award-winning films. On average 75 films are sent to international film festivals every year and 40-45 bag prestigious awards. Sukhdev, Mushir Ahmed, N.S. Thapa, S.N.S. Sastry, Loksen Lalwani, B.D. Garga, Clem Baptista, Fali Bilimoria, Mani Kaul and a host of others have thus made a mark in the world of documentary cinema. But John Grierson, the father of the modern documentary, is reported to have warned that 'the Films Division is falling prey to some of the cheap film festivals of the Western affluent countries... of getting prizes for having caught the sickness of some of the frustrated countries in the West.'

While the Films Division has gained world-wide recognition, it has woefully failed the country in the area of development communication. It is much too centralised a body to turn out films meaningful to the millions in the rural areas. A study carried out by the Indian Institute of Mass Communication, New Delhi, has revealed that only 10% of the films produced between 1975 and 1978 were primarily oriented to the rural classes, which make up 76% of the population. The study also found that the frequency of screening of films in villages was low. It concluded that the level of recall of films in villages among village folk was low because of the lack of socio-economic or cultural relevance of the films' backdrops to villagers' surroundings, complicated technique, an overload of statistics, difficult language and rapid speed of commentary.

During the late seventies and early eighties several independent documentary producers like Mani Kaul (The Nomad Puppeteer, Arrival), Loksen Lalvani (Burning Stone, They call Me Chamar) and others made sensitive documentaries for the Films Division. By the mideighties, however, the clear trend among independent film-makers, was to go in for private sponsorships, or to seek support from the NFDC and other sources. The focus of attention of the young filmmakers, in particular, was marginalized groups in Indian cities. Anand Patwardhan, for instance, focussed attention on political opposition led by Jayaprakash Narayan to the Indira Gandhi regime (Waves of Revolution, Prisoners of Conscience) and the plight of Bombay's slum-dwellers (Hamara Shaker), and Pradeep Dixit documented the two-year-long strike of 250,000 textile workers of the same city (Although the City Looks Quiet). Patwardhan has gone on to document the movement against the Narmada Dam (Narmada Story), and the rise of Hindutva in his trilogy (In Memory of Friends, In the Name of God, and Father, Son and Holy War). He has also made A Time to Rise, a scathing expose of the exploitation of Sikh farm labour in Canada, with assistance from the National Film Board of Canada. Patwardhan has had to go to the courts in appeal against the censors for almost every documentary of his.

Rajan Palit, a cameraman-director trained at the FTII, Pune turned the searchlight on the exploited weavers of Bhivandi, and went on to boldly record the struggle of the peasants of Baliapal to stop the government from converting their region into a missile site, in Voices from Baliapal. The film is co-directed by Vasudha Joshi.

Bhopal has been the subject of a number of independently produced documentaries. Perhaps the most soul-searching has been Bhopal: Beyond Genocide made by Tapan Bose, Suhasini Mulay and Salim Sheikh. A similar social concern is reflected in Man Versus Man, a sympathetic portrayal of Calcutta's rickshaw-pullers by Sashi Anand, and in Famine '87 by Sanjiv Shah, and an Indian Story on the Bhagalpur blindings.

Women film-makers (such as the six young women of Delhi's Mediastorm) have turned attention on the Deorala sati tragedy of Roop Kumar, in From the Burning Embers. Suhasini Mulay has directed two documentaries, Pani and Chithi, Deepa Dhanraj questions the family planning campaign in Something Like A War and Chandita Mukerjee demythologises the Working Woman in Totanama.

The Films Division has supported several feature-length documentaries. Some of these include Benegal's three hour film on Satyajit Ray, Jabbar Patel's film on Indian Drama and Theatre, Prakash Jha's Parampara (on the guru-shishya tradition in various styles of Indian dance), Girish Karnad's Kanak Purandara (on the Bhakti traditon in Karnataka), and Tapan Sinha's two one-hour featurettes: Manas and The Story of TIblu, and Mani Kaul's feature film Siddeshwari.

CENTRAL BOARD OF FILM CERTIFICATION

It is a certifying body which certifies all Indian and foreign films—feature, short and long films prior to their exhibition. It has an advisory panel consisting of nine eminent people from various fields. It has it's headquarters in Bombay and regional offices at Bombay, Bangalore, Madras, Cuttak, Calcutta, Hyderabad, New Delhi, and Thirvananthpuram.

It works according to the principles of Cinematograph Act 1952 and guidance provided under cinematograph made to allow a challenge of any decision of the Board. For this, one needs to file an appeal with the Film Certification Appellate Tribunal (FCAT), which has been functioning from March 1984. It has its headquarters in New Delhi.

The films are previewed for the purpose of certification and the reports are treated as confidential. The central board of film censors has to come out with specific reasons when it asks for cuts in a film and it must also furnish the particulars of guidelines under which cuts are sought to be effected to the film producer. The films are certified as 'V' for unrestricted exhibition, 'A' for public exhibition restricted to adults only, 'UA' for unrestricted public exhibition subject to parental guidance for children below the age of 12 and 'S' for public exhibition restricted to specialised audiences such as business groups, sportsmen, doctors, handicapped people etc.

The board may ban a film or refuse to give it a certificate if certain suggested deletions in visuals and sounds are not made.

The film censorship is justified in the interest of the people and society as a whole, because the art and the media are abided by the restrictions imparied by the law in the interest of the integrity and sovereignty of India. Our constitutions has sanctioned restrictions on the fundamental right of freedom of speech and expression.

Therefore, restrictions imposed on the arts and media are in the interest of the society.

The decisions or certifications by censor board are also challenged many times by individuals, pressure groups or organisations for passing some vulgar dances and dialogues, for intention of disrespecting a community or an eminent leader of the country. For example, a film 'Dil Ka Doctor', 'Satyam Shivam Sundarum', 'Ram Teri Ganga Maili'. 'Nikaah' were charged for either vulgarity or disrespecting a minority community. Thus, film can be banned even after the certification of the censor board.

Guidelines to Board of Censors

In exercise of the powers conferred by Sub-section (2) of Section 5-B of the Cinemetograph Act, 1952 (37 of 1952), the Central Government hereby directs that in sanctioning films for public exhibition, the Board of Film Censors shall be guided by the following principles:

1. The objectives of film censorship will be to ensure that:

    (i) the medium of film remains responsible and sensitive to the values and standards of society;

    (ii) artistic expression and creative freedom are not unduly curbed; and

    (iii) censorship is responsive to social change.

2. In pursuance of the above objectives, the Board of Film Censors shall ensure that:

    (i) anti-social activities such as violence are not glorified or justified.

    (ii) the modus operandi of criminals or other visuals or words likely to incite the commission of any offense, are not depicted.

    (iii) pointless or avoidable sense of violence, cruelty and horror are not shown;

    (iv) the sovereignty and integrity of Indian is not called in question;

    (v) human sensibilities are not offended by vulgarity, obscenity and depravity.

    (vi)   visuals or words contemptuous of racial, religious or other groups are not presented.

    (vii) the security of state is not jeopardised or endangered.

    (viii) public order is not endangered.

    (ix) friendly relations with foreign states are not strained.

    (x) visuals or words involving defamation or contempt of court are not presented.

3. The Board of Film Censors shall also ensure that the film:

    (i) is judged on its entirety from the point of view of its overall impact, and

    (ii) is examined in the light of contemporary standards of the country and the people to which the film relates.

4. Films that meet the above mentioned criteria but are considered unsuitable for exhibition to non-adults shall be certified for exhibition to adult audiences only.

In the beginning, *i.e.* in thirties and forties censorship boards were particularly sensitive to nudity, passionate or suggestive love making, women in a state of drunkenness, anything that might show the white man in bad light and any reference to political activity or ideology.

National Film Development Corporation (NFDC)

It was established in 1980 with the objective of promoting Cinema good cinema. It produces and finances films, oversees matter concerning export of Indian films, import of foreign films and their distribution, import of relevant technology and the production and distribution of recorded video cassettes. The NFDC provides financial support under its Theatre Financing Scheme. The NFDC has made inroads into the programming of small screen. The metro and other channels on Doordarshan telecast serials produced or financed by the NFDC. It offers perhaps the sole example of an institution which handles so many film-related activities of such a diverse and complex nature under one roof.

Directorate of Film Festival

It was set up in 1973 under the Ministry of Information and Broadcasting to promote good cinema and Indian Films. It organises national and international film festivals in India. The Directorate gives away the National Film Awards. Under the Cultural Exchange Programme (CEP), the Directorate arranges film weeks for the people in India. Similarly, it holds India film weeks abroad.

Children's Film Society, India (CFSI)

It was established in 1955 with the objective of producing and distributing films which provide 'clean and healthy entertainment' for children and young people. It produces animation films and dubs foreign cartoon films for children in Hindi, which are very popular on Doordarshan.

Film Archives

It is a media unit of the Ministry of Information and Broadcasting. It was established in 1964 with its headquarters in Pune and with three regional offices at Bangalore, Calcutta and Thiruvananthapuram. It preserves films, audio and video footage, and also does documentation and research on films in India and even some foreign languages. It plays a pivotal role in sensitising the film viewing public to the nuances of film making. It also organises screening of films to audiences to selected cities.

Films and Development

Both fictional and non-fictional films can convey development messages effectively. The immense popularity of films have made them a powerful disseminator of values and ideas. Therefore, they can be harnessed as an important agent for social change and national development.

Today, Indian cinema has advanced both, technically and artistically. It has a history Every day millions of people go to see films. Therefore, it can be used as the most powerful and potential weapon for development of a nation.

Films conveying development messages are usually produced by government. These are in the forms of newsreels, documentaries, instructional films, industrial films, and promotional films. The main objective of these productions is to promote the existing government and their various development efforts. Films for special occasions are also produced. For example, to commemorate independence day, army or navy day, in remembrance of a national hero.

Government also produces films for supporting special campaigns like road safety, save water, save electricity, cleanliness, rural health, prevention of AIDs and so on. Government sometimes resorts to producing theatrical films because it remains a popular form of entertainment. Development messages are shown in to these films which involve life dramas like the efforts of a person on individuals to improve his community people related to the development of a nation, the birth of a nation, fighting all odds to overcome obstacles to development, etc. For example, production of films like, 'Sardar' highlighted the role played by Sardar in making of Independent India which was financed by Gujarat Government. 'Manthan' was produced by Milk Co-operative societies of Anand and National Dairy Development Board to let people known how development practitioner has to fight all odds to overcome obstacles to development.

The criticism of the films produced with development message is that these films tend to be very serious and frequently neglect the importance of the entertainment value to ensure large viewerships. For example, documentaries rarely have strong entertainment appeal. In fact, most of the time they do not have mass appeal. Government must seek ways to improve their development messages through films.

Many a times, traditional characters or folklore heroes are used to convey development messages through films. For example in the form of Bhavai or Puppet play or Nautanki.

Thus, there is a need to formulate new strategies to enhance the capabilities of films to disseminate development messages more effectively.

CHILDREN'S CINEMA

Children's Cinema is which entertains children. If we want to create a new cinema consciousness in our people, we should seek to offer a new cinema to our children. In countries like France, Russia, Czech, Slovakia and Britain, children's films are produced regularly. They provide children with approximately one new film every month. They hold children's shows at fixed hours in a week at a nominal admission charges.

India produces highest numbers, *i.e.* more than 700 feature films every year, it can produce exclusively children's feature films and documents reflecting on our cultural heritage, scientific achievements in the world, adventurous stories of children, children and their relationships and so on. India is far behind in the production of children's cinema and the state is very discouraging.

Children's film society has so far limited its function to producing animation films and dabbing foreign cartoon films and some serials for children in Hindi.

Many Hindi films get adult thoughts and dialogues delivered by children. Children are shown in serious emotional drama. This does not convey any message to young viewers. Films should be altered to suit the needs and interests of the children. The film 'Chota Chetan' could be said to be the children's film.

Children's films should present good examples of normal behaviour and characters that react in a correct manner. These films can be exhibited in schools, villages and labour areas through mobile vans so that a large number of children can take advantage of these films.

As expressed by Goswami, "Making films for children is a harder task than making films for adults. The producer has to take great care at every step. Only the best should be shown to children. Their whole life can be adversely affected if they see the wrong films in the formative state of their mental development."

IMPACT OF FILMS

In the last fifty years, cinema has become not only a serious art form but a field of study by itself. Continuous advancement in film technology and high level of conceptualization of the film take viewer to the world outside his day-to-day world providing entertainment, which has made cinema a popular medium of masses.

Indian educationists and sociologists have shown a surprising lack of interest in the film as an educational force and a social challenge. Hardly any academic, systematic scientific studies have been undertaken on the social and psychological impact of the films in India.

There is no data available on the systematic use of the documentary and the feature film in social education programmes in India. However, experiences in Canada, USA, and USSR indicate that documentaries and films have contributed to bringing about a better social order and in building up a national community having common thinking about the nation.

Many social scientists have shared their informal experiences and observation regarding the impact that films have created.

According to Bhola, "Cinema being a composite art has been responsible for popularizing music, dance, painting, literature among the common people and in India to a very large extent for the popularization of Hindi in Non Hindi speaking south of India".

Films have a hypnotic influence on most children and adults. They imitate the heroes and heroines. They indulge in day dreaming and fantasy and when it increases, children become unable to accept the hard realities of life. Apart from these, films create fear, terror, sorrow and pathos, love and passion, thrill, excitement and stimulation. People suffer from hang over after watching a film. Thus, films have a dynamic influence on people which ultimately affects the society as a whole.

Most films implicitly subscribe to the view that the highest goals in life are power, money, luxury, public adulation and one can use any means to achieve these goals. Thus, most of the films glorify false patterns of life.

There have been few studies on effects of violence and sex in specific films on children and youth. When we want to know the impact of films, one has to look at how stories of cinema affect the actual life of the people.

The main reasons for going to see films have been to learn about the world of ideas and things, to forget and get away to escape, to pass time, to relieve boredom, to impress others.

Having seen a film serves as a means of social integration as it shows that an individual is a part of the mainstream cultural activities of his reference group. Having seen film in first week of it's release is a minor form of prestige. People tend to use scenes from films as analogies to real life situations, or use dialogue from movies as a common means of expression understood by all.

In eighties and early nineties, there had been a decline in the movie going population due to the availability of VCR and Cable Television across all socio-economic groups. The increasing cost of going to the movies has made movie going a much more elitist activity, whereas, television absorbs the interest of those with lower socio-economic status.

Films as mass media continue to play an important role in leisure pattern of our society. Despite television, many people today go to the theatre to see the films to enjoy the photography and music and sound effects, whenever they have leisure time. Some enjoy it on television, whereas, some watch it on video at their own convenience, without being under the pressure of following the time schedule of a theatre or television.

Many foreign films are also being shown in theatres as well as on television. Many feel that these films pose a threat to our cultural identity. These films help people to know the culture, values, people of the world. As a result, they are able to select their value system with more wisdom and maturity, because cultural openness also contributes to the development of mind.

The films affected television also. The film directors and producers turned to television to produce either mythologicals like Mahabharata and Ramayan or soap operas like Buniyaad, Rajni, Nukkad, and Swabhimaan. Tele films, were also produced, such as 'Janam' and 'Phir Teri Kahani Yad Aye', etc. In Indian cinema, the awareness of social relevance was very much there till recently. Gradually, due to various reasons a rampant commercialization overtook this awareness. As a result, none of the people's injustices or inequalities nor any of the country's burning problems like population explosion, black marketing, industrial unrest and lack of civic sense received more than a cursory attention from film makers. The film censor board is largely responsible for this.

It has inhibited social and political themes regarding them as an act of blasphemy. If a film maker insists on focusing on social ills, the causes have to be away from politics and authority. This consorial attitude is not only absorbed and initiating but, it is dangerous for a democratic country like India.

Films have been the medium for revolutionists who want to express their revolt. For example, film like 'Fire' has depicted the life of the lesbians or a film like 'Diara' has well depicted the feelings of yunuch. The film 'Inquilaab' concluded with the idea of uprooting the existing political system in order to have society free of corruption, exploitation and inequality.

ailability of TV, cable TV and Video, cinema became middle class homes, Entertainment values became in feature film. Apart from feature films, song and dance sequences from them such as 'Chitrahaar', 'Chitramala' and 'Rangoli' became very popular. Many other types of cinema - quizes came on Doordarshan and Satellite channels beamed to India, for which also quiz books began to be available in market. Cinema thus became a national craze and obsession on TV.

The great potentialities of the film for education, instruction and training in agriculture, industry and other fields are not yet widely appreciated or exploited in India, where the cinema is generally regarded as an entertainment medium. Although documentary and educational films are produced in India, their circulation is usually limited to large cities and their near by towns. Thus, there is a need to fully exploit the formal use of films for education.

Obscenity and Violence in Films

Obscenity and violence in commercial cinema or most of the feature films has become a burning problem of the present times which has acquired great urgency. Most of the popular films produced today in our country are subverting the country's culture, morality and it's cohesion. By projecting fantasy world, these films encourage expectations of the viewers and kind of behaviour which is not in congruence with the prevailing cultural environment. As a result, people are led to violence and socially disruptive tendencies.

Most of the films endorse social evils like dowery, bigamy, role stereotypes, pragmatism and domination of anti social elements and so on. Films being powerful and popular medium having, strong reality dimension in it's presentation, encourages adolescents and youth in resorting to crime, violence and taking law into one's own hands.

Many people dealing with the maintenance of law and order and the administration of criminal justice, have expressed that most criminals are deeply influenced by popular feature films depicting crime and violence. These films have contributed significantly to the growing violence against women. The styles of eve-teasing, molestation and rape in films are imitated in a similar manner.

Women are being more and more portrayed as sex objects in the films. They are used to include the element of vulgarity in films by making them to show suggestive gestures, and nudity and to entertain the audience with cheap, vulgar dances and songs. Their costumes or dresses are shown vulgarly in the name of modernity.

Unfortunately, law is also not able to define vulgarity and obscenity in films clearly. This leaves many doors open for the film makers to exploit these elements fully to make their film popular at box office. The guidelines by the government did forbid more than six minutes of violence in a film but hardly any film had violence to be shown for such a short period, laws of censorship are not followed strictly and the interpretation of scenes of violence and obscenity are left to the whims of the members of the censor board. Many socially and culturally concerned citizens have tried to oppose these by filing public interest litigation but hardly anything fruitful has come out of it.

Print media has brought out the cases of violence among adolescents and youth where they were motivated to commit crime or become violent after seeing a film having lot of violence. However, no research data is available in this 'regard'. Violence is being shown as entertainment. The film producers show violence in increasingly gruesome and sickening manner. Technological advancements are being used to make violent scenes more graphic.

MAG study, observed that very often the violence depicted on screen is unnecessary. These scenes should be limited and with strong justification, such as, a criminal or a wrong doer must be punished. Films are having irrelevant and unnecessary violent scenes because of profit motive. There is no art or culture depicted through it.

Many people dealing with the maintenance of law and order and the administration of criminal justice, have expressed that most criminals are deeply influenced by popular feature films depicting crime and violence. These films have contributed significantly to the growing violence against women. The styles of eve-teasing, molestation and rape in films are imitated in a similar manner.

The crisis with the Indian film industry today is not financial but cultural.

Improving Quality of Films

There is a growing concern about the deteriorating quality of majority of feature films, in our country due to the inclusion of the elements like vulgarity, obscenity, violence and other means of cheap entertainment. Least concern is shown by the film makers about the impact these kind of films can create on the society.

Although the efforts are being made for improving themes, treatments and techniques of Indian feature films, much remains to be done to improve the quality of these films. Indian films should become more socially purposeful, so that being the most popular and powerful mass medium, they can contribute to the development of the society.

Government should make policies which encourage production of quality films, facilitate their distribution and exhibition.

The formulation of a film policy is not optional: it is imperative. Technology and commerce have made film available. But film is not just any commercial product or technological gadget. Film is a cultural commodity. If we fail to articulate our film policy on the development needs of our people, we may still have the means to reach out to all of them, but no clear vision of what might constitute good, healthy, socially useful films.

As pointed out by Kumar, "the high taxation rates and the stringent rules for licensing of cinema houses give the impression that cinema is an undesirable activity which needs to be kept at an adequate distance from the social life of the community". However, government has set up National Film Development Corporation to finance production of good films, Directorate of Film festivals, National Film Archives, National Center of Films for Children and Young people and instituted National Film Awards to boost production of good cinema. International Film Festival of India held in many cities have provided opportunities to the film lovers to be exposed to outstanding films of other countries.

To continue these efforts of promoting film as an art form, the working group has recommended the establishment of the Chalchitra Akadami, Sangeet Natak Academi, and the Lalit Kala Akadami. It has also recommended the setting up of a film Educational Advisory Service for inculcating a critical attitude towards cinema in schools and colleges as well as a Film Information and Documentation Centre, a National Film Museum, and a children's Film Centre.

Media education should become integral part of curriculum and film education, a part of media education. This can help youngsters to fully appreciate the movies they watch so that they can protect themselves against any harmful influences films might have and understand the social role of a film maker. This type of education through curriculum can go long way in improving the quality of films in future. At higher level, film production should be offered as a discipline by itself, where not only the training in technical aspects is imparted but the qualitative and affective aspects of films are also taught. This can produce film makers who are better aware of their responsibilities towards society.

Research trends in communication reveal that very few studies have been conducted in India on film utilization by the viewers. These types of research studies are necessary as they throw light on the significance of films in the life of the people. Government should encourage such research by funding them.

Censorship should be tighten up to prevent the glorification of crime and violence in feature films. More and more incentives in the form of finances, facilities, tax rebates etc. should be provided to encourage the production of films of high artistic quality.

Advantages of Films

Films as mass medium have similar advantages as television as far as motion and manipulation of time are concerned. Motion is essential for comprehending certain concepts and messages. For example, science experiments, operation of machines or industrial plants can be shown effectively with motion. Both the media show few hours long event in few minutes.

The emotional impact left by films helps in shaping personal and social attitudes. They present the situation in a dramatic, recreation form which brings reality also and assures the involvement of the viewer and leaves emotional impact. Films preserve modern sense of privacy and anonymity. Man has longed for invisibility and the absence of responsibility it confers, and film satisfies precisely this with. In watching a film we view a magically reproduced world while remaining invisible to it.

Film is a versatile medium. If lends itself to instructional use in both large and small groups, and for individual study. Technically, film allows a wider range of colors than video, further more, the colors vary more in terms of hue and portray a greater range of contrast then television. This holds viewers attention better than video or television.

Films provide for viewing of phenomena at extremely close range or from a vast distance, which is not possible in television.

Films can be used for variety of purposes such as entertainment, education, persuasion, changing motivation and opinions. The messages conveyed through films are retained better due to it's reality element. They allow for a creative production approach. It is possible to make different language and cultural versions of a film.

Limitations of Films

The main limitation of the films is its fixed pace. They move at a fixed pace, some viewers are likely to fall behind, if they are unable to keep pace with the pace of the film. Since films are mostly the dramatized presentation, there are chances of sophisticated treatment or exaggerated version of a situation or issue. For example, if an adolescent has seen a film with generation gap theme, it is likely that he will take this melodrama in a literary sense and feel that he also has to face many problems due to generation gap in his relationship with his parents or teachers.

It is very difficult to define the limits of what is "controversial" in films. For example, the film "Aandhi" was banned during the emergency period in India. It was labelled as controversial film. When released, people did not find anything controversial or objectionable in the film.

The commercial films are made with the audience's preference in mind, but there is hardly any feedback mechanism.

The production of film or a replication of a film are costly, and require huge amount of finances. It requires highly sophisticated equipment for production as well as projection.

Film production also requires trained personnel such as Director, Photographer, Sound effects expert, musician, editor, etc. once the film production is complete, it is very expensive to make any changes in the film.

Each film requires individual distribution network, which requires investment of large amount of money and time.

ADVENT OF FILM MAKING

Chroniclers mention that the motion picture originated when Edison invented the kinetoscope in 1899. Combining his kinetoscope with his photographs and recording, he showed the first synchronised sound film in Paris in 1902, when silent movie theatres had become popular in the world. Griffith developed the story technique in movies. Forest's vacuum tube provided the amplification for the first talking motion picture in 1927. Thus it took more than 30 years for the flat, black and white silent flicks to be transformed into sound films.

Combining story, pictures, motion, drama, emotions, dialogue and voice modulation with the potency of visual presentation, the cinema has become the darling of all communication media. This is evident from the fact that people, despite the physical inconveniences involved in going to a cinema house, throng and jostle in queues for obtaining tickets. Although TV and video provide most of the ingredients within the home with all the comforts that it can provide, people still prefer to see pictures on wide screens in crowded halls. In the times of silent pictures tbe spectators used to involve themselves vocally. Now, in the case of talkies, they are drawn into emotional relationships with the characters, silently empathising with them and sharing their anguish and happy moments. By portraying identifiable local environment, local character, local problems and locally tried out solutions, the film can cause more animation and produce viewer's affinity.

From the point of view of aesthetics, the art of cinema is called the art of all arts, absorbing other arts ranging from dance and drama to novels and short stories, from art to architecture. Cinema is most persuasive. Seeing provides the most direct communication to the mind and images do not need to be translated to be understood. Hence, a film can be enjoyed despite the viewer's ignorance of the language employed in the dialogue or narration. This, however, could act as a detrimental factor sometimes and adversely affect the people, especially young children and those persons who are innately prone to the influence of evil, sex or violence. For this reason films are censored judiciously and creatively.

Beginning of Film Making in India

India took to film making in the early years of this century, for her people had known and practised the Six Arts and Nine Muses from time immemorial. The sculptures in Khajuraho and Chidambaram depict successive stances of dance figures which, says an eminent authority, can come to life when filmed and edited properly. Even the paintings of manuscript illustrations show in their drawings the progressive stages of motion. And the film is not very different. It is an improvement upon the static arts by the addition of motion. Indian tradition of song and dance, and even the exotic strain of her plastic and graphic arts, admirably lent themselves to the need of the cinema. It is no wonder that this art was easily acquired at the initial stages and adapted to the Indian environment.

In India, immediately after the first film was viewed in Bombay in 1896, film making experiments were started by Harischandra Sawe Bhatvadekar in Bombay and Hiralal Sen in Calcutta. Both imported movie cameras and made films; the former on wrestling matches and the Hanging Gardens, Bombay, and the latter on theatrical performances. The production of a feature film, that is a full length film, however, took some more time and it was in 1913 that Dadasaheb Phalke, the Father of Indian Cinema, screened his first film, Harishchandra, depicting the story of a great legendary votary of truth. Inspired by a Western film, Love of Christ, he struck on this puranic story which had all the elements of a box-office hit. As there were no female artists or heroines, nor playback singers, it was a male actor who had to don the sari and play the role of Taramati, the wife of Harishchandra. The players had to also sing themselves. Nonetheless the initial success of the first film was so great that the cashbox money had to be carried in a bullock cart. And right since that year, 70 years ago, the people of India have been cinema struck. It is, however, an irony of fate that this totally dedicated Father of the Indian Cinema died a pauper, but not before he had laid the foundation of the Indian cinema.

The twenties saw the all-round proliferation of the Indian cinema. Even during that decade, India was producing more films than Great Britain. In Bengal, P. C. Barua, Dhiren Ganguly and Debaki Bose had made their mark. Bombay did not lag behind. Chandulal Shah's Gunasundri became the 'signpost of the time'. And so did Himansu Rai's Indo. German internationally known film Light of Asia. This era was also dominated by Shantaram in Maharashtra and K. Subramanyam in Tamil Nadu. Most of the films related to religious, historical and social topics stunts and humorous situations added colour to the pictures.

Some Landmarks

The next landmark in the history of Indian cinema was the release of the first Indian talkie on 14 March 1931. This feat was accomplished within two years of the screening of Universal Pictures talkie film Melody of Love. Produced by Ardeshir Irani, this so called 'the living and breathing too' Indian talking film, created a rage. Talkies burgeoned forth in the same year in many other languages. This marked the growth of language films in the country and films came to be made in various centres as far away as Lahore (then in India), Madras, Calcutta and Kolhapur. Exploiting the operatic tradition in Indian drama and folk theatre, songs began to dominate Indian films. Inder Sabha, a picture of Madan Theatres, included as many as 59 songs. Gradually, playback singers emerged and music directors became more important than even the singer actors.

In India the silent era did not die with the advent of talkies, but petered to exinction in 1934. The Treasure (or Khazana) was the last film in this series. The first silent film of social relevance was Untouchable, produced in 1933 by British India Film Co.

The next landmark in the history of Indian cinema was also provided by Ardeshir Irani in his colour film Kisan Kanya. This added a new dimension to film making in India. In the context of the Indian situation, it was surprising that the earliest talkies were either film versions of stage plays or fantasies with mythological: background or famous love legends like Laila Majnu or Shirin Farhad, because all these themes were already well known and popular among the masses. With musical embellishments they were bound to be hits.

The first artistic masterpiece based on popular mythological legend about Rama and Sita was produced in 1934. Directed by Debaki Bose, it was shown at the Venice Film Festival. Owing to British censorship, socio-political themes had to be camouflaged in the garb of mythological or folklore fantasies. The first symbolic fantasy produced in our country was Amrit Manthan directed by Shantaram. In course of time, Indian films started reflecting social themes consistent with the socio-political climate of the country. In this series there were films on saints carrying sound reform messages. These included Dharmatma and Duniya Na Mane (directed by Shantaram) and a most realistic drama Aurat directed by Mehboob Khan. Then appeared towards the close of the British period in 1945 some trend-setting films by newcomer amateurs comprising a film directed by Chetan Anand called Neecha Nagar (an impressionistic and experimental representation of a progressive social theme) which won an award at Cannes Film Festival, and a more realistic film about Bengal famine, Dharti Ke Lal (acclaimed alike in USA, USSR, UK and France) by K. A. Abbas.

Another direction was laid by the emergence of the studio system around New Theatres in Calcutta, Bombay Talkies in Bombay; Prabhat Films in Pune, Pancholi Studios in Lahore (now in Pakistan) and many others. Notwithstanding language barriers, these centres operated as all-India enterprises. This trend was however reversed during World War II. The regional cinema was still-born, except in the south where it had dug its roots.

During World War II the shortage of goods led to a roaring black market. The newly emerged rich class which reaped the harvest started luring the stars away from studios with fantastic fees. This led to the ending of the era of studio production. The number of cinema-goers expanded. The same period marked the shifting of themes from social and religious ones to more hedonistic entertainment. Star fees and production costs started climbing steeply. The cinema had fast becoming a big money and box-office oriented game.

The redeeming feature of the war situation was, however, the export of Indian films to South and South East Asia, West Asia and East Africa where it later came to represent heights of entertainment. This feat was accomplished with the introduction of high professionalism in the realm of song and dance sequences and elements of melodrama.

Film as Publicity Agent

Another trend promoted during the Second World War was the wider application of film. The medium came to be recognised as a

agent for publicity as also an activist in bringing about
n or behavioural changes. A beginning was also made to use
it for advertising, youth and child welfare and documentary purposes.
The film became a multipurpose publicity agent.

FILM A MEDIUM OF COMMUNICATION

Communication is automatically assumed that there are two
parties involved in it, the one who communicates, and the other one
to whom it is communicated. In the case of feature film the director
or the maker of the film is the communicator and the observer or the
audience is the one to whom he communicates. Thus film, like all
other art forms, and medium of communications, forges the
relationships between the creator and the consumer, the artist and the
observer. This relationship leads us to delve in a bit more deeply into
the nature of communication that a film can make to its audience.

The very word 'communication' pre-empts the word 'language'.
There can be no communication without a language. Language has
two sides—the functional and the artistic. The first aspect deals
merely with the expressions of a feeling and the second aspect puts
the finer touches to it. Thus the first one deals with content, the
second, with the form. Film language started with the functional. The
very first movie showed a train coming in to halt at a platform. There
was nothing very artistic about it; a mere reproduction of a mundane
fact was the idea. Later, the language of the film gained sophistication
until film evolved a unique language of its own. The main medium of
this language is the camera. Each camera shot is like a sentence,
which, when arranged systematically, produces the idea which the
creator of the film wants to make. Camera acts as the eye of the
director—we see what the camera wants us to see. The camera can
be objective or subjective. In an objective camera, 'a rose is a rose
is a rose' *i.e.*, for instance, when we see a girl standing beside a bed
of roses, the flowers can be made to appear as a mere prop to the
whole scene, just a part of the landscape, nothing more. On the other
hand, if the camera is subjective, the same rose can be made to
signify 'love' and then the flower becomes at the same time the

signified and the signifier. But whatever the aim of the director, he can make the audience see whatever he wants them to see. Of course there is scope of reading a film from different perspective, but still, basically it remains a 'controlled' media. The other medium of the film is the sound. As we all know, the first of the films started as silent movies, when there was no sound. Later when sound was invented, film became an 'audio-visual' medium rather than a mere 'visual' medium. But even then, we must acknowledge the supremacy of the camera over the sound. Some of Charlie Chaplin's master-pieces were made as silent films after the advent of sound. As stated at the beginning of this article—the question of communication in a film is between the director and the audience and we see the film as the director wants us to see. It has evolved its own symbols, syntaxes etc. of which we can give an instance from the Ray masterpiece of Pather Panchali. After the death of her daughter Durga, mother Sarbajaya is seen sitting in front of the oven which has an overflowing pan on it. This pan signifies the mental turmoil she is undergoing due to her daughter's death. This is a typical example of film language where the camera can speak without the use of any words.

Film as a medium of expression is also a very manifested medium, which leaves very little scope for imagination. Thus it can communicate more directly than any other forms of art. Hitler banned Eisenstein's Battleship Potemkin because he was afraid that the film might influence the Nazis to anti-war sentiments. Before the age of the movie, literature, to some extent had the same kind of influence over men, but its appeal was restricted to the lettered intellectuals. After the movie came into being, gradually it took over this role from literature, mainly for two reasons. The first reason as stated earlier is its being more manifested. Cinema takes you there, inside the space—right into the specific place, time, even inside the inner recesses of the psyche, if necessary. For instance, in Ray's Charulata the audience can travel inside Charu's bedroom, share her lonely middays there, her garden, even her plans to renovate the same garden with Amal, simply because the camera moves into these places, and with it, the audience. Thus they can identify directly with the situation, and react more intensely to it than any other form of communicative art like drama, dance, song, etc. This can never happen with literature which remains basically an intellectual exercise.

The second reason for the cinema having more influence over the consumer is because of its ability to reach a wider mass. Because film is a recorded art, and also because it can be reproduced, film can reach the masses in a way no other forms of communication can. A film can be shown at the same time all over India and attended by millions of people at the same time. Not so with drama, where the audience is limited in number, and literature, painting, music etc. which is still reserved for the elite few. Film also integrates the audience so much because of its naturalistic way of presentation. Acting, again with the aid of camera, can achieve the height of natural behaviours in a film. An actor acts with the whole body, from his eyelids to his toes. In Ray's Devi when the father-in-law touches the feet of the daughter-in-law, believing her to be the reincarnation of Goddess Kali herself, the camera moves to the toes of the girl, and we see her curling in her toes with embarrassment for this bizarre behaviour. This acting can never be done in drama. Add to this acting style the landscapes, colour, etc. and the whole medium achieves a realistic proportion which leaves little scope of taxing the imagination or the intellect. Hence, even the least intellectual person can be integrated into the scope of film viewing.

Apart from the language of the film, its forms and also its mass appeal, there is a deeper aspect *i.e.* how and where its potential lies. The politics of the film determines how the film relates to the rest of the world. According to James Monaco, there are actually two aspects of it—when the film relates to the society we may call it 'sociopolitics' and when it is relating to the individual, we may call it the 'psycopolitics' of the film. Because of its popularity, the film has tremendous sociopolitical value. The film JFK might serve as an example. This film about John F Kennedy's assassination created such a controversy in the USA that the CIA has had to re-open the case for investigation years after the case had been officially 'closed'. Film can even change the world we operate. It can change the culture of a country, or at least effect it. On the other hand, film reflects the cultural tradition of a country. That is why a film made in Hollywood and a film made in Bombay differs in treatment though the subject may be the same. The Hollywood movie Madame Bovary and Ketan Mehta's Maya Memsaab stands example to this. In the latter, the film has been Indianized to make it more acceptable to the Indian audience. As for examples how films change or affect the culture of a country, eve-teasing has become a social problem in urban India. It is commonly believed to be the outcome of watching too many Hindi Mainstream movies where the hero is often shown outraging the girl and thereby winning her love at the end. Thus film here is affecting the social behaviour of a country. In the same Bombay films, family as an institution always gets precedence over the individual's problems. This is a reflection of the Indian social operation, where family is still regarded as an important institution. In the film Masoom by Shekhar Kapoor, the wife accepts her husband's illegitimate child inside her family rather than breaking away herself because she would rather not do that and jeopardize the institution itself. Film therefore has a direct communication with society and also has the power to analyse and explain the structure to us.

Indian audience has a very typical characteristic when it comes to viewing the films. It seems that the early oral tradition of narration is still on, except that instead of listening to the narration of the tale, they now both listen to it and watch it at the same time—the main objective being getting a grasp of the story line. This accounts for the narrative structure of our mainstream film, where every film has a story, with a beginning, a middle and an end. The end usually conforms to the usual requisites of the social norm, such as the rebel hero gets a place in the society, or a job and lives happily thereafter. The heroin is invariable a housewife who 'takes care' of the family or, if she is not married, falls in love with a man so that she can marry him and have a family to take care of. Due to its oral narrative structure, each film has a moral at the end. Usually the 'good' triumphs over the 'evil' and the 'good' non-conformist or rebel hero is given a place in the mainstream society as a reward of his goodness. Thus he is being integrated into the social values because a person who is a rebel is a threat to the prevailing value system and the narrator—in this case the director—cannot allow that because his job is to uphold those values. That is why a prostitute who has many men in her life but loves one dies in Mukaddar Ka Sikandar and the one who is faithful to one man only (she lives with—him as man and wife) gets to marry the hero in Tawaif. In the blockbuster Sholay, the man who is in love with the widow and is loved in turn has to die so that the norms of social acceptance are not outraged. The reverse of this is seen in the much publicized film Khalnayika where an interesting bit of film language is being used. The anti-heroin, as long as she is accepted by the family, is seen wearing a saree. At the end, when she is recognized by the family as what she is, and she enters the screen to murder the couple and take away their children, she is seen wearing a two-piece men's suit. This serves to alienate her, both from the Mainstream of social norm and also from the plot; she is killed off at the end. This killing is necessary because no Indian woman can be allowed to plan destruction of a family or plan such an 'unfeminine' thing as murder—the unfeminine part being the planning rather than the act because she is killed by the mother of the children herself. Thus the shift in dressing style also serves to desexualize her. But the later *i.e.*, the mother of the children, is redeemed inspite of the killing because she does it to save her children.

Another unique feature of the Indian audience is their perception of the film as a 'mixed entertainment medium' where many mediums come together, tales, drama, dance, songs, colour, to name a few. Film as a serious medium of communication is an idea yet alien to the mass of this country. Of course, the possibilities have been explored by a handful of serious film makers, but their numbers remain a few and attract lesser number of audience. To name a few, Ray's Sadgati deals with the problem of un-touchability. Govind Nihalani's Chakra shows the problems of a woman living in a Bombay ghetto, a life of misery, poverty, drug, prostitution and her attempis to come out of that life and subsequent failure. Coming back to the mainstream, precisely because of this entertainment value, the films have a mass appeal which can be exploited propedy to get across a message. Raj Kapoor was among the first to realize this potential of Mainstream films, along with Guru Dutt and their films blended both entertainment and serious messages which never deterred their popularity. Shree 420, Awara, Mera Nam Joker, of the former and Pyasa of the latter bears ample proof of that. These films have got specific ideological communications without losing their entertainment value which accounts for their immense popularity. In recent days we may site examples like Anjali where the problem of a retarded child in society and her family is dealt with in an apparent light vein. Same can be said about Rudali where the setting of the story is shifted from the misery of Bihar to the more exotic Rajasthan to make it more appealing. But the main content of the film deals with the outrageous custom of professional mourners and the problem of prostitution. Salam Bombay reveals the misery of child labour in the same straight narrative manner. In Hollywood the film generating a lot of interest is Steven Spielberg's JURRASIC PARK. It is a science fantasy aimed at the younger audience, but it has negated fundamentalism in such as way which we can make some use of. The plot suggests that civilization, which has come too long a way through evolution, can never gain anything except destruction if it ever tries to look back, thus negating the ideology of fundamentalism.

Film can also communicate, more directly, through other genres of film making, like documentaries, docu-features, committed films and so on. But that is another scope of study. This is undoubtedly true that whatever the type of film, it certainly communicates something—as the relationship is between the creator and the consumer. The dialectics of realism and film expressionism should also be taken into account—between the film's power to mimic reality and its power to change it. There is scope of controversy to accept film as an medium of art, but it certainly does two things— it attempts to mimic reality (mimesis) and it brings about catharsis (through identification) among the audience. The communication depends on the style of making, though. When made in a realistic style, the director brings the audience and the film nearer; when he uses expressionisms of various forms of language, he distances the audience from the film and it becomes an exercise of the intellect. But either way, a film has a dynamic relationship with the audience. Each film, major or minor, has something to communicate and acts in one or more of the three ways, To quote James Monaco; "Ontologically; because the medium of film itself tends to deconstruct the traditional values of the culture; mimetically because any film either reflects reality or recreates it...; inherently, because the intense communicative nature of film gives to the relationship between film and observer a natural political dimension."

⊓

12

Cinema After Independence

If India attained a pre-eminent position in any single visual art after Independence it was film making. It shot up to become the top in the world and still retains that pinnacled position. In 1983, over 800 feature films were certified for public 'exhibition mostly in colour and a few in black and white. This number was nearly four times what India was producing immediately after Independence. Languagewise, Telugu topped the list followed by films in Hindi and Malayalam. Trailing behind were films in Bengali, Gujarati and Marathi. Within the film industry the most significant development that has taken place during this period is the acceleration of film making in south India. Both in terms of the number of cinema halls, and in respect of the number of pictures produced, the south has forged ahead to take the lead from the well-entrenched traditional centre of Bombay. Over the years more than 17000 films have been produced in India. More than 13 million Indians go to the :movies every day, sometimes trudging miles to the nearest movie hall.

Yet this enormous structure caters essentially for urban and suburban people, who represent only one-fifth of the total population. The number of cinema houses where films can be screened are 11682 including the touring talkies. These cinema houses are unevenly distributed and obviously well below the world average.

Milestones in the Growth of Cinema

Many milestones marked the overall growth of cinema in the country since Independence. The Government showed concern about the balanced development of the cinema which had become a ag and multi-star industry. To this end, it appointed the Film Enquiry Committee whose recommendations resulted in the foundation of some basic institutions like Films Division of India, Film Finance Corporation and Children's Film Society in the sixties. In their own way these institutions including a growing number of talented producers and directors have cumulatively given a shot in the arm to the film industry.

The Films Division set up by the Ministry of Information and Broadcasting in 1948 gave a boost to documentary films and upgraded it professionally and technically. In 1975 the National Films Development Corporation was constituted, which was activated in 1980 and the Film. Finance Corporation and the Indian Motion Picture Export Corporation were amalgamated with it. The Corporation plays a vital role. Its function is to plan, promote and organise an integrated and efficient development of the industry in accordance with the national economic policy and objectives.. Its broad range of activities covers the handling of the import and export of feature films, allocation and distribution of raw stock and equipment used by the industry, distribution and exhibition of films through the existing network, and undertaking a programme of construction of a chain of national theatres, promotion of quality films, research and development in film equipment and raw stock. Recently the Corporation has taken an innovative step in deciding to finance the production of featurettes, *i.e.* films of approximately half an hour to one hour duration. These can be shown on TV networks in India and abroad.

Film as a Change Agent

The film is motion, picture, sound, theatre and school all packed in one. That is why it can communicate effectively, create better impact than other mass media and draw hundreds and thousands of viewers including the illiterates, workers and villagers. Even the elite and urbanites swarm cine halls or glue to their seats at home near video-cum-TV sets. The film being visual reality and a universal language cutting across cultural barriers, film exponents advocate that a socially relevant cinema can prove to be the best activist.

Taking the example of India as a developing country where less than five per cent of the population buy or read newspapers and books, the talkie film is perhaps the only popular form of culture available to a large number of the common people. The contact of most of the people with prose is the dialogue that they hear in pictures, the only poetry that enriches their lives is the poetry of film lyrics, and their models for style, fashion and mannerisms are the celluloid heroes. Many experts therefore think that the film can educate and inspire, motivate and change their attitudes. To use the communication language, the film in the hands of good script writers and directors can function not only to spread a common filmy language but act as a social monitor and a gatekeeper as well. Like any magazine or newspaper, it can be effectively investigatory and expository. More than any other media it can tellingly project social angularities and injustices, forcibly portray the moods and attitudes of alienated and wayward youngsters, emotionally and incisively depict what poverty is and how farmers, workers, woman and the poor and down-trodden eke out their existence. Recent feature and TV films show that given wise direction, the film without becoming didactive or ceasing to be an entertainer, can expose the black marketeer, the corrupt politician, the anti-social, industrialist or a trade union dada. the 'yes minister' bureaucrative teaser and social parasite. Not only in this respect but positively it can stimulate values of good life and citizenship as also participatory virtues of developmental activities. Through characterisation, demonstration and depiction of scenes and situations, it can even directly help to sell the concepts and norms of national or emotional integration, dignity of labour, the bare-foot doctor or engineer, an understanding spouse and the pulls of extra-marital relations. Documentary experts say that within the constraints of creative reality, even these films can reflect their country's development aspirations and strivings and even the failings and achievements of its people.

In some African, Asian or communist countries there are few individual film makers classified as new-wave film makers, who have set in motion the movement for the socially relevant cinema. This the effort to use the power of the film medium not only to entertain, but to educate and influence the life pattern of viewers. As a change agent its potentiality has started manifesting to reach wider audience, to persuade them and to get their acceptance. The commercial cinema has also started reflecting some of these new trends and offbeat themes of great social significance.

Commercial Cinema

The cinema after Independence in India was predominantly commercial so far as feature films were concerned. The star system, high budgets, escapism, concoction of popular entertainment ingredients, and abundance of music, song anddance were generally the characteristics of this cinema. Circumstances like inflation, overcrowding, dislocated life, social tension, rampant unemployment, disillusionment and youth alienation encouraged film makers to resort to fantasies and escapist or entertaining themes for their pictures. Starting with Sholay and graduating from certain films like Kache Dhage and Reshma Aur Shera, Indian heroes started having an image of a Robin Hood, Garth or Tarzan. The films had revenge as the theme with accompanying attributes of fighting violence. As one critic points out "the dividing lines between art and industry, between north and south, between the moghul and the maverick became hazier than before, movies more than any of the arts provided a spectacle that enthralled, exasperated and appalled in excess." Multi-crore budgeting registered ascendence in Naseeb and Kranti and reached its culmination in Razia Sultan, which also sought to outdo any other picture in respect of grandiose of sets and costumes..

Reaction to this trend however found a manifestation both in the form of the evolution of a new wave or art cinema and the appearance of new directions in commercial cinema itself.

A new trend in film making was born first in Calcutta and then in sporadic waves in other centres of film production in the south. The impact of international film festivals, the institution of film awards, documentary cinema. and the influence of famous film makers from abroad like Jean Renoir (France), Frank Capra (Hollywood), V.I. Pudovkin (USSR) were some of the forces which contributed to the quest for an alternative cinema. These new trend films were made at low costs, outside the main stream of commercial cinema. Their dominant characteristics were their social concern, purposefulness, realism, narrative style. exclusion of unrelated song and dance routines and fights and other familiar devices of the commercial package. Their acceptance by the intelligent and cultivated audiences in the country and the high praise which some of the really good new trend films won abroad brought a much needed self-confidence to adventurous or innovative film makers. The Film Finance Corporation and its successor the National Films Development Corporation provided institutional aid to the otherwise individualistic trend among young film makers. Some notable proponents of this new wave cinema, also called socially relevant cinema or alternative cinema, were Satyajit Ray, K. A. Abbas, Balraj Sahni, Raj Kapoor, Shyam Benegal. Mrinal Sen, Basu Chatterjee, M. S. Sathyu, Utpalendu Chakraborty, Pattabhi Rama Reddy, Adoor Gopalakrishnan, Govind Nihalani, Girish Karnad and B. V. Karanth. This trend was, however, beset with difficulties. Important among these were lack of finance and exhibition halts, direct confrontation with influential commercial cinema and their monoply distributors, and extreme individualism in communication appeals and entertainment techniques by sophisticated aesthetics. Yet, with assistance from Film Finance Corporation and other means, some prize winning films like Ghare Baire and Paar have been produced. Mrinal Sen, who is regarded as one of the Third World's most experienced and internationally renowned radical film makers, has produced new films that win prize after prize. From Ek Din Pratidin to Khandar is a saga of laurel winning in film making. He himself says that cinema should not hibernate and many a film maker with his way of thinking besides India's film 'Wizard Satyajit Ray, have been experimenting with the medium to find a new analysis on the growing explosive social situations around them. The films Chokh by Utpalendu Chakraborty and Damul by Prakash Jha are described as models of possible alternative cinema, for it is cinema of hope. It is advocated that a good film is one that should depict the odds against the best of life and yet seek to transcend them and affirm that these odds should not choke the indomitable spirit of the men, women and children of a society. Ardh Satya is considered the new cinema's biggest hit. It deals with the inequitous system of justice through the story of a sadistic policeman. It is heartening that old masters of new cinema continue to work With increasing maturity and younger film makers are exploring newer subjects and styles with growing confidence.

While the movement for the new cinema in India is still on, though with diffcrent intensity and dimensions in different regions, there are some discernible new directions manifested in the commercial cinema itself. Reaction against high budgeting was visible when Hrishikesh Mukherjee carried on the New Theatres tradition with some success. The films of Basu Chatterjee, Rajnigandha and Chhotisi Baat with their humorous insights into the ordinary daily life of people, proved that such movies could also attract crowds. Films like Love Story and Ek Dujje Ke Liye, costing one-tenth of the high price-tagged pictures, almost shattered the concept that multicrore and multi-star pictures would essentially be box-office hits. A change in acting style scemed to be obvious. A new line of heroes and heroines have started emerging who seek to play their roles as actors and actresses and not just stars. Another thing that has emerged is the return of love stories and adoption of offbeat themes including women's lib, extramarital relations, estrangement between parents and children and the lives of coal miners. Pictures like Arth, Souten, Dard Ka Rista, Talaq, Mandi, Do Dishayen, Devta, Mayuri and Kalka have proved that such pictures have started having more appeal to the changing tastes and moods of cine goers. Film makers have stopped depicting women as objects of sex exploitation or male chauvinism. A set of films dubbed as feminine genre are gaining popularity. These films present women as equal citizens and individuals in their own right. In Arth, two women, a wife and a lover, move from emotional dependence on a man to the freedom of rebuilding their lives on their own. Subha sought to find justification for a woman to seek fulfilment in her career even at the cost of her marital security. The movie

Mujhe Insaf Chahiye depicts the story of a liberated woman in all her trials and turbulations including her angry cry for justice.

Yet another trend visible in the commercial cinema is an occasional effort at light comedies like Chupke Chupke, Khatta Mitha, Naram Garam and Kissi se na Kehna. These efforts only show that reasonable thematic experimentation or innovativeness in film-making in India can be tried without box-office debacle.

The taste of cinema goors seems to be changing also in respect of overpadding of chaotic song and dance sequences. This is discernible in cinema halls when viewers walk out when such scenes are being shown.

Some of the film critics today maintain that the real trend centres in the commercial cinemas are the regional films. While the previous monopoly of artistic Bengali films and of the commercial Hindi films has gone down, the regional cinema in Malayalam, Kannada, Telugu and other southern languages is coming into its own. Young directors and new stars are emerging in these regions. Even in competitions the winners are dominantly from regional cinema. However, a recent avalanche of semi-pornographic and blue films from the south, adroitly side-stepping the censor's regulations, constitute an alarming trend.

Documentary in India

India is forging ahead even in the field of documentary films, news reels, cartoon films and quickies which are all different visual instruments of public information, education and instruction, motivation and attitude changes. Defined originally as creative treatment of actuality, today documentary and information films include those which deal with significant historical, social, scientific or economic subjects, photographed in actual occurance or reenacted, and the emphasis is more on factual content than on entertainment. These films record contemporary history and present fitmic reports on the social and economic progress of a country.

Starting modestly when the Films Division of the Ministry of Information and Broadcasting was set up in 1948, India is currently having an annual production of 104 short films. In 1983-84 the Films Division produced 143 documentary films including 40 produced by independent producers.

In India the State governments, public undertakings and private enterprises can also produce documentaries. If they are within the maximum length of 2000 feet, these films can be released on theatrical circuits only through the Films Division. Production assignments can be also given to independent producers, and annually about 40 to 50 films are produced that way.

India has many well known documentary film makers both in the public and private sectors. They have made both individually and collectively, significant contributions to the development of Indian documentaries and animated films. Produced by Films Division many of these films have obtained international and national awards. Many independent producers outside Films Division have also made docmnentary films of merit and received awards for their films.

Documentaries and news reels are exhibited in all cinema houses and at each performance; the rental is one per cent of the average weekly collections. Every week one news reel and two short films are released at all important centres. The Films Division also supplies prints on loan to Government departments, semi-government educational and charitable institutions, hospitals, social welfare organisations and individuals. This is done through its distribution branch offices as well as through th~ regional and field publicity units of the Directorate of Field Publicity. For non-commercial shows films are loaned. free of charge.

The documentary film movement has a bright future in India. Other than the number of good film makers in the country, there are also sponsoring organisations which realise the importance of documentary films as a powerful and effective visual medium for depicting creative actuality of our changing social scenes and ecology.

The Government on its own part is looking forward to having more such films on technology, science, envirenment, ecology, places of pilgrimage, hill stations, sports, folk music, folk dances and other varieties of art and culture from various parts of the country.

Many Miles to Go

Whatever may be the quality of our motion pictures, they continue to be popular. The video and TV boom has further boosted their importance and craze. TV films have added a new dimension and it is significant that the first TV film (Sadgati) was made by Satyajit Ray and more such films are being produced by other eminent film makers. Good films for children is another branch which needs to be further activised and diversified. To this end, the Children's Film Society the main producing agency, is being keyed up.

India is an exporter of films especially to those areas where Indians or Asians live in fairly large numbers. It is heartening that package marketing interests and tastes of the internal audience has started being reflected in the widening range of current themes and their improving treatments. Participation in various national and international film festivals is helping to infuse new trends and techniques among the more professionally alert film makers, actors and technicians. Yet, some communication experts still believe that apart from popular entertainment ingredients, creativity and aesthetics, Indian films should become more socially purposeful. They should rid of their irrelevant paddings or trappings and professionally unedifying constituents to have a more ennobling impact on the youth and illiterate persons, without becoming pedantic or shedding individual creativity or professional merit.

At present there are, however, some inbuilt handicaps in the film industry. Apart from the firmness of censors and the new danger from video piracy, the most important hurdle in the way of this popular visual medium reaching a vast majority of people is scarcity of cinema houses and exhibition facilities. Very few of the existing cinema theatres have proximity to deep and distant places of rural India. Although Field Publicity units of the Central and State governments do try to fill in the gap, the total number of cinema seats is much less than 2/5th of UNESCO's minimum norm. From the point of view of adequate and sophisticated technology the 16 mm, 8 mm super and wide screen technologies need to be improved. The position in respect of raw material and studio equipment also needs to be further geared up. Government activisation and the efforts of the National Films Development Corporation and other media organisations as also innovative film makers both in the field of commercial and new cinema, have pushed the medium and industry well ahead. But our films have many miles to go as yet in the direction of professional, communication and technical excellence, creative visual impact, wholesome entertainment, aesthetics and international marketability.

This task of the Indian cinema, in becoming a booming industry, a more persuasive and socially relevant change agent, technically well equipped and a decent package offering wholesome entertainment and good music, places a tremendous responsibility upon the industry and on those who operate and direct it, as also on the governing media institutions and censors.

❐

13

New Trends in Cinema

THE BACKDROP

The years preceding the dawn of cinema in India were witness to the growth of musical dramas (sangeet natak), the Parsi theatre, the drama companies of Madras, and the jatra in Bengal. Music, dance, song were an integral part of these performing traditions; this was the heritage of Sanskrit drama and later popular folk performing traditions such as the ram lila, the ras lila, the nautanki and the thirukoothu. In painting, the calendar art of Raja Ravi Varma and others was well known and stage sets incorporated some of the designs and colours of this new art form.

So, when the first 'cinematographic exhibitions' of the Lumiere Brothers were held in Bombay on July 7, 1896, Indian dramatists, photographers, magicians, musicians and singers say in them great potential for the re-telling of Indian myths and folklore. The Times of India advertised these early exhibitions as the marvel of the country, the wonder of the world." The 'exhibitions' included 'living photographic pictures' in 'life-sized reproductions' of the arrival of a train, of workers leaving a factory, of a sea-bath, and of ladies and soldiers on wheels. The exhibitions continued to draw crowds to four shows daily for over two months. Meanwhile, a British cinematographer held exhibitions of a similar kind in Calcutta, then the capital of British India. It is significant that the cinema had its beginnings in India almost at the same time as in other major film-producing countries. Indeed, barely six months after the first Lumiere Brothers' cinematograph projected moving pictures on to a screen in a Paris basement, and two years after Edison's invention of the Kinetoscope in New York.

Among the numerous crowds that watched the first screenings at Bombay's Watson Hotel with utmost fascination was a photographer named Harishchandra S. Bhatvadekar (alias Save Dada). He ordered for a moving picture camera from London, and when it arrived took it along to a wrestling match, and shot the match live (Two Wrestlers). He soon acquired a projector and processing equipment. To him must go the credit of shooting one of the earliest Indian newsreels, Return of Wrangler Paranjpe, which recorded the triumphant welcome in December 1901 accorded to R.P. Paranjpe, an Indian student who had won honours in mathematics at Cambridge. Another Bhatwadekar short was A Man and His Monkey. Jag Mohan, the historian of the Indian documentary, credits Bhatwadekar with being 'the father of the Indian factual film'. However, it is likely that the first Indian short films were Coconut Fair and Our Indian Empire, both made and exhibited in 1897 by unknown English camera persons.

Just as Indian photographers and studios proliferated soon after the introduction of the camera in 1840, so the arrival of the motion picture attracted a large number of business people, artists and craftspeople into film production and exhibition. Photographers in particular took to the new enterprise with enthusiasm. They turned out such items as Poona Races, Train Arriving at Bombay Station, Tilak's Visit to Calcutta, Bathing Ghats at Benaras, Great Bengal Partition Movement, and Terrible Hyderabad Floods. Some of them became professional showmen taking their equipment all over the country and holding exhibitions even in remote towns and villages. The first rural travelling cinemas had begun operating by the end of the twenties. On May 18, 1912, R.G. Tomey filmed a Marathi stage play, Pundalik, while it was being acted out. The play was based on the legend of a famous Maharashtrian saint. Tomey's screen version gave India its first feature film; though some film historians like to credit Dadasaheb Phalke's Rajah Harishchandra, which was made a full year later, with being Indian cinema's first feature.

The Pioneers

'The cinema is an invention without a future', declared Louis Lumiere who together with his brother, Auguste, pioneered what was to develop into an international cultural industry. The Lumiere brothers were the inventors of the 'cinematographe', a compact and portable machine with which a few adjustments could be used as a camera or projector or printing machine. As professional photographers themselves, cinema for them was no more than an extension of photography; hence they sought to capture events from a static position and therefore from a single point of view, in brief actualities such as the arrival of a train, a train leaving the station, workers leaving a factory, a sea bath, ladies and soldiers on wheels. Like still photographs, these 'living photographic pictures' were attempts to reproduce reality. They narrated no story, but reproduced a place, time and atmosphere. These brief moving reproductions were therefore termed 'actualities.'

It was another pioneer, the French magician Georges Melies, who was to revolutionise the cinema from being a 'photoplay' to a mass medium for the creation of fantasies and dreams. Several of his creations had the words 'nightmare' or 'dream' in their titles. He used elaborate sets and editing techniques to make science fiction films like Voyage to the Moon (1902).

So while the Lumiere brothers laid the foundation of realism in cinema, Melies pointed the way to 'expressionism' and to the magic 'of cinema. The Lumiere's realism introduced cinema to the 'mise en scene' while Melies pioneered the technique of 'stop motion photography' to create magical special effects in his many 'trick films.' Elaborate stage sets and special effects were the hallmarks of his films. It is this historical tension between traditions of realism and traditions of expressionism that is at the heart of the aesthetics of cinema.

Realism and Soviet Cinema

The cinema of realism climaxed in the work of the early Russian film-makers, especially that of V. I. Pudovkin and Sergei

Eisenstein. Eisenstein was not only a prolific filmmaker of the Revolution, but also a film theorist. His 'materialist' approach to the form of cinema is exemplified in his masterpieces, Battleship Potemkin, Ivan the Terrible and others. Both Pudovkin and Eisenstein theorised extensively about the concept and practice of 'montage'. Pudovkin (who directed Mother) identified five basic types of montage: contrast, parallelism, symbolism, simultaneity and lietmotif. He developed a theory of the interaction between shots variously called 'relational editing' or 'linkage.' Eisenstein, on the other hand, saw the relationship between shots as a collision rather than a linkage, and further refined the theory to deal with the relationships between elements of individual shots as well as the whole shots themselves. This he called the 'montage of attractions.' Other early Soviet filmmakers and theorists include Lev Kuleshov, Vertov (Kino Eye) and Dovzhenko (Earth): a major concern of the film-makers of the early Soviet cinema was ideology and the socialist state.' Their films had the appearance of a documentary style.

Evolution of Language

Thus, before becoming the means of expression familiar to us, cinema was a simple means of mechanical recording, preserving, and reproducing moving visual spectacles whether of life, of the theatre, or even of small mises-en-scene, which were specially prepared and which, in the final analysis, remained theatrical. It was only when the cinema confronted the problems of narration, particularly in the years between 1910 and 1915 when films like Quo Vadis?, Enoch Arden, The Battle of Gettysburg and Birth of a Nation were made, did film language start inventing its own vocabulary to describe its techniques and procedures.

The pioneers of film language were Melies, E.S. Porter and D.W. Griffith who "cared little about the symbolic, philosophical or human message of their films", but who were ace story-tellers. Melies it was, for instance, who invented 'double exposure', the device of 'multiple exposures' with a mask and a dark backdrop, the 'dissolve' and the 'fade in', and the 'pan shot.'

Melies was present at the Lumiere brothers' exhibition of the cinematograph. In fact, he offered to buy up the machine. As a theatre owner and magician he believed he could make his magic shows more lively with a projector. Accordingly, he bought a projector from an English photographer and used it for his magic shows. He turned the projector into a simple camera to record objects in motion. Once it so happened that the camera jammed and so goes the legend it was this accident that led to his discovery of 'quick' and 'slow' motion of 'stop-motion', and also of the 'fade' and 'dissolve.'

Melies' masterpieces were Cinderella and A Trip to the Moon-the first perhaps to combine paintings with studio-sets. This technique was later perfected by the German expressionists. Melies regarded film-making as an extension of his career as a magician. Most of his work was destroyed during World War II; the few films that have survived reveal a film-maker who resorted to photographic tricks, to 'enchantments' and to actuality recording to create his movie magic. Edwin S. Porter, who made the first story film, The Great Train Robbery, was deeply influenced by Melies.

The first occurrences of some other procedures of filmic language are attributed to the same pioneers as also to the Englishmen G.A. Smith and J. Williamson, and to the Russian, Sergei Eisenstein. The procedures are: the 'close-up', the 'pan shot', the 'tracking shot', 'parallel montage', and 'interlaced' or 'alternate montage.' Of these, the most significant and the most revolutionary was montage, derived initially from the masterpieces of D.W. Griffith. Indeed, it was montage that "gave birth to film as an art, setting it apart from mere animated photography; in short, creating a language" (Andre Malraux). Alfred Hitchcock and Jean-Luc Godard developed film language further with the introduction of new types of shots and camera and cutting techniques.

Dadasaheb Phalke

One of the pioneers of the silent feature film in India was Dhundiraj Govind Phalke (alias Dadasaheb Phalke), a Bombay printer, painter and magician. It is reported that he was converted to cinematography when he saw the film, Life of Christ, at a Christmas cinema show. The idea of a similar full-length feature on the life of Lord Krishna took hold of him, and he made it his life's ambition. But financial stringency and the blatant unwillingness of women, even prostitutes, to act in his films, were crucial issues he would have to contend with through his long career as a film-maker. He broke ground in 1913 with Rajah Harischandra. So successful did it prove with audiences in all parts of the country (though it was hardly noticed by the English-language press) that Phalke went on to make more than a hundred films including short films and full length features. His most popular features were Savitri, Lanka Dahan, Sinhasta Mela, Krishna Janma, and Bhasmasur Mohini. The young man whom Phalke selected to play the women in his films was A. Salunke, a restaurant cook "with slender features and hands."

Only a few scattered fragments of Phalke's silent films are extant. "The overall structure of each film is forever lost, but the fragments show a fine pictorial sense and remarkable technical resourcefulness. Like another magician who became a film pioneer, George Melies, Phalke was a special effects genius. He explored a vast range of techniques, including animation. He experimented with colour, via tinting and toning."

But the religious (or 'mythological') genre held little appeal for some of the other filmmakers of the twenties and thirties. D.G. Ganguly of Calcutta specialised in satirical comedies like England Returned (1921) and Barrister's Wife, Chandulal Shah of Bombay in films dealing with social problems-Gun Sundari (English title: Why Husbands Go Astray), Typist Girl (1918), and Himansu Rai, sponsored by the Germans, made the brilliant films, The Light of Asia (1925), Shiraz (1926), A Throw of Dice (1929), and Karma (1934) which immortalized the actress Devika Rani.

In South India, as in most other parts of the country (with the exception perhaps of Kerala), the mythological genre held sway. The foundation for a flourishing film industry in South India was laid by

R. Nataraja Mudaliar, a businessman trained in cinematography in Poona. In 1917 he set up his own Indian Film Company and by 1923 had made six silent films-all based on mythological characters from the epics. The first was Keechaka Vadha (1917); the others included Draupadi (1919), Lava Kusha (1920), Markandaya (1922) and Mayil Havana (1923). The films carried inter-titles in English and Indian languages.

During the Silent Era (1896-1930) over a thousand films were made in India; however, only ten of them survive, now restored and preserved in the Pune archives. Meanwhile, American and European films continued to grow in popularity, though a major source of worry for the Imperial Government was that they would corrupt Indian minds in 1917, the European Association warned the Government against a film called The Serpentine Dance, which was certainly calculated to bring the white men and women into low esteem in the Indian mind.

Arrival of Talkies

The films of the Silent Era did not 'talk' but they were never watched in 'silence.' Dialogue was presented through inter-titles, which were often in English, and two or three Indian languages. Almost every film had a background score, which ran through the length of the film. The score was 'live', and helped to dramatise the narrative. Sometimes there was only a piano accompaniment, but there were several films where a violin, a harmonium, tablas and other musical instruments could be added.

The 'Talkies Era' was set in motion by The Melody of Love (1929), the first 'talkie' to be screened in India. The first Indian talkie Alam Ara (1931) directed by Ardeshir Irani, was released two years later. The premiere was a proud occasion at the Majestic theatre in Bombay, with the Governor as the chief guest. It included seven songs, so enchanted was the director with the novelty of sound Indra Sabha, which was released the following year, had 70 songs. Though the novelty has long worn off, the enchantment remains to this day. No commercial film dare cutting out song-and-dance sequences altogether, except in rare cases such as B.R. Chopra's Kannoon and K.A. Abbas' Munna (1954). Hindi films dominated right from the start: from 1931 to 1947, over 6,590 Hindi films were produced, while from 1947 to 1987, around 5,074 films were released.

Studio System

With many new hands now needed for the production of films, which was gradually developing into a small industry, the "studio system" made its appearance in Bombay, Calcutta and Madras. In Bombay, V. Shantaram and three others set up the Prabhat Film Co., and went on to roll out films at regular intervals. Shantaram himself directed most of the films. Among his outstanding films were: Ayodhyacha Raja (1932), Sant Tukaram (1936), Amar Jyoti (1936), Duniya Na Mane (the Marathi version was entitled Kunkii), and Admi. The Prabhat Film Co. later moved to Pune on the site where the Film and Television Institute of India now stands.

Led by Himanshu Rai, the Bombay Talkies (established in 1935) flourished as much as Prabhat, turning out three mythological films a year. The Imperial Film Co., another minor Bombay film venture, produced over seven features annually. Wadia Movietone, established by J.B.H. Wadia and his brother Homi, produced 130 films, with J.B.H. himself writing several of the screenplays. The credit for making the first railroad thriller shot on location (Toofan Mail, 1932) and the first film on Hindu-Muslim unity Jai Bharat, 1936) must go to the Wadias.

In Calcutta, the foremost Studio Company was the New Theatre Co., which under the baton of B.N. Sircar and Dhiren Ganguli produced Chandidas (1932), Devdas (1936), and Mukti (1939). K.c. Barua's Devdas, was made in Hindi and Bengali, and introduced audiences to Bimal Roy, the cameraman who was to go on to make his own films, notably the classic Do Bigha Zameen (1953), and also to the immortal voice of Kundanlal Saigal.

Studios were opened in Madras, Salem and Coimbatore, but it was the Madras United Artists' Corporation under the leadership of

K. Subrahmanyam, that turned to film-making in Tamil, Telugu and Malayalam. The southern studios, just as the Madras Studios do today, produced films also in Hindi.

Era of Movie Stars

During the forties, however, the big companies lost their hold on the studio system. Shantaram left Prabhat in 1941 to make films under his own banner. So did Mehboob Khan and others. This gave rise to the 'star system', the 'formula' film and the injection of 'black' money into the film world-three inter-related evils which have beset the commercial cinema ever since. Shantaram with the help of the writer K.A. Abbas, made Journey of Dr. Kotnis, a war-effort film, Dharti Ke Lal, and others. Sohrab Modi's films (notably Pukar) and Mehboob Khan's Mother India, Roti were box-office draws. Gemini Studios' Chandralekha was the greatest Tamil draw in the south, and later in the entire country when the Hindi version was released. Still later, an English version was distributed overseas. It was a spectacular song and dance extravaganza. Its music appeared to anticipate the 'fusion' of the post-MTV Hindi film such as Hum Aapke Hain Koun. The songs are based on Carnatic, Hindusthani, Bharatnatyam, Latin American and Portuguese folk music, as well as the Struass Waltz, each distinct and standing on its own, with barely any background score attempting to interlink anything, just periods of silence.' A significant event at the close of the forties was the starting of the Calcutta Film Society by Satyajit Ray.

Satyajit Ray

It was not until 1954, however, that Ray could ring up the curtain on his career as a film director. He followed up his Apu Trilogy-Father Panchali (1954), Aparajito (1957) and Apur Sansar (1959),-with such masterpieces as Jalsaghar (1958), Devi (1969), Teen Kanya (1961), Charulata (1964), Nayak (1966), Gupy Gyne Bagha Byne (1968), a fantasy musical, Aranyer Din Ratri (1970), Seemabadha (1971), Sonar Kella (1974), Ashani Sanket (1973), Ghare Bhaire (1985), Ganasatru (1989), and Aguntak (1991). Shatranj

Ke Khilari (1977) was Ray's only Hindi feature. Ray's documentaries include the moving Rabindranath Tagore, a one-hour documentary narrated by Ray himself, and Sikkim (1980). "Ray's work traces the essential outline of the middle class in modern India. More'importantly, it is an affirmation of faith in the human being," says Chidananda Das Gupta, a film maker in his own right and author of several books on Indian cinema.

Golden Age

During the fifties and sixties, Sohrab Modi and Mehboob Khan continued their film making ventures. But with a difference-the films were all in colour. Modi's Jhansi Ki Rani (1953) was India's first colour feature; it flopped at the box-office. But they had now to compete with two other stalwarts in Indian cinema. The first was Raj Kapoor who began his career as a clapper-boy in Bombay Talkies; the second, Guru Dutt. Raj Kapoor acted in and directed his own films-Awara, Barsaat, Shri 420, Sangam, and Mera Naam Joker. In the seventies he directed the phenomenal success Bobby, and later the controversial Satyam Shivam Sundaram, and Ram Teri Ganga Maili.

Guru Dutt excelled in delineating the tragic mood in films like Kagaz Ke Phool, Baazi, Pyaasa, and Sahib Bibi Aur Gulam. Kamal Amrohi's studies of Uttar Pradesh's elite, Mahal, Dawa and Pakeezah belonged to the same period.

The two great money-spinners of the decade after independence were V. Shantaram's Jhanak Jhanak Payal Baje (1955) and Mehboob Khan's Mother India (1957). Shantaram's film had a record run of 104 weeks at a single cinema theatre in Bombay. It was basically a song and-dance extravaganza in technicolor, featuring Sandhya and Gopikrishna. The colourful decor, costumes, locations and dances accompanied by lilting music gave the cue to Indian film-makers that a story could be dispensed with if such light entertainment were provided in full measure. Mother India, on the other hand, showed that a mother's suffering and sacrifice could touch the hearts of millions in India.

The sixties saw Mughal-e-Azam (1960)-a costume epic dependent on luxurious sets, dance and music sequences, and easy flowing Urdu dialogue for its success. It set the pace for films with a Moghul background. In 1961 Ganga Jamna introduced the figure of the wronged man turning into a dacoit as also the stock-characters of contemporary Hindi cinema-two brothers, one a law-keeper, the other a law-breaker. Raj Kapoor's Sangam (1964) started the trend of shooting on foreign locations, the necessity of a smooth camera technique and in terms of plot, made the friendship between two males (Yaarana) and their falling out over a woman as a result of circumstances, everlasting on the screen.

Angry Young Man

The seventies began with Bobby (1973) proving how big a draw the portrayal of young love on the Indian screen could be. But perhaps the greatest spectacular of post-independence cinema has been Sholay (1975).14 Shot in 70 mm and moving at a rapid-fire pace, it glorified the stocky and lovable dacoit chief, Amjad Khan. For the next decade or so excessive violence became the norm of the mainstream Hindi cinema. Amar Akbar Anthony (1977) was in the same mode, and so was Muqaddar-ka-Sikandar (1978). In the eighties the box office draw was disco and music and dance sequences tied together with dollops of vendetta and romance. Feroz Khan's Qurbani remained the pace-setter for this genre.

But during the nineties, the family drama genre, with the usual ingredients of romance, song, dance and endless arguments about what it means to be 'Indian', promised to be the main attraction, despite the phenomenal growth of television channels. Sooraj Barjatya's Hum Apke Hain Koun ('Forever Yours' in English, Anbaalayam' in Tamil) and Aditya Chopra's Dilwale Dulhaniya Le Jayenge were runaway successes at the box office, helped along by savvy marketing strategies, and the strict monitoring of cable operators attempts to screen pirated versions; so were Yash Chopra's Dil To Paagal Hai, Pardes, Border and Rangeela. Besides, David Dhawan's wafer-thin comedies-cum-romances (Hero No.1, Judwaa, Coolie No.1 and

Gharwali Baharwali) breathed new life into the ailing Bombay film industry. The decade was marked by a revival of the mainstream Hindi and Tamil cinema and the return of audiences to the big screen.

New Wave Films

What is termed the 'New. Wave' in the history of Indian cinema is not the 'nouvelle vogue' of French cinema with which Bresson, Godard and other experimental filmmakers were associated in the fifties and sixties. In the Indian context, the terms are rather loosely used to describe the deliberately realist and non-commercial style of film making that sometimes experiments with form and content. Its roots are in IPTA theatre, the realist novel, and European cinema (especially Russian, French and Italian). It eschews the escapist Hollywood and the Bombay film traditions, and is concerned more with real-life issues of Indian society than with just entertainment. Other terms used to talk about this cinema are 'alternative', 'parallel', and even 'another' cinema.

The establishment of the Film Finance Corporation (FFC) in 1960 raised the expectations of serious film-makers though they were wary of the terms of the loans provided by it. The FFC began in a business-like manner giving loans only to established filmmakers. But from 1968 onwards, low-budget ventures by young filmmakers too began to be granted loans. Mrinal Sen's Bhuvan Shome (1969) set the trend for the 'New Wave' Indian film. Bhuvan Shome was filmed on location with a small cast, "simple in structure though rich in resonance", breaking from the 'formula' film. It made a mark as a commercial success, and won the year's Best Feature Film, Best Actor, and Best Director awards; it won laurels abroad too. Like Ray, Mrinal Sen continued to turn out films at regular intervals. His prolific work includes: Baishey Shravan, Akash Kusum, Interview, Padatik, Chorus, Ek Din Pratidin, Parashuram, Mrigaya, Ek Adhuri Kahani, Ek Din Achanak, and Genesis.

Then came Basu Chatterji with Sara Akaash, scripted and directed by him, with camera work by KK Mahajan. Chatterji whose forte has been ridicule of the 'formula' film has gone on to make Rajnigandha (1974), Chhoti Si Baat (1975), Chitchor (1976), Swami (1977) and TV serials likeRajani.

In 1973, two FFC-aided films broke new ground. The FFC is now the NFDC, the National Film Development Corporation. Avtar Kaul's 27 Down was a paen to railway lore and mystique in the outward form of a love story. It won the year's Best Hindi feature award and later an award at the Locarno festival. Of a different genre was M.S. Sathyu's Garam Hawa (1973) which told the story of India's partition through the eyes of a Muslim family in Agra. FFC assisted in funding the making of more than a hundred films, many of which did not reach the box-office. Notable among these have been Kumar Shahani's Maya Darpan, and Tarang, and Mani Kaul's Uski Roti, Ashad Ka Ek Din, Duvidha ('... they do not form a trilogy. They are about women yes, aspects of women, that's all'), Satah Se Utha Admi (on Muktibodh, the Hindi poet) and Siddheshwari, a tribute to the thumri singer.

Middle Cinema

Hindi cinema, dominated in the 1970s by the Sippys, Hrishikesh Mukherjee, B.R. Ishara and Vijay Anand, was jolted out of its wits when Shyam Benegal assisted by Blaze Enterprises, shot into prominence with Ankur (1974), and later with Nishant (1975), Manthan, Bhumika (1977), Kondura (1977) and Junoon (1979). Benegal turned his back on the standard Kalyug and Aaradhana (1981) genre, injecting a dose of caste-politics into his first three films. He was closely associated with the making of Govind Nihalani's Aakrosh (1980), a political film about the exploitation of illiterate Mivasis Ardh Satya (1984), Party (an expose of the upper middle class), and his TV serial on the partition of India, Tamas, have been significant successes.

While the films of Mrinal Sen, Mani Kaul and Kumar Shahani did not fare very well at the box office, those of the 'middle cinema' reaped a good harvest. Saeed Mirza's Albert Pinto Ko Gussa Kyon

Aata Hai, Mohan Joshi Hazir Ho, and Salim Langde Pe Mat Ro, Rabindra Dharmaraj's Chakra, and Ketan Mehta's Bhavni Bhavai (in Gujarati and Hindi), Mirch Masala, and later Maya Memsahib, and Sardar, started a trend in the making of socially conscious and political films which were entertaining as well. Both the New Wave and the Middle Cinema wilted under the impact of multi-channel television, 'commercial cinema', the commercialization of the National Film Development Corporation (NFDC), and above all the abysmal lack of exhibition outlets. The gradual decline of the Film Society movement too had a role in the fading away of 'parallel cinema.'

Second New Wave

As the century drew to a close, there was a revival of the New Wave spirit, with some assistance from the NFDC, Doordarshan, overseas TV companies such as Channel Four of Britain, and private financiers. Some termed this revival the 'Second New Wave', even though most of the film makers involved in the revival were also part of the first New Wave. Mani Kaul (Nazar, The Idiot, Siddeshwari), Shyam Benegal (The Making of the Mahatma, Mammo, ... Saatvan Ka Ghoda, Sardari Begum), Saeed Mirza [Naseem (1996)], Adoor Gopalakrishnan [Kathapurusharn (1995)], Girish Kasaravalli [Mane (1996)], Thai Saheb (1998), Govind Nihalani [Hazaar Chourasi Ki Maa (1998)], Kumar Shahani [Chaar Adhyay (1997)] and others in different regional languages of the country helped keep the spark of 'alternative' cinema alive. The establishment of the National Centre for Children and Young People (NCYP) provided an impetus to the making of films targeted at Indian youth.

Perhaps the most significant development for Indian cinema in recent years has been the long-awaited status of an 'industry' accorded to it by the new BJP-led government. Film makers can now obtain loans from nationalised banks and insure their products and personnel with the national insuran:e companies. It is hoped that such a status will wean the industry from dependence on 'black money.'

Regional Cinema

At the national level, films in Hindi made in Bombay and Madras, continue to reign supreme. During the 1990s, however, some films made in the languages of the South, either re-made or dubbed in Hindi, have found a good market. Mani Ratnam's Roja, Bombay, and Border, are examples of such films.

Several Hollywood films too began to be dubbed in Hindi, beginning with Jurassic Park, Schindler's List, Pretty Woman and The Lion King, though not all of them managed to succeed at the box-office. The various Hollywood companies such as Columbia, MGM, Twentieth Century Fox, Paramount and Disney have a significant presence in Bombay and other large cities. A recent trend is the production of a few Indian films in English, such as The Making of the Mahatma, and English August. Yet another trend is the making of films on India-related themes by NRI film-makers such as Mira Nair (Bombay, Mississippi Masala, Kamasutra) and Deepa Mehta (Fire, Earth, Water).

Marathi Cinema

Indian cinema had its beginnings in Maharashtra. The first two Indian feature films, Pundalik and Rajah Harishchandra, were unmistakably Maharashtrian in form and substance. The traditions of the Marathi stage were followed closely. The mythological genre was clearly dominant in the early Marathi cinema, but there were historical and social themes taken up as well. Indeed, the mythologicals invariably carried social messages, in the manner of popular folk traditions such as ram leela, krishna leela, and keertans. The first studios for making films in Marathi were established in Kolhapur, Nashik and Pune.

Baburao Painter made mythological films like Sairandhri and Vatsala Haran, historicals. like Sinhagad, and a remarkable social realist film, Savkari Pash, which told the tale of a Marathi peasant family in the context of the exploitation of poor illiterate farmers by moneylenders.

But it was Prabhat Talkies' Sant Tukaram (directed by Damle-Fatehlala) that won plaudits at home and abroad; the film represented Indian cinema at the 1937 Venice Film Festival. This and other films produced by Prabhat Talkies have inspired Marathi cinema over the years. The first studios, however, were set up in Kolhapur-the Maharashtra Film Co. by Baburao Painter who together with Anandrao, pioneered the silent film era in Western India. Sardar Balasaheb Yadav, the owner of Chhatrapati Cinetone, also in Kolhapur, made mythologicals like Kurukshetra (1933), with draperies and other paraphernalia provided by Baburao Painter after he had wound up his own studio.

Bhalachandra Gopal Pendharkar (better known as Bhalji Pendharkar) of Jaiprabha Studios, also in Kolhapur, made over 50 films, including nine silent films which he wrote, produced and directed himself. Pendharkar was a journalist, a stage actor, a translator, but above all a nationalist. The cinema for him was a weapon to serve his country, to add to her, glory and to enhance the reputation of everything Indian. He made both mythological and historical films, as also films on social issues, to further these goals. In Shyamsundar (1932), for instance, Lord Krishna is a revolutionary out to destroy the evil Kansa. His oeuvre includes Meethbhakar (1949), Saadhi Mansi (1965) and Taambdi Maati (1969); Dada Khondke debuted as an actor in the last film.

The films of Master Vinayak who worked in collaboration with P.K. Atre, were brilliant social satires of the forties. The foremost director of the 1950s was Raja Paranjpe, who collaborated with the poet and screenplay writer, G.D. Madgulkar. The role of literary figures in the making of Marathi films climaxed in the work of P.L. Deshpande. In these hands cinema lost much of its visual character and was turned into a literary and verbose product. A significant film of the fifties was Anant Mane's Sangtye Aika, based on the life of a popular contemporary actress. The film ran for over 130 weeks in a Pune theatre. Mane's other box-office triumphs were Aboli (1953), Martini and DhatkiJaoo.

The few films that were produced during the sixties and early seventies were formula films-either of the tamasha or the family drama genres. Dada Khondke made his debut as a director in 1971 with Songadya, and followed it up with a string of successes. His racy comedies laced with double entrende, his khakhi shorts which barely held up, his chaplinesque walk, and catchy lyrics and folksy music, provided a heady mix at a time when violence and gang wars reigned supreme in the Hindi cinema.

The eighties and nineties saw some welcome trends in both the popular and parallel streams of Marathi cinema. The renaissance came about mainly because of the 'entertainment tax refund scheme' (ETRS) introduced by the State Government in 1975. Under this scheme, a film-maker had only to make a second film to get a refund of upto 80 per cent of the entertainment tax collected by the State Government from his or her first film.

In the early Marathi cinema, men of letters were collaborators, but in recent years they have turned into film-makers in their own right. Jabbar Patel, a pediatrician by profession, is easily the most eminent among them. Scripted by Vijay Tendulkar, his first venture Saamna (Confrontation) is about the changing scene of rural Maharashtra, dominated as it has been all these years by sugar barons and power-politics. The second, Jait Re Jait, deals with tribal life, and the third Simhasan (Throne), is a political satire on the goings-on in Maharashtra politics. His Umbartha (Subah in Hindi) based on the novel by Shanta Misal, has a feminist theme.

Films based on well-known Marathi stage successes have also proved popular. Ghasiram Kotwal and Shantata Court Chalu Ahe by Vijay Tendulkar, the latter directed by Satyadev Dube and shot by Govind Nihalani, are cases in point. Other outstanding films of the eighties include Sarvasakshi (Omnipresent) directed by Ramdas Phutane, 22nd June 1887, directed by Chinoo and Jayoo Patwardhan, and Raj Dutt's Devki Nandan Gopala, a biographical film on the life of Gadge Maharaj, a modern saint.

Ramdas Phutane went on to make a film based on a Marathi drama, Down with Festivals, and Shriram Lagoo, a veteran stage actor and director, made his debut as a film director with Zaakol (Omnious Shadow). Vijaya Mehta, Arvind Deshpande and Amol Palekar, three big names of the Marathi stage, have also entered the world of cinema, Mehta as a director, Deshpande as an actor, and Palekar as both an actor and director. Mehta's film ventures include Smriti Chitre and Rao Sahib, while Palekar has directed Bangarwadi and Daayra.

In 1991, a record 29 films were made but the only real box-office hit was Vijay Kondke's Maherchi- Saadi which set off a trend in family dramas. Despite being a remake of the 1983 Gujarat film Mahimni Chunnari, it proved to be such a phenomenal success (it ran in Pune's Prabhat theatre for more than a year) that even films by Sachin (Ayatya Gharat Gharoba) and Mahesh Kothare Jivalaga) could not hold the audiences.

At the end of the nineties, Marathi cinema was gasping for survival, with only nine films produced in 1996, and 10 in 1997. The era of Dada Khondke came to an end with his passing away in early 1998. Shravani Deodhar's Sarkarnama (1997) focussed on political corruption, while Nachiket and Jayoo Patwardhan's Limited Manuski (1996) used slapstick to satirise middle-class values. Other remarkable films of the time were Arun Khopkar's Katha Don Ganpathivanchi (1996). Sumitra Bhave and Sunil Sukhtankar's Doghi (1996), Ramesh Deo's Senani (1996), and Piaj Lagnachi (1997). However, it appears that Marathi cinema will get a new lease of life with the State Government offering to subsidise 15 films every year, to the tune of Rs. 1.6 million for each venture, and the Central Government assuring the grant of the status of an 'industry' to film making.

Gujarati Cinema

The first Gujarati film was a short feature entitled Mumbaini Sethani, released on April 9, 1932, while the first full-length feature was Narsinh Mehto. Other early films included Sati Savitri, and Char

Jamai. As in other parts of the country, Gujarati films had to compete with Hindi films made in Bombay and Madras, because of the small number of theatres. So until the early seventies, only 130 Gujarati films had been made, the most remarkable being Kantilala Rathod's masterpiece Kanku. However, even Kanku could be released only in one theatre for just a week.

Then came the film 'boom' consequent upon the State government's generosity in granting sudsidies and in exempting films produced in studios within the State, from entertainment tax. As many as 40 films were produced each year during the 1970, but less than 30 during the 1980s, though the quality of films was rather indifferent. Popular Gujarati cinema has been largely based on mythology, folk tales and novels.

Some graduates of the Film and Television Institute, Pune, have set up a film cooperative called Sanchar. Sanchar's first venture, Bhavni Bhavai, made in 16 mm and shot on location and directed by Ketan Mehta, won a national film award and the acclaim of critics. So has Mirch Masala. The spirit of Kanku and Kashi No Dikro returned to Gujarati cinema between 1980 and 1985 (the 'golden period' of Gujarati cinema), but for the next decade or so mythologicals and folk dramas continued to dominate. Gujarati cinema received a boost at the close of twentieth century with a string of blockbusters by Govindbhai Patel, the foremost being Unchi Medi Na Uncha Mol (1996) and Desh Re Joya Dada Pardesh (1997). Like Hum Aapke Hain Koun and Dilwale Dulhaniya Le Jayenge, Patel's films are in the family drama genre, with the focus on the joint family system and the search for an Indian identity.

Bengali Cinema

The Bengali cinema has been dominated for over three decades now by Satyajit Ray, Mrinal Sen, Tapan Sinha and Ritwik Ghatak. Ghatak died in 1976, and Satyajit Ray in 1993. Talented young film makers who have joined the ranks of the 'parallel' cinema in recent years include Purnendu Pattrea, Buddhadeb Dasgupta, Utpalendu

Chakravorty, Nitish Mukherjee, Gautam Chakravorty, Gautam Bose and Aparna Sen. But since all of them work at their art like lone wolves there's no 'movement' worth the name to provide them the support that comes from a cooperative effort.

The result is that their films win laurels abroad, but can find few exhibitors at home. The Nandan Film Centre in Calcutta has now come to their rescue. The Centre has exhibition and documentation facilities, conducts seminars and workshops which draw film-makers from all over the country. The Satyajit Ray Film and Television Institute, and the Film Studies programme at Jadavpur University have given further impetus to the Bengali film industry.

Buddhadeb Dasgupta launched his career as a director with Dooratwa (Distance) (1978), a close look at middle class mores in contemporary Calcutta through the story of a young lecturer's disillusion with leftist politics; Neem Annapurna (Bitter Morsel) followed a year later, and Grihayuddha (The Civil War) in 1982, the latter focusing on the inevitability of class conflict. Andhi Galli (Blind Alley) (1985), a film in Hindi, explored the erosion of Bengali youth's values against the backdrop of police 'encounters' of the 1970s for bumping off young leftists. He returned to Bengali with Phera (The Return) (1987).

Utpalendu Chakravorty made his debut with a documentary Mukti Chai and a feature on bonded labour Moyna Tadanta (Post Mortem), both of which have won national film awards. He went on to make Chokh (The Eye) (1982), Debshishu (Child God) (1985), Phansi (1989), the tragic tale of a professional hangman, Chandanneer (The Nest of Rhythm) (1989), a musical, and Kanna (1989), a documentary on a Bharat Natyam dancer.

Gautam Ghose made documentaries (New Earth, Chains, Bondage, Hungry Autumn) before he started directing feature films in Bengali, Hindi and Telugu. His first feature was a Telugu film Maa Bhoomi (Motherland) (1979), which focussed attention on the Telangana peasant uprising in Andhra in the early forties. Dhakal

(Occupation) (1981) told the story (in Bengali) of a gypsy woman's struggle to keep her land against the local landlord who is in collusion with the district officer. The Hindi feature Paar (The Crossing) (1984) told the dramatic tale of survival of a poverty-stricken couple, while the Bengali Antarjali Yatra (The Voyage Beyond) (1987) drew attention to the practice of sati.

Other filmmakers of note include: Aparna Sen (36 Chowringhee Lane, Paroma, Sati, and Picnic), Raja Mitra (EkitJiban), Sandip Ray (Himghar), Nitish Mukherjee (Ekdin Surya, Nayan Shyama and Rabidar), and Purnananda Pattrea (Streer Patra, Chentra Tamsukha, and Malancha).

Telugu Cinema

In terms of the number of films produced no state has been as prolific as Andhra. Most of the Telugu films made are pot-boilers of Hindi cinema, loaded with song and dance sequences. Mythologicals, folk love fantasies, socials and crime thrillers dominate. The first Telugu talkie was H.M. Reddi's Bhakta Prahlad (1932); Reddi's Grihalakkshmi (1937) was a path-breaking film: it broke away from the tradition of using grandhikam in dialogue and employed a colloquial spoken style. From the 1930s onwards, Telugu films were made in Rajahmundry, Vizagapatlnam, Madras and even Kolhapur. Some of the classics of early Telugu cinema are: G. Ramabrahman's Mala Pillai Raita, K.V. Reddi's Bhakta Potana, Yogi Vemana, Chittoor V. Nagaiah's Thaiagaiah and B.N. Reddi's Malleswari.

Shyam Senegal with Anuragham, Mrinal Sen with Oka Cori Katha did try to break into Telegu films but without much success. B.S. Narayana has won national and international acclaim with his two features, Oorummadi Bratukulu, a naturalistic film about the struggle of the poor, and Nammajjanam, which deals with the suicide of a young bride who is the victim of rape. Two other outstanding films are Ravindran's Harijan and Gautam Ghose's Maa Bhoomi, which focus on the plight of the have-nots in an exploitative situation.

Telegu cinema shot into the limelight in 1981 with K. Viswanath's Sankarabaranam, which bagged the Golden Lotus for Mass Entertainer with Aesthetic Values. In 1989, his Sevarna Kamalam was selected for the Indian Panorama. Vishwanath went on to make several other films, such as Sita Mahalakshmi, President Peramma, Saptapadi, Subalekha, and Sagar Sangamam. Among the other directors worthy of mention are K.V. Reddi, L.V. Prasad, Dasari Narayana Rao, K. Raghavendra Rao and U. Vishveshwara Rao.The big crop of films each year in Andhra is the State Government's support. It is perhaps the only State Government that ploughs back about 7% of the receipts from entertainment tax into the film industry. The Andhra Pradesh State Film Development Corporation supports films made in Telugu.

Tamil Cinema

Chennai has been a centre for film production in Hindi and the South Indian languages, from the early years of Indian cinema. Several silent features based on the mythology and the puranas were produced, and proved to be very popular among the masses. The first silent film was Keechakavatham (The Extermination of Keechakan) (1916), a mythological, and the first talkie Kalidas (1931) contained no fewer than 50 songs. Tamil cinema was seen as an extension of the popular performing arts such as company drama, therukoothu, the circus and wrestling. The repertoire of the (drama) companies was limited to a few mythologicals, written as musicals. The stories were standardised as a series of songs. In keeping with the tradition of company drama, the talkies carried a large number of songs and placed less emphasis on dialogue. Right from the beginnings of Tamil cinema, the Brahmin elite despised cinema Oust as it did company dramas and therukoothu (folk street theatre), regarding it as 'low culture', in contrast to Bharatnatyam and Carnatic music which constituted 'high culture.' The first three phases of Tamil cinema, according to one analyst, were *(i)* the puranic, mythological and folklore period (1931-50), *(ii)* the melodramatic story period (1951-75), and *(iii)* the partly realistic anti-sentimental stories period (1951-75).

The perspective is of course elitist; realism is seen as the ideal towards which cinema must aspire. The 'parallel' cinema, which was marked by social realism, had its influence on the Tamil cinema of the late seventies. The pioneers were K. Balachander, Bharathi Raja, Mahendran, Balu Mahendra, Dorai, Jayabharati, Bhagyaraj, Rudraiyyaand H.A. Kaja. Mahendran's UtharipookalandDorai's Past continued the realistic genre started by the late Bhim Singh's Sila Narangalil Sila Manithangal, which challenged the myth of the ideal heroine. Bharathi Raja set the trend of locating films in villages, and Mahendra gave the villagers 'solidity, depth and relevance' in his 16 Vayadinile. There was a radical move away from the dialogue-oriented film, as in J. Mahendran's Mullum Malarum and the co-operative venture of some young people under the leadership of Robert and Rajasekaran, Oru Thalai Ragam. The demise of film-star and Chjef Minister M.G. Ramachandran in 1988, and the ouster of Jayalalitha as Chief Minister has not affected film production though some studios have closed and attendance has fallen, owing to cable, the Sun and Vijay TV channels (JJ TV has folded temporarily), and Sun Movies, the round-the-clock film TV channel of the Sun TV group. Mani Ratnam, lliayarajah and A. R. Rehman have put Tamil cinema on the all India map.

Malayalam Cinema

The seventies were the 'golden' period of Malayalam cinema. The pioneers of the 'parallel' cinema in Kerala were Adoor Gopala-krishnan, G. Aravindan, John Abraham and Shaji. Gopalakrishnan's oeuvre includes some finely crafted narratives made over the last two decades: Swayamvaram, Kodiyettam (1977), Elipathyatn (Mousetrap) (1981), Mukhamukham (Face to Face) (1984), Anantaram (1987), Mathilukal (1989), Vidheyan (1993), and Kathapurusham (1995).

Malayalam films have had the largest representation at the Indian Panorama of our international film festivals since the seventies. Film co-operatives (like Chitralekha), film societies (like Odessa), and loyal audiences have been the major reasons for the steady growth of Malayalam cinema. Besides, the State Government has set up a film complex. in Trivandrum and provides subsidies to established film-makers.

The other film makers who have made valuable contributions in terms of form and content, include: Vasudevan Nair (Nirrnalayam Bandhanarri), P. A Backer (Kabani Nadi Chuvannappot), Padmarajan (Peuyazhiambalam and Kallan Pavithran), V.R. Gopinath (Greesham), John Abraham (AmmaAriyan Letter to Mother; Cheriyachante Krogra Krithyangal The Wicked Deeds of Chediyachan, Sivan (Yagarri), and K.R. Mohanam (Ashwa Thamd) and Shaji (Piravi). K.G. George Gourney's End), Lenin Rajendran (A Tale of the Past), K. Ravindran's (Ore Tahvool Pakshigal and Varikuzha), are some of the other distinguished directors. The films that stood out in the early nineties were Shaji N Karun's Swaham, Hariharan's Parinayam and Padmakumar's Sammohanam, and in the mid-nineties T. V.Chandran's Ormakalundayirrikanam, Hari Kumar's Sukrutham, and Lohitdas' Bhootakannadi (Magnifying Glass). Jeyraj, the maker of Deshdanam, won the Best Film Award for his Kaliyattam in 1998.

Kannada Cinema

Perhaps the earliest film in Kannada was Bhakta Dhruva (1934), but Kannada cinema really took off only after the mid-fifties under the leadership of Dr. Raaj Kumar. Its heyday was of course the 1970s when one daring film after another challenged the status quo.

The State Government of Karnataka was perhaps the first to encourage the regional cinema by offering generous subsidies, and granting tax exemptions to films made in Kannada. In the space of two decades, Kannada cinema began to wrest national awards. Sarnskara (1970), Vansha Vriksha (1971), Kaadu (1973), Chomana Dudi (1975) and Hamse Geethe won national and international acclaim.

The ventures of Puttanna Siddhalingayya and Raaj Kumar which attempted to blend art with popular entertainment proved successful at the box office.

The 'new wave' has receded in Karnataka as elsewhere in the country, with Karanth and Girish Karnad leaving the State, and the new film-makers taking to big-budget films. M.S. Sathyu oiGaram Hawa and Bara (Famine) fame made two big-budget Kannada films- Kanneshwara Rama and Chitegu Chinte-and Girish Karnad Ondanondu Kaladalii and Tabaliyu Neenade Magane (jointly with Karanth). P. Lankesh's Pallavi too made a mark. But it has been Girish Kasaravalli who remains the foremost director now with a wholecorpus of visually arresting films-Ghattashradha, Aakramana Mooru Darigallu, Mane, and Thai Sahib (1997) to his credit.

Oriya Cinema

Perhaps the first film to be made in Oriya was Sitavivah in 1934. As in the cinema of the other Indian languages, the early Oriya films were for the most part mythological. TIme was when Oriya films matched the popularity of Bengali films. Notable films up to the fifties were: Lalita, Mahalakshmi Puja, DasyuRatnakar and Parinam. Mrinal Sen made Matira Manisha in Oriya, a film based upon Kalandi Charan Panigraha's Oriya novel of the pre-Independence period. One of the most popular films of the 1960s was Prabhat Mukherji's Nua Bou, replete with songs; the lead role played by the veteran Dhira Biswal.

Around 16 feature films are made each year in Orissa, which has only one film laboratory, namely, the Prasad Kalinga Film Laboratories. A clutch of Oriya film makers of the last two decades, most of them alumni of the Film and Television Institute of India, have made a valuable contribution to Oriya cinema. One of the most distinguished is A.K.Bir, whose work includes Aadi Mimansa, Lavanya Preeti, Aranyaka and Shasha Drusht (The Last Vision). Nirad Mahapatra, an FTII alumni, has been relentless in his scrutiny of the Oriya family system in films like Maya Miriga (The Illusion) (1983). Other film makers like Sagir Ahmed have focussed on children who grow up without love and care in Dhaare Aalua (1983), and Prafulla Mohanty on child marriage in Bhanga (Broken Slate) (1987). Manmohan Mahapatra has given us a whole range of sensitive yet incisive films on traditions and practices in urban and rural Orissa: Sita Raati (Winner's Night) (1982), Neerabadha Jhada (The Silent

Storm) (1984), Klanta Aparaha (Tired Afternoon) (1986), Majhi
Pahacha (The Middle Step) (1987), and Trisandhya (1988).

Punjabi Cinema

Prior to partition, Punjabi films were made in Bombay and
Lahore where modern studios hummed with activity. There were
three studios in Lahore (punjab Film Company, United Players and
Kamla Movietone) established during the silent era. Himanshu Rai's
Love of a Mughal Prince was made in the Lahore studios, but the
most successful was A.R. Kardar (who owned United Players) who
made around nine silent films, with English titles such as Golden
Dagger, Brave Heart, Serpent, Shepherd, Mysterious Eagle and
Wandering Dancer. The English titles invariably had alternative titles
in Punjabi. The Victim, for example, was called Bhukh nu Bhog,
Wooing Nightingale bore the Punjabi title Bol Tu Bulbul, Jewelled
Arrow was Poonam nu Chand, in Punjabi, and The Dancing Girl had
the creative title Gutter nu Gulab. However, the 'talkies' in the early
1930s and later the partition brought an end to the Lahore ventures.
The first Punjabi film, K.D. Mehra's Sheila (1935), inspired by
Tolstoy's Resurrection, was premiered at the Corinthian Theatre in
Calcutta; Mehra's Heer Sayal, based on Warris Shah's Heer Ranjha,
the immortal tale of young love, revived the studios of Lahore,
though only until the partition.

Dalsukh Pancholi (GulBakawli and Yamla Jat), Roshan Lal
Shorey (Chaman) (1948) and Roop Shorey (Mangti, Dulla Bhatti,
Koel and Tarzan Ki Beti) contributed much to Punjabi cinema during
the post-partition years. Bombay became the hub of Punjabi cinema
after the partition, but Pakistan's ban on Indian films, the further
division of the state of Punjab, and above all the competition from
Hindi films dealt a deathly blow to Punjabi films. Devotional films
(Nanak Nam Jahaz Hai, Nanak Dhukia Sab Sansar, DhannaJat, Dukh
Banjan Tera Nam, Man Jeeta Jag Jeet, and Sherni) proved to be a big
draw during the years of the Green Revolution, followed closely by
years of fear and terrorism. Other films worthy of note are: Virendra's
Sarpanch and Lamberdarni, Dharmakumar's Daaj, Peepat's Chann
Pardesi (1980) and Vijay Tandon's Kachehari (1993).

Assamese and other North-eastern Films

Cinema in Assam and the North-east has received much attention at national film festivals in recent years. The state film development corporations have provided the primary impetus for this growth of interest in indigenous cinema. For instance, active support from the State-run Assam Film Finance and Development Corporation has played a vital role. It provides loans to talented film-makers, and has plans of establishing a chain of 'Janata halls' for regular exhibition of films. Mobile cinemas are also being encouraged by exemption from entertainment taxes. The first Assamese film was Jyotiprasad Agarwala's Joymati, released in 1935. Agarwala later madeIndra Malati, but received little recognition. He is believed to have been the first director to introduce playback singing in Indian cinema.

The following two decades saw a crop of films by Rohini Kumar Barua, Parvati Barua and Phani Sharma. In 1955 Piyali Phukan won a national award. In the sixties, the best known film-makers were Bhupen Hazarika, Padma Barua, Abdul Mazid, Attul Baroli and Manoranjan Sur. By the end of the eighties, however, film production had slumped. In 1986 only 11 films were made, and only eight in the following year. But this too is creditable since the whole state has only one government owned studio and minimal infrastructure. Most post-production work has to be completed in laboratories in Calcutta, Bombay or Madras. Exhibition theatres do not number more than 143 in the entire state.

Jahanu Barua and Bhabendranath Saikia have now put Assamese cinema on the international festival circuit. Saikia's major films include Sandhya Rag, Anirban, Agnisaan, and Kolahal (1988), and Barua's are: Apamopa (1979), Papori (1985), Halodhia Choraye Boodhan (1987), Bannai (1989) and Hkhagoroloi Bohu Door (1996). Halodhia Choraye Boodhan won the Golden Lotus in 1988 and also the Grand Prix for Best Film and Best Actor at Locarno.

Barua and Saikia are in the tradition of 'new wave' Indian cinema. They strive for an authentic portrayal of the village ethos, of the struggle of men and women against oppression and exploitation.

Other film makers of note in Assam include Siba Thakur (Asouta Prahof), Padum Barua (Ganga Chilaner Pakhi), Jones Mohalia, Gautam Bora, Mirdul Gupta and Hemanta Das.

Manipuri Cinema

Around ten films have been produced so far in the Manipuri tongue, with the first film made in 1972. Perhaps the most acclaimed Manipuri film has been Imagi Ningthem (My Son, My Precious) (1981), directed by Aribam $yam Sharma. It won the Grand Prix at Nantes, France, in 1981. The film weaves a sensitive tale of a boy who, following his unmarried mother's death in childbirth, is brought up by his grandfather. The boy's father is traced by the local school teacher, and is found to be married; but his wife is only too happy to adopt the boy as her own. Among the other Manipuri films of note are: Matamgi Manipur (1972), Ngak-ke-ko Ngangse (1974), Lamja Parusaram (1975), Khuttang Lamjet (1979), Olangthagee Wangmadasoo (1980), Khonjel (1981), and Wangma Wangma (1982). The Manipuri film is basically Meitei in content, theme and behaviour, though not mainly in form and style. The Meitei film is Imphal-based and middle-class in outlook and temper. And the middle-class mind is what constitutes the 'Manipuri mind.'

A small number of films have also been made in the other languages of the north-east, such as Khasis Manik Raiting (Mamk, the Miserable), and Lawei Ha Ki Kti Jong Ngi.

❑

14
The Foreign Entertainment

Although the advent of sound tended to nationalize film and reduce film's claim to being an international art as in the days of the silent movie, the current popularity of foreign films in America and the even more widespread distribution of American films in foreign markets demonstrate the primary role played by a film's visual elements, and the lesser importance of language as a communications device. In fact, when a motion picture is subtitled for distribution in a foreign market, the subtitles convey little more than one-third of the dialog. Yet the meaning of the film is seldom, if ever, impaired, and its beauty is often enhanced.

The USIA film Years of Lightning, Day of Drums (1964) illustrates the lesser role played by verbal language in motion pictures, even in a non theatrical film. Approximately 40 percent of the film uses neither dialog nor narration. Designed as a tribute to John F. Kennedy and as a vehicle to bolster confidence that the work Kennedy had begun would continue after his death, the film presents the six facets of the New Frontier, interlacing such programs as the Alliance for Progress, Civil Rights, and the Peace Corps, with sequences depicting the funeral. These funeral sequences are largely wordless, with the sound track carrying natural sound: the heavy footsteps of the marchers, the more staccato hoofbeats of the horses, and the steady, muffled drumbeat. Yet no words are necessary during these sequences. Death and bereavement are not uniquely American experiences. The styles of burial and mourning may vary from country to country, but the loss occasioned by death is a constant. Similarly, the scenes depicting the parades and enthusiastic crowds that greeted Kennedy on his international speaking tours need little narration—save the words spoken by Kennedy himself. The human face is the human face; closeups of Kennedy's face, or of a nameless Filipino's or Costa Rican's, demand no verbal interpretation. Assembled from stock footage, Years of Lightning, Day of Drums, by sharing Kennedy's death with the foreign viewer, shares his political achievement and America's aspirations.

A note of warning: Film is probably the most powerful propaganda medium yet devised. As a consequence, its potential for aiding or injuring civilization is enormous. In addition to supplying a verbal message through dialog, narration, or subtitles, the film provides an instantaneous, accompanying visual message-supplying the viewer with a picture to bulwark what has been learned through language. Thus, the imagination need not conjure a mental image to accompany the words; the viewer leaves the theater complete with a concept and its substantiation. If a picture is worth 1,000 words, a picture together with three or four carefully chosen words is worth 10,000 words. Makers of television commercials know this; so does anyone who has ever thought carefully about this compelling and utterly contemporary medium of communication.

In the past, American motion pictures have been associated with Hollywood. Persons desiring careers in the film industry saw and followed one road-and that road led to the golden West. But the situation has changed today. There are many roads leading to important and satisfying work in films, and not all end in Hollywood, as this chapter will reveal.

The Entertainment Film

Hollywood: 1945-1965. The late 1940s were boom years for Hollywood. At the close of 1946, box office revenues from United States movie theaters totaled a record $1.7 billion-compared with $1.2 billion in 1953, and $904 million in 1963. During 1949, more than 90 million tickets were sold weekly in American movie houses-compared with 45 million paid admissions each week in 1956, and 21 million in 1968. Again during 1949, the major studios-among them Metro-Goldwyn-Mayer, Twentieth Century Fox, Columbia Pictures,

RKO, and Warner Brothers-released 411 new motion pictures, compared with 296 released in 1954, 235 in 1959, and 203 in 1963. Administered by the men who had established them, the major companies offered such escapist films as the horror-thriller The Beast with Five Fingers (1946) and the slick romantic comedy June Bride (1948), along with such provocative and candid films as The Best Years of Our Lives (1946) and Crossfire (1947) to a receptive and apparently uncritical American audience.

But then several events caused the near collapse of the Hollywood movie empire. First, television rocketed into prominence—almost replacing the motion picture as a medium of mass entertainment. Successful prime-time network television series attract between 30 million and 50 million viewers—a number roughly double that of movie tickets sold weekly in 1968. And second, as a consequence of action taken by the federal government in the early 1950s, the major companies were forced to sell their chains of movie theaters—thus denying the studios an automatic outlet for their products regardless of intrinsic merit. In noisy desperation, Hollywood turned to the wide screen, undertook longer and more expensive film productions with star-studded casts, made use of more "adult" subject matter, advocated increases in ticket prices, started to produce 30 and 60 minute filmed series for television, and began selling already exhibited movies to the television industry. Between 1955 and 1958, Hollywood sold almost 9000 pre-1948 feature films to television, and by 1960 the major studios were vying with each other for sale of films produced since 1948.

The first of these retaliatory measures, the wide screen, has been called the most significant innovation in film technology since the advent of sound. Until the appearance of the first wide-screen motion picture, The Robe (a $5 million Cinemascope film produced and distributed by Twentieth Century Fox in 1953), the standard screen shape had been a rectangle 20 feet wide and 15 feet high; this represents a ratio of 4 to 3, or 1.33: 1-a proportion determined by the width of the film and going back to Thomas Edison and the Kinetoscope. The new wide screen changed the ratio to anything from 2.62: 1 to 1.66: 1, with Cinemascope settling at 2.55: 1. Regardless of trade name and varying dimensions, however, most new screens are at least twice as wide as they are high.

Initial critical reactions to the wide screen were mixed, with some filmmakers insisting that the new screen size signaled the end of the closeup and rendered established directorial and cutting techniques ineffective. In time, however, the advantages and possibilities of the wide screen became apparent to filmmakers, who have used its inclusiveness to achieve a naturalness and spontaneity, arid its new dimensions to experiment with new kinds of visual compositions and new uses of the closeup.

In response to the wide screen and as a further effort to bring the American public back into the movie theaters, Hollywood began to produce longer and more expensive movies with casts of thousands and an abundance of well-known stars. Often, best-selling novels or successful dramas that called for copious action and spectacle provided the "story" for these productions—as in The Ten Commandments (1956), Raintree County (1957), El Cid (1961), and Cleopatra (1963).

During these years, the already complex machinery needed to produce a Hollywood picture was becoming even more complex, with producers, directors, writers, actors, cameramen, editors, stunt men and women, script consultants, script personnel, costumers, set designers, wardrobe assistants, prop men, lighting technicians, makeup artists, carpenters, actors' agents, painters, publicists, and gossip columnists composing the Hollywood scene. Overseeing the vast collective enterprise that movie making had become were the studio presidents and executive producers men like Jesse L. Lasky, David O. Selznick, Samuel Goldwyn, and Darryl Zanuck, who exercised ultimate authority over script, stars, and budget.

The Foreign Film

Italy. If Hollywood chose to ignore, by and large, the realities of the post World War II world, that was not true of Italian filmmakers. Responding to the grim reality of a war-torn, impoverished Italy, Roberto Rossellini directed Open City (1945)—the first important film shot in a style quickly dubbed by the critics as neorealism. Combining stock newsreel footage with his own film (shot chiefly on the streets of Rome and scratched to resemble newsreels), Rossellini depicted the hardships endured by Italians during the Nazi occupation and their courageous resistance. To heighten the authenticity gained by actual locations and natural lighting, he 'used only a handful of professional actors whom he encouraged to ad lib, and chose ordinary Roman citizens as supporting players. Although none of these techniques in isolation was new, none had been used so successfully together before; and Open City became, as the film historian Arthur Knight has said, "the key film in the entire neorealist Italian revival."

Equally as personal and visually intense, and equally as concerned with social realism, are two early films by Vittorio De Sica. In Shoeshine (1946), De Sica portrays the lives of a group of homeless Roman boys involved in the corrupt underworld of the Italian black market. Bicycle Thief (1947) treats the relationship between a father (played by a factory mechanic) and his son (played by a Roman newsboy) who together try to beat the apparently insurmountable odds occasioned by unemployment, poverty, and corruption.

Other directors central to this movement are Luigi Zampa (To Live in Peace, 1946; Angelina, 1947), Giuseppe De Santis (The Tragic Hunt, 1947), and Alberto Lattuada (Without Pity, 1947). Within a five year span, neorealism began to die out, its force vitiated by postwar recovery and renewed prosperity.

In recent. years, amid a rash of conventional and often sensational films, the work of two masterful directors has emerged. Described as "second generation realists," Federico Fellini (La Dolce Vita, 1960; 8½, 1962; Juliet of the Spirits, 1965; Satyricon, 1970; Amarcord, 1974) and Michelangelo Antonioni (L'Avventura, 1959; La Notte, 1960; The Red Desert, 1964; Blow-Up, 1966; The Passenger, 1975) have little in common except a compulsion to use the surfaces, rituals, and hidden recesses of contemporary existence as theme and subject matter, and a proven ability to use improvisation as an effective cinematic technique.

France

Suffering lack of funds and the shifting patronage of the French government, French filmmakers in the late 1940s and early 1950s were engaged in the production of drab imitations of American gangster films; sensational melodramas; film noir (the film of despair, represented by such works as Clouzot's Manon, 1959; Clement's Les let Interdits, 1952); films based on successful or distinguished fiction (Symphonie Pastorale, 1946; Devil in the Flesh, 1947; L'Idiot, 1947); Jilms embodying existential doctrine (Les Jeux Sont Faits, 1947; Cocteau's Orphee, 1950); films exploiting sex (initiated by Roger Vadim's And God Created Women, 1956); and a few individualistic works, such as the comedies of Jacques Tati (M. Hulot's Holiday, 1953; and Man Oncle, 1958) and Robert Bresson's Les Dames du Bois de Boulogne (1944), and Journal d'un Cure de Campagne (1951).

But then, in 1958-1959, the New Wave erupted on the French film scene, with 'Francois Truffaut's Les Quatre Cents Coups and Alain Resnais' Hiroshima Mon Amour winning awards at the 1959 Cannes Film Festival. Other films that heralded the New Wave are Claude Chabrol's Le Beau Serge (1958), Louis Malle's Les Amants (1958), and Jean-Luc Godard's Breathless (1959). Although heterogeneous and resistant of labels in the manner of all creative artists, these New Wave directors do share many cinematic ideals as well as an outlet for these ideals in the influential film journal Cahiers du Cinema. Truffaut, Godard, and Chabrol had been film critics in the early 1950s, and they continued to write interestingly of the cinema. Describing his own procedures, Truffaut has said, I start with a very imperfect script, in which there are certain elements that please and stimulate me. Characters that strike some chord of response in me. A theme that lets me "talk about" something I want to film. As I work I find I am eliminating all the scenes of story transition and explanation. So it can happen that when the film is done, it is completely different from what it was proposed to say in the first place. The shooting of the film is that sort of adventure.

In Breathless, Godard took his camera onto the Paris streets. Using a hand-held Arritlex and a three-page script outline by Truffaut, Godard allowed the camera to follow the actions and reactions of Michel (a small-time gangster, played by Jean-Paul Belmondo) and his American girl friend (played by Jean Seberg), depicting a life devoid of logic or purpose.

Although the New Wave has dissipated itself (by 1964, Cannes was denigrating the very movement it had applauded five years earlier), these films and their directors have made great and irrevocable contributions to cinema art—in particular, in the imaginative and "free" camera work that characterizes New Wave films, in the encouragement of a liberated acting style dependent on improvisation and self-portraiture rather than on self-conscious or stagey performance, on the fanciful use of silent film techniques, on the absence of conventional plotting and continuity, and on a moving away from a cinema grounded in literature and drama to one that uses the strengths of the film medium to make its own powerful, highly cinematic statements.

England

Films like Blue Scar (1948) and The Brave Don't Cry (1952), both depicting the life of coal miners; Chance of a Lifetime (1950), set in a small Gloucestershire factory; and such short films as Lindsay Anderson's Every Day Except Christmas (1957), concerning workers at Covent Garden, and Karel Reisz's We Are the Lambeth Boys (1958), in which a boys' club in London furnishes the principal locale, prefigure the realism of British theatrical films in the late 1950s.

Room at the Top (1958) was the first in a remarkable series of outspoken realistic films to gain widespread critical attention. Soon, motion pictures like Saturday Night and Sunday Morning (1960), A Taste of Honey (1961), The Loneliness of the Long-Distance Runner

(1962), A Kind of Loving (1962), Billy Liar (1963), Morgan (1966), The Leather Boys (1963), and This Sporting Life (1962) had established the reputations of their directors—Karel Reisz, Tony Richardson, John Schlesinger, Sidney Furie, Lindsay Anderson—and the significance of the British feature film. Describing their work as "free cinema," these directors brought to the screen a penetrating social realism focused on the English working class, preparing the way for the Beatles (who themselves are featured in Richard Lester's A Hard Day's Night, 1964; and Help!, 1965) and the ascendancy of Liverpool over Pall Mall.

Other Countries

In Soviet Russia, film production is not only nationalized but the work of individual studios like Lenfilm, in Leningrad, and Mosfilm, in Moscow, is closely supervised by a specially designated state committee. Not unexpectedly, therefore, many Soviet feature films have either implicit or explicit social messages, like the strongly chauvinistic The Turbulent Years (1960). But there are also films that focus on personal crises and solutions rather than on social problems. Among them are the previously mentioned The Cranes Are Flying (1957), Clear Sky (1961), I'm Twenty (1965), and such adaptations of literary classics as Sergei Youtkevich's Othello (1955) and Grigori Kozintsev's Don Quixote (1957) and Hamlet (1963).

Although the Polish film industry is also nationalized, Polish filmmakers have produced a sizable body of sensitive and cinematically expert films. Many, like The Last Stage (1948) and Five Boys of Barska Street (1954), depict Poland's immediate past (World War II, the Nazi occupation, concentration camps, and the politically troubled postwar years) with a frank and searching realism. Andrzej Wajda's Ashes and Diamonds (1958) provides a good example. Set in the late 1940s, the film depicts as its hero a basically a political young man who, acting upon orders from a right-wing political group, kills a Communist leader and is killed, in turn, by agents of the state.

A later film by Wajda, Innocent Sorcerers (1960), eschews any overt political concern, depicting the aimless, amoral, unsentimental existence of worldly and bored Warsaw young people, and shows the influence of the New Wave in both subject matter and treatment. Other important Polish directors are Roman Polanski (Knife in the Water, 1962), Andrzej Munk (Eroica, 1957), Jerzy Kawalerowicz (Mother Joan of the Angels, 1961), and Kazimierz Kutz (A Pearl in the Crown, 1972).

Although, as in Poland, the Czechoslovakian film industry is nationalized, a young group of Czech filmmakers has been producing some significant movies since the early 1960s—like Jan Nemac's Diamonds of the Night (1964) and Milos Forman's Peter and Pavla (1964) and The Loves of a Blonde (1965). But when Soviet intervention put an end to the increasing liberalization of the Czech government in 1968, the much-heralded "new Czechoslovak film" also died. Directors like Forman, Kadar, Barabas, and taborsky no longer work in Czechoslovakia.

In Sweden, recent filmmaking has been dominated by Ingmar Baergman, who uses film to explore such abstract and eternal problems as the meaning of life and death (The Seventh Seal, 1956), the nature of truth (The Magician, 1958), and man's tragic inability to communicate (The Silence, 1963, and Cries and Whispers, 1972).

The Japanese film has becbme best known to American audiences through the work of Akira Kurosawa. Like Bergman, Kurosawa depicts elemental problems and passions using highly stylized, historical settings to underscore the timelessness of his themes. Rashomon (which won the Grand Prize at the Venice Film Festival in 1951) concerns the nature of truth, while Throne of Blood (1957), like Macbeth after which it is patterned, depicts the breaking down of morality through greed. Also drawing upon Japan's rich history of legend and strict social order, the films of Kenji Mizoguchi (Ugetsu, 1953, and Sansho the Bailiff, 1954) nevertheless transcend nationality. But Japan has not neglected contemporary settings and subjects, as Kurosawa's Drunken Angel (1948), Imai's Stained Image (1953), Toyoda's Wheat Whistle (1955) and Ozu's Tokyo Story (1953) attest.

Recent Developments in the American Film

American Experimental Film Makers. While Hollywood in the 1940s and 1950s persevered in its chosen course, determinedly oblivious to innovations in European filmmaking, a segment of the American movie-going public was well aware of their importance. Excited by the new techniques and possibilities for film, dismayed at the impersonality and inanity of most Hollywood movies, and aware that film is as much an art form as the novel, dance, or painting, numerous young Americans turned to film to give shape to their feelings and ideas, as their predecessors (and many of their contemporaries) had chosen the more conventional vehicles of drama, fiction, poetry, painting, or sculpture.

Much of the credit for publicizing and organizing the work and esthetic doctrines of America's experimental filmmakers goes to Jonas Mekas, himself a filmmaker, in addition to being a publisher and editor of Film Culture, occasional film critic for the Village Voice, and organizer of the Film Makers' Cooperative and Distribution Center. In describing his own work and that of other independent filmmakers, Mekas has said:

Our movies come from our hearts—our little movies, not the Hollywood movies. Our movies are like extensions of our own pulse, of our heartbeat, of our eyes, our fingertips; they are so personal, so unambitious in their movement, in their use of light, their imagery. We want to surround this earth with our film frames and warm it up-until it begins to move.

Of extreme importance to the experimental filmmakers is the unambitiousness and intensely personal nature of their films, as described by Mekas. In many instances, desire and budget dictate that the film be the result of one person who functions as producer, director, cameraman, editor, and often distributor. The actors are often friends, and usually non-professionals. Most films ate done on 16 mm. And, as in the New Wave films, there is an absence of chronological continuity and carefully plotted story lines, along with considerable use of improvisation and emphasis on spontaneous action and reaction rather than upon stagey performance.

As the New Wave is a convenient rubric that lumps together highly individualistic directors, so the New American Cinema Group— "a free organization of independent filmmakers dedicated to the support of the men and women giving their vision to the filmic art"- is a convenient label, embracing filmmakers with divergent purposes,. talents, and methods. But, like the New Wave directors, the New American Cinema Group shares an outlet for its views, the magazine *Film Culture*, and evinces a common hatred and a common enthusiasm. As the French directors rebelled against film's prior dependency on literature and rejoiced in the cinema as an art form with its own esthetic, so the New American Cinema rebels against all that is unimaginative, standardized, and hopelessly phony about Hollywood and celebrates, too, the film as an art form.

Among the more notable experimental filmmakers are Jonas Mekas (Guns of the Trees, The Brig), Stan VanDerBeek (Mankinda, Skullduggery, Summit, Breathdeath), Stan Brakage (Dog Star Man, Window Water Baby Moving, Scenes from Under Childhood), Bruce Conner (A Movie, Cosmic Ray, Liberty Crown), Kenneth Anger (Scorpio Rising, Inauguration of the Pleasure Dome), Gregory Markopoulos (Twice a Man, Serenity, Ming Green), Charles Boultenhouse (Handwritten, Dionysius), Shirley Clarke (The Connection, Skyscraper, The Cool World), and, of course, Andy Warhol and Paul Morrissey.

Parodying Hollywood's film factories with his own Factory, Hollywood's star system with his own superstars, Hollywood's trumped-up and ultimately phony retailing of sex and sex goddesses in Screen Test, and Hollywood's bad guys, good guys and Westerns in Horse, Warhol has been enormously and unabashedly prolific and successful. In all his films, whether in the early "documentaries" like Empire, Sleep, and Eat, or in the later "feature" films, Kitchen, The Chelsea Girls, My Hustler, Bike Boy, and Lonesome Cowboys, Warhol's constant subject has been the film itself. Even as producer for Morrissey's films, notably the highly successful Trash, Warhol's personality and vision dominate. Using a variety of techniques, from a static camera focused on one object for more than eight hours, to cinema verite pushed to an extreme, to employing two screens and running two films simultaneously, Warhol has drawn attention through technique and subject matter to the film as product and substance, reveling in and revealing its particular properties as a physical entity.

The many purposes and styles of American experimental films range from social criticism using documentary techniques to embodiments of the subconscious through surrealism and myth to psychedelic experiments with light and color. At their best, the films of the avant garde are exciting, fresh, sensitive, and fully able to transmit their maker's vision. At their worst, they are very bad indeed—as bad as the worst products of any art form—as trivial and boring, for example, as the worst Hollywood movie.

Hollywood: 1965-1978

In 1950, when a consent decree put teeth into a court decision calling for the major motion picture studios to sell their theater chains, a monopoly was broken up that had linked production with distribution and had fostered the exhibition of American motion pictures regardless of quality. And when this blow to Hollywood was followed by the ascendancy of television in the American economy and the American home, Hollywood began to retrench. In addition to cutting back on production, the major studios dropped contract actors, directors, and writers at option time. In 1950, there were 474 actors, 147 writers, and 99 directors under contract to the major studios; in 1955, there were 209 actors, 67 writers, and 79 directors; in 1960, there were 139 actors, 48 writers, and 24 directors. Three studios—RKO, Republic, and Monogram—stopped production entirely. And approximately 6000 movie houses closed their doors.

Into these troubled waters stepped the independent producers. Some of the independent production companies were formed by the stars themselves—among them Burt Lancaster, Frank Sinatra, Kirk

Douglas, and Bob Hope. Other independent companies were started by directors—William Wyler, Alfred Hitchcock, Elia Kazan, and Otto Preminger. Some had been producers, like Sam Spiegel and Arthur Hornblow. Still others had been writers, like Richard Brooks, Joseph Mankiewicz, and Robert Rossen. In itself, the independent production company was not a new commodity in Hollywood. But the independent producer had never made any significant inroads in the Hollywood system. until the 1950s. At that time, the major studios, having involved themselves in fewer productions, began increasingly to finance and then distribute films made by the independent production company. Gradually, therefore, the studios began to function like United Artists, which had been started in 1919 as a releasing company without studio facilities.

By accepting the lesser role of financier, promoter, and distributor, even at times leasing their own facilities to the independent production companies, the major studios relinquished artistic control over the films they were underwriting. Control passed to the independent producer, creating a situation that allowed a film to have a style impressed on it by those who made it rather than by a studio boss overseeing a dozen or more films simultaneously.

Although not all the motion pictures produced by the independent companies have been artistic or commercial successes, a good many independent productions are of outstanding quality and have increased the prestige of the Hollywood movie both here and abroad. Seven of the nine films winning Oscars as Best Motion Picture of the Year between 1954 and 1962 were produced by independents: On the Waterfront (1954), Marty (1955), Around the World in Eighty Days (1956), The Bridge on the River Kwai (1957), The Apartment (1960), West Side Story (1961), and Lawrence of Arabia (1962). Other successful independents have been The Diary of Anne Frank (1959), The Hustler (1961), Advise and Consent (1962), Guess Who's Coming to Dinner (1967), In the Heat of the Night (1967), The Graduate (1967), Bonnie and Clyde (1967), Easy Rider (1969), and Rocky (1977).

And, in turn, the more interesting and stimulating movies have been bringing American audiences back into the movie houses, but with a difference: The Opinion Research Corporation of Princeton, New Jersey, reported that in 1975 persons under 24 years of age comprised approximately 60 percent of the movie audience and that 88 percent of that audience was under 40 years of age. W. R. Simons & Associates reported that 31.7 percent of adult men and 28.8 percent of adult women attended the movies once or more in the average month (defined as "frequent" movie-going) in 1977. Persons who have attended college are more than twice as likely to see movies as those without a high school diploma. This means that movies are less a mass medium than an elitist medium—that is, less a form of mass art than of high art. In the inevitable rearrangement caused by displacement, television has become the mass medium. The two media, however, are intertwined. A recent Gallup poll found that 63 per cent of the population is interested in viewing movies at home, 19 per cent because they dislike going to theaters.

In the 1970s, however, the Hollywood epic was reborn. As in the 1930s, the public sought refuge from a declining economy in movie theaters. Films such as Star Wars, Close Encounters of the Third Kind, The Godfather, and The Exorcist, with star-studded casts and big-budget effects, drew crowds in numbers unprecedented since the advent of television. Box office grosses in 1976, for example, amounted to $2.4 billion, the largest ever, although only 186 films were released, far below the average total of 373 films per year in the 1950s and 445 in the 1940s. Ironically, film producers were using television to lure audiences, spending well over $98 million in 1977 for advertising on local and network levels.

To accommodate the new audiences and the new movies, 16,800 movie screens were in operation in the United States in December, 1976. Of this total, 13,000 were in indoor or "hardtop" theaters and 3,800 were in drive-ins. From 1972 to 1976 indoor screens increased by 21.5 percent and drive-in screens by 2.7 percent. In all there were approximately 700 circuits, each with four or more theaters, operating about 53 percent of all movie houses. The remaining movie theaters were owned and operated by 6,800 individuals or companies.

Within the past few years, elaborate movie palaces of the 1920s and 1930s, such as Times Square's Paramount, Roxy, Capitol, and State, have been torn down. Approximately 243 new theaters, both indoor and outdoor, were either opened, announced, or placed under construction in 1976. The day of the multiauditorium theater was at hand. Most were twin-auditorium theaters, but some had three, four, and even six auditoriums. Along with these more ambitious projects were an ever increasing number of minitheaters, deluxe houses with audience capacities of 150 to 400 persons and relatively inexpensive to construct and operate. Of these 243 new projects, approximately 35 percent were in shopping centers, continuing a trend that had begun in 1962.

At present, American motion pictures continue to dominate the world market, being preferred in most countries to the indigenous product. It is estimated that American films take up 60 percent of the world motion picture playing time, occupying 67 percent of motion picture screen time in England, 55 percent in Italy, 33 percent in France, and as high as 90 percent in other countries with less developed film industries.

The International Movie

Part of the life style that characterizes the new Hollywood concerns the international movie. A step toward internationalization occurred in the 1950s. The independent producers, not being shackled to particular film studios, made movies in Europe and other foreign locations in order to profit from cheaper labor costs and national subsidies, to use actual locales, and to please the movie stars themselves who, by establishing residence in a foreign country, could avoid paying U.S. income tax on money earned while working abroad.

At present, changed tax laws and increased foreign labor costs have reduced the advantages of filming in foreign locations. But the transporting of Hollywood actors, directors, cameramen, and all the assorted personnel connected with movie production continues, and this trans Atlantic and trans-Pacific traffic has helped to return movie making to its international beginnings. The new mobility of contemporary moviemakers has been aided tremendously by certain technological developments. Lightweight cameras and sound recording equipment, as well as ministudios capable of being airlifted, are allowing movie producers to set up shooting where whim and geography dictate.

Further, such elements as the directors and writers, as well as the financial backing and distribution arrangements, have done their share to internationalize the industry. For example, Blow-Up, which won the 1967 Cannes Film Festival Golden Palm Award, was an English entry, with an Italian director (Antonioni), produced for MGM. Taking Off, which won the 1971 Cannes Jury Special Prize, was a United States entry directed by the Czech director Milos Forman. The 1966 Berlin Festival winner was a British entry, Cul-de-Sac, made by the Polish director Roman Polanski, who also directed Rosemary's Baby. The list could go on and on. Even such an American movie as Bonnie and Clyde was almost a French product. Its American writers, Robert Benton and David Newman, wrote the screenplay first for Francois Truffaut. When Truffaut rejected the script (he was then filming Fahrenheit 451), Benton and Newman approached Jean-Luc Godard, who was interested but ultimately decided against undertaking the project. And it was only at this time that Warren Beatty began negotiations, finally buying the script for $75,000.

The many film festivals prevalent today are additional evidence of the internationalism of the film industry. Festivals in Cannes, Berlin, Venice, San Sebastian, New York, Moscow, Montreal, Cork, Chicago, and Mexico have provided showcases for films from every nation and a meeting and market place for actors, directors, writers, and producers.

The Documentary Film

In both England and America, the documentary film came of age in the 1930s through direct patronage by national governments, and matured, still under government auspices, during the troubled years of World War II. Perhaps this is not surprising, as a documentary's purpose is always partially social—setting forth public and private crises and victories, showing us where man has been and what, inevitably, man will become unless proper action is taken.

In England, the earliest documentaries are associated with the Empire Market Board Film Unit, headed by John Grierson. Grierson's first film, Drifters (1929), shot on location on the North Sea, portrays the daily existence of the herring fishermen. When the EMB Film Unit was shifted to the General Post Office in 1933, Grierson and the film unit continued the production of quality documentaries, including Weather Forecast (1934), Song of Ceylon (1934), Coal Face (1935), Night Mail (1936), and North Sea (1938). "By the time the war broke out," Arthur Knight writes, "the British documentary movement—headed by men like Paul Rotha, Stuart Legg, Basil Wright, Harry Watt, Alberto Cavalcanti, Arthur Elton and Edgar Anstey—had achieved a worldwide reputation and inspired scores of directors outside England to attempt documentary movements in their own countries."

World War II gave impetus to increased documentary film production, ranging from training films for United States service personnel to informative films for a civilian population needing instruction in wartime procedures. As well, Hollywood directors like John Huston, William Wyler, and John Ford began making films for the military. San Pietro (1944), Memphis Belle (1944), and Battle of Midway (1944) are memorable documentaries filmed on and around World War II's battlegrounds.

In England, the documentary filmmakers, now working under the aegis of the Ministry of Information, also turned their attention to wartime subjects, producing such films as London Can Take It (1940), depicting London during a Nazi air raid; Target for Tonight (1941), documenting an air force bombing mission; and Desert Victory (1942), an account of the North African campaign. Early in the war, the English independent film studios were mobilized to

produce training films as well as to continue in the production of
feature films. As Arthur Knight has observed, "for the first time, the
documentary and fiction filmmakers of Britain joined forces. Some,
like Alberto Cavalcanti and Harry Watt, moved from documentary to
fiction; while fiction directors like John Boulting, Thorold Dickinson
and Carol Reed became, at least for the time, documentalists."

Basic to many recent documentaries is a problematic cinema
technique known as cinema verite, spontaneous cinema, or direct
cinema. The term cinema verite applies to film that uses the camera
to record reality in an unbiased and unmanipulated way. In presenting
the essence of a situation, the director does not work from a
preconceived shooting script, and, to all intents and purposes, does
not direct—if by directing one means organizing and, controlling
what happens before the camera. By making use of the new lightweight
cameras and recording equipment, the filmmaker goes into the field
where he or she, and camera, act as witnesses and scribes. The
intent is to provide either minimal or no interpretation and to retain
the spontaneity and natural characteristics of the actual event.

In practice, documentary films exhibiting pure cinema verite
are hard to find. Either consciously or unconsciously, most filmmakers
impose an interpretation on their subject matter through in-camera
editing, or editing after the film has been shot. Others "edit" reality
before any filming occurs by carefully selecting the persons and
objects to be photographed and only then applying cinema—verite
filming techniques. For example, Chronique d'un Ete, by Jean Rouch
and Edgar Morin, shows evidence of rather stringent preshooting
"editing," although the most effective parts of the film result from the
characters behaving in ways that could not have been predicted
beforehand.

In contrast, Showman and The Beatles provide good examples
of pure cinema verite. Directed and produced by Albert and David
Maysles, these films have been criticized for their superficiality.
But, the Maysleses contend, their vow has been to avoid interfering
with the subject during filming; any superficiality, therefore, is

inherent in the subject and is inevitably part of the truth that the film depicts.

Robert Drew, Richard Leacock, Donald Pennebaker, and Gregory Shuker have produced many outstanding documentary films under the label The Drew Associates. On the Pole depicts the ambitions, anguish, and ultimate failure of an Indianapolis race-car driver named Eddie Sachs. Primary concerns the Hubert Humphrey—John F. Kennedy primary contest in Wisconsin. Crisis depicts the Robert Kennedy—Governor Wallace fight over the token integration of the Alabama schools. The Chair is about an effort to prevent a young black from going to the electric chair. Jane is a film portrait of Jane Fonda on the opening night of an unsuccessful play.

Other notable documentaries include Lionel Rogosin's On the Bowery, filmed on location in New York City, and Frederick Wiseman's controversial Titicut Follies, High School, and Hospital. Still others are Allan King's Warrendale which concerns the treatment of emotionally disturbed children, and Frank Simon's The Queen, on a "Miss America" contest for transvestites.

In recent years, television has provided a ready market for documentaries. A fine example of a television documentary, and one that also makes use of cinema verite techniques, is "Royal Family," produced by a consortium of BBC and England's independent television companies and shown on American television. Richard Cawston served as producer-director, working with an eight-person crew throughout an almost full year of shooting forty-three hours of film. Cawston has attributed the success of this film to the royal family's freedom to talk without restraint, ad-libbing in front of the cameras, in the knowledge that Queen Elizabeth and Prince Philip had the right to veto any sections they found unacceptable in retrospect. "I decided it could be done only with some sense of humor and with a sort of cinema-verite technique," Cawston has said. "Therefore, nothing was really rehearsed. We would discuss beforehand what would happen, and then simply shoot it. It worked out very well."

Other television documentaries are considerably shorter and understandably more humble in subject matter and technique, ranging from film accounts of war maneuvers in Vietnam to Charles Kuralt's "On the Road" segments for CBS News. The television news magazines, like "Chronolog," and timely news specials provide excellent documentaries on such subjects as a U.S. Olympic sky-diving team and a Stone Age New Guinea tribe, photographed with precision and sensitivity by a team of Japanese cinematographers. Other outstanding documentaries have been ABC's Cousteau and National Geographic series and "Sadat: Action Biography"; Public Broadcasting Laboratory's "Birth and Death"; CBS's "Hunger in America" and "The Selling of the Pentagon"; and NBC's "Pensions: The Broken Promise."

Arthur Knight has conjectured that in the near future regional filmmakers may be celebrating their region through film as, traditionally, novelists, poets, and musicians have done. Certainly, the field for documentary production is wide open. Invariably, it seems, truth is stranger and more interesting than fiction. As a purveyor of facts and feelings, as a conveyor of an increasingly important photographic reality, and as a molder of public opinion, the documentary film is a powerful force in modern communications.

FILMS FOR INDUSTRY, GOVERNMENT AND EDUCATION

This is a mushrooming industry in which an estimated 1200 firms are at work in the United States, producing pictures on a multiplicity of topics for showing to industrial and sales groups, schools and universities, government and community organizations, the armed forces, and professional and religious bodies. These firms might be compared to the hundreds of small trade journals in the magazine field. Few of them are major organizations, but in the mass they form an influential channel for communicating information and ideas.

Non-theatrical filmmaking is heavily financed by American industry, which has found in this type of motion picture a highly

effective means for presenting its purposes, methods, and achievements. Approximately 15,000 non-theatrical films are produced each
year. Most are on 16 mm film, the standard size for projection by
small and portable machines. A few of the more elaborate are made
on 35 mm, some even for widescreen projection. This total includes
some 9400 business and industrial pictures, 1900 government films,
1700 educational films, 250 for medical and health use, 300 for
community organizations, and 150 religious films. Nearly $1.5 billion
is being spent annually to produce these films and for other audiovisual
aids, such as filmstrips, slides, and equipment.

The price of making and distributing a good company film
averages nearly $150,000, with some major productions exceeding
$500,000. As many as 200 prints are made for some films to satisfy
the demand. The average total audience for such a film is estimated
to be 1.5 million. Many educational and instructional films are
produced on far smaller budgets, some of them only a few thousand
dollars, and are shown to more limited audiences.

Production of educational and informational films began with
the development of the 16 mm portable projector in 1923. At present
more than 750,000 projectors are in use in the United States, mostly
in schools and businesses, but also in clubs, libraries, homes, and
churches.

A large proportion of these non-theatrical films are available for
use by organizations and private citizens free of charge. The cost is
underwritten by business organizations as part of their institutional
public relations budget; by federal, state, and local governments; by
social or economic organizations that seek to present educational
material in their particular fields; or by tax-supported institutions
such as public libraries or adult education schools. There are 2600
film libraries in the United States distributing 16 mm films. The H. W.
Wilson Educational Film Guide lists more than 20,000 films that can
be borrowed.

□

15

The Control Over Cinema

FILM AS A CONTEMPORARY ART FORM

It is only in recent times that the cinema has come to be looked upon as a serious art form worthy of study at the university level. While accepting an Honorary Doctorate from the Jadavpur University in 1980, Satyajit Ray made a strong plea for including the teaching of cinema as part of the educational curriculum. Only two universities, Jadavpur and Calcutta, have a Master's level programme in Film Studies. Most other universities have fullfledged departments of Communication/Journalism where brief courses in film appreciation are taught as part of the discipline of Communication. Government institutes like the Film and Television Institute of India, Pune, the Madras Film Institute, and the Satyajit Ray Film and Television Institute, Calcutta, and private institutes like the Xavier Institute of Communications, Bombay, and Chitrabani, Calcutta, offer diploma programmes in film production.

The popular attitude to cinema as a means of mass entertainment has its origin in the type of films made up to the fifties in India. Satyajit Ray told the Working Group that 'the works of the early film makers suffered from a low level of conception, as right from the beginning cinema in India was aimed at the lowest common denominator and became primarily concerned with providing entertainment. Even when well-known writers became involved with cinema, they deliberately changed the quality of their writing. It is only in the last decade or so that intellectuals have begun associating actively with the making of films and thereby raised the status of cinema to an art form'.

The Control Over Cinema

The Government's attitude too has reinforced the popular view that cinema is a means of cheap entertainment. As the Working Group's Report notes: 'One of the major factors which has impeded the growth of cinema as an art form and as a medium of cultural expression is that despite a history of about 70 years of film-making, cinema in India continues to be treated almost as a sub-culture. This general attitude seems to permeate the total spectrum of the Government's policies towards cinema. The high taxation rates and the stringent rules for licensing of cinema houses gives the impression that cinema is an undesirable activity, which needs to be kept at an adequate distance from the social life of the community. At the same time, it must be acknowledged that the Government has set up a Directorate of Film Festivals, a National Film Institute, a National Film Archive, the NFDC, and instituted National Film Awards to give a fillip to cinema. The film society movement indirectly supported by the Government has spread to many cities, making it possible for film lovers to be exposed to outstanding films of other countries. To continue these efforts at promoting film as an art form, the Working Group has recommended the establishment of the Chalachitra Akademi, on the lines of the Sahitya Akademi, the Sangeet Natak Akademi and the Lalit Kala Akademi. It has also recommended the setting up of a Film Educational Advisory Service for inculcating a critical attitude towards cinema in schools and colleges as well as a Film Information and Documentation Centre, a National Film Museum, and a Children's Film Centre.

The cinema is the art of today, just as drama was in earlier ages. It is, as Pudovkin, the Russian theorist of film wrote in 1933: 'a synthesis of each and every element—the oral, the visual, the philosophical; it is our opportunity to translate the world in all its lines and shadows into a new art form that has succeeded and will supersede all the older arts, for it is the supreme medium in which we can express today and tomorrow.'

on Society

ns 'impact', 'cinema' and 'society' are extremely
h too comprehensive to take at surface-value.

The term .-.pact' is frequently used synonymously with 'effect'
and 'influence' but its connotative meanings point to an effect or
influence that is deep and long-lasting. These terms also suggest that
the influence is one powerful force upon—a passive inorganic receptor.
A further complication arises when one realises that an 'impact' can
be weak, moderate or strong, that it can relate to the psychological,
social, economic, cultural, political and even physical. The reality is
that it is well-nigh impossible to look at 'impact' of cinema or any
other media in isolation from social life.

The term 'cinema' is equally complex today, with television,
video, cable and satellite TV vying with each other to screen films on
the small screen. Further, does the term refer to films shown on the
big screen alone? Or, does 'cinema' refer to the whole industry of
film production, distribution and exhibition, as well as the marketing
of different genres of films whether for the big screen or the small
screen? That is a huge field, and to analyse its 'impact' on 'society'
is a daunting task for any researcher. Moreover, there are so many
genres of cinema, each genre perhaps having an 'impact' of its own.
'Horror films', for instance, might have the impact of frightening
viewers, and slapstick comedies of entertaining and relaxing them.
Kung-fu and karate films might offer a 'cathartic' experience, leading
to a purgation of the emotions of pity and fear. The third term
'society' is an infinitely more complex phenomenon. The term takes
within its compass all social institutions (such as the family, the
school, the university, the state, the legislature, the class and caste-
systems, religion, culture, political and economic institutions, etc.).
How does one assess the 'impact' of 'cinema' on such an all-
encompassing phenomenon? If therefore seems that the 'impact' of
'cinema' on 'society' is a very tricky subject for study. For several
decades now, 'impact' or 'effects' studies have been conducted
(though mostly in laboratory settings), but these have been narrow

psychological studies on the 'effects' of violence and sex in specific films on specific groups such as school children, college and university youth. Most such studies have been carried out in the United States. In India, the Indian Institute of Mass Communication, New Delhi, conducted a 'sociological' study on the 'Effects of Cinema.' The first research study on the influence of Hindi Cinema on Bombay Youth was conducted by Panna Shah in 1948.

More interesting perhaps would be to look at the politics and economics of cinema, of the relationship between the stories of the cinema with the actual lives of the people, or how audiences use and incorporate cinema in their daily lives.

Ethics of Cinema

While censorship is imposed by the authorities and the law, the matter of 'ethics' is imposed by individuals on themselves. Some communication professionals like advertisers and public relations practitioners have drawn up 'Codes of Ethics' for themselves. Film producers in India have not yet done so; nor have journalists. The Censor Board (now known as the Central Board of Film Certification) has been provided 'guidelines' for certifying films.

The need for ethics in cinema and the other mass media arises from the fear that children and sensitive adults might be harmfully influenced by certain portrayals and actions. Film makers must be concerned about the possible influence on individuals and groups of their artistic efforts. For instance, the stereotypical portrayal of women and minorities in Indian films could help to reinforce cultural stereotypes rather than stimulate new thinking about their roles in society. Few are the films that show women as intelligent, independent and hard working; fewer still are the films that show minority communities in a positive light. This is where 'ethics' comes in: a concern for the sensitivities of audiences and the nation's cultural pluralism. Unethical practices would include the insertion of 'adult sequences' in films meant for family viewing; the insertion (by cinema exhibitors) of pornographic sequences in films that have been already censored; the portrayal of excessive violence for minutes on end, when such portrayal is irrelevant and unnecessary; titillating bedroom and 'rain' sequences when they are not germane to the plot. It is unethical to use scenes in film posters, which do not exist in the film itself.

Film Censorship

Film Censorship was set in motion in India when the Cinematograph Act of 1918 was made law from May 1920. It allowed the exhibition of films only after they had been certified as suitable for public exhibition. However, the exhibition of a firm could be suspended and its certificate annulled in any Province on the authority of the District Magistrate or Commissioner of Police, pending the order of the Provincial Government, which could un-certify the film for the whole or part of the Province.

Censor Boards were accordingly set up in Bombay, Calcutta, Madras, Rangoon and Lahore. All members of the Boards were appointed by the Government. They consisted of the Commissioner of Police, the Collector of Customs, a member of the Indian Educational Services, and three prominent citizens representing the Hindu, Muslim and other communities.

Prior to the Act of 1918, total freedom did exist for the Indian film-maker and exhibitor, though some control was exercised under the Indian Penal Code and the Criminal Procedure Code. These were primarily concerned with obscenity, the wounding of religious sentiments, or inciting disaffection against the Government. Under the Act, the control was made more rigid and effective countrywide.

In the early days of censorship the Boards were "particularly sensitive to nudity" passionate or suggestive lovemaking, women in a state of drunkenness, anything that might show the white man in bad light, scenes of Western women in any contact with Oriental men and of course, any reference to political activity or ideology."

Amendments to the Act of 1918 in later years made film censorship a function of the Provincial Governments. By far the largest number of films exhibited in India from the 1920s was American and the British Government resented their influence.

In October 1927 an Indian Cinematograph Committee was appointed with an Indian, T. Rangachariar, as Chairman. It observed in its Report submitted two years later that censorship is certainly necessary in India, and is the only effective method of preventing the import, production and public exhibition of films which might demoralise morals, hurt religious susceptibilities or excite communal or racial animosities. But the coming of the talkies in India introduced new elements into censorship, and the Report was shelved.

During the war-years censorship was strictly enforced particularly with regard to political allusions. By Independence film making had become a losing proposition, and on June 30,1949 an All India Cinema Protect Day was held to protest against the government's taxation policy. That crippling taxation policy is still the greatest restraint on film making in India. 60% of the gross collections go as entertainment tax to the coffers of State Governments.

The Cinematograph Act of 1952 continued the British tradition of severe censorship of films that made any references to the political situation or to communal groups. The guidelines of the Act are lifted almost entirely from the Hays Code, named after Will Hays, once Post-master General of U.S.A. While the Code has been scrapped abroad, the censors here still continue to swear by it.

In 1969, the Khosla Commission was appointed to report on the whole film industry. It recommended an autonomous Censor Board without any official government controls, the examination of a film as a whole and the inclusion of kissing, nudity and violence, if they were integral to the theme. The Government reluctantly accepted the Report, and in 1974 a Bill was introduced in the Lok Sabha. However, the clamping of the emergency soon led to even stricter control by the Government. The guidelines by the government now forbade more than six minutes of violence in a film, though Sholay was cleared at the behest of the Centre. Indeed, the whims of the I & B Ministry decided which films should be given' A' or 'V' Certificates. Political satires like Kissa Kursi Ka were banned.

The Janata regime appointed a Working Group on National Film Policy. The Working Group's Report has criticised the rigid approach of the film censors against the exposure of corruption in the police and the Government's political leadership. Such an approach, says the Report, prevents creative film-makers from portraying social reality as it exists. Cinema, like literature, has to be given the freedom to make social and political comment, if it is to fulfil its function as a catalyst of social change. The Group has also opposed the Government's issuing of guidelines, and its acting as an appellate body. It suggests that the only aspect of censorship requiring the Government's guidelines is the sovereignty of the State, the security of the State, and friendly relations with foreign countries.

Rationale of Censorship. All citizens, says Article 19(1) and (2) of the Constitution, shall have the right to freedom of speech and expression, and then goes on to add, 'Nothing in this clause shall affect the operation of any existing law, or prevent the State from making any law, in so far as such law imposes reasonable restrictions on the exercise of the right conferred by the said clause in the interests of the sovereignty and integrity of India, the security of State, decency or morality, or in relation to contempt of court, defamation or incitement to an office.'

This is the key to the laws of censorship in the media in India. Reasonable restrictions on the fundamental right of freedom of speech and expression are sanctioned by the constitution. The State is therefore justified in imposing restrictions on the arts and the media. However, the restrictions imposed must be 'reasonable' and whether they are reasonable or not has to be decided by the courts.

K.A. Abbas challenged the censorship of films in general and pre-censorship in particular in the Supreme Court in November 1969. In its verdict delivered on September 24,1970, the Supreme Court said that 'censorship in India (and pre-censorship is no different in quality) has full justification in the field of exhibition of films. We need not generalize about other forms of speech and expression here for each such fundamental right has a different content and importance.'

'The censorship imposed on the making and exhibition of films is in the interest of society. If the regulations venture into something, which goes beyond this legitimate opening to restrictions, they can be questioned on the ground that a legitimate power is being abused. We hold, therefore, that censorship of films, including prior restraint, is justified under our constitution.

Central Board of Film Certification (CBFC)

The Central Board of Film Censors (since June 1,1983 renamed the 'Central Board of Film Certification') has been set up by the Central Government under the powers granted it by the Cinematograph Act (1952) and the Cinematograph (Censorship) Rules 1958. The Board is headed by a chairman, appointed by the Central Government and is assisted by not more than nine members. (This number has now been increased to 12-35 members; this has been done to facilitate the opening of more regional offices). Presently, there are offices at Mumbai, Chennai, Kolkata and Trivandrum, with Bombay as the headquarters.

Advisory Panels

Advisory Panels are constituted at each regional office by the Central Government, which also decides, in consultation with the CBFC, the number of panel members for each office. The members are appointed by the Central Government in consultation with the CBFC. However, the Central Government may dispense with such consultation in the case of members whose number does not exceed one-third of the total number. The members are appointed for a period of two years and may be re-appointed after the expiry of the term. The Central Government reserves the power to remove a member before the completion of the term. The member is entitled to a consultancy fee of Rs. 50/-for previewing a film or attending a meeting.

How Films are Censored? A film producer has, in the first place, to submit an application for a certificate to the CBFC. The fee charged is Rs. 100 per reel. The Examining Committee consists of a member from the Advisory Panel and an examining officer in the case of a short film, while in the case of a feature film four members from the Advisory panel and an examining officer. The film to be examined must be complete in every sense, with the background music and all sound effects duly recorded on the film itself.

Under the Amendment Act, 1983, all previews of films for the purpose of certification and the reports and records related to it, will be treated as confidential. The names of members of the Examining Committee will not be disclosed to any official or non-official entrusted with the preview of a particular film or to any other person including the applicant or his representative. The applicant or his representative will not be allowed to be present inside the preview theatre.

This 'confidentiality clause' has been introduced to counter a judgement of the Madras High Court, which stated that the CFBC must specify the guideline under which a film has been refused a certificate. Said the Court on February 7, 1983 in the case between Ramakrishna Cine Studio and the CBFC: 'The Central Board of Film Censors has to come out with specific reasons when it asks for cuts in a film and it must also furnish the particulars of guidelines under which cuts are sought to be effected to the film producer. If for any reason, the members of Committees (Examining or Revising) felt that any particular portion of film has to be cut, there could not be any 'confidentiality' about these opinions especially when the privilege was not claimed on the ground of public interest.'

The CBFC had directed the deletion of shots of President Reagan and Tamil Nadu Chief Minister M.G. Ramachandran, in a Telugu film starring N.T. Rama Rao, and produced by the Ramakrishna Cine Studio. The Court observed that by no stretch of the imagination could it be said to offend against public order, decency or morality under the Act, and the procedure followed by the Board was far from satisfactory.

Examining Committee

The recommendations of all the members of the Examining Committee are sent by the Examining Officer to the Chairman of the CBFC within three days of the preview. Within the next seven days, the producer is informed about the Certificate issued. Under the Cinematograph Act of 1952, films were certified 'U' (for unrestricted exhibition), and 'A' (for public exhibition restricted to adults only). But according to the new amendment, two more categories have been introduced. The first is 'UA' (for unrestricted public exhibition subject to parental guidance for children below the age of 12), and the second is 'S' (for public exhibition restricted to specialized audiences such as doctors, etc.)

The Board may, of course, ban a film or refuse to give it a certificate unless certain deletions in visuals and sounds are made. It may also offer to grant a 'U' instead of an 'A' provided suggested deletions are agreed to. In some cases where the Examining Committee is divided or where the producer makes a request for a reconsideration of the decision arrived at, a Revising Committee takes a second look at the film.

Revising Committee

The Revising Committee, under the new directives, consists of a chairman and not more than nine members selected from the Advisory Panel by the Chairman. No member of the Examining Committee can sit on the Revising Committee of the same film. It is stipulated that within three days of seeing the film, the recommendation of all the members have to be sent by the presiding officer to the chairman of the CBFC. Appeals against the CBFC's decisions are heard by the Film Certification Appellate Tribunal (FCAT) which was constituted in 1984. The Tribunal sits in New Delhi.

But the possession of a 'censor certificate' does not necessarily ensure the smooth exhibition of films throughout the country. Petitions can be filed in High Courts seeking a ban on a film. For instance, a private organisation had sought to ban Attenborough's Gandhi in a

Jhansi Magistrates court. In another case, the Allahabad High Court served notices on the writer, director and artistes of Andha Kanon directing them to show cause why action should not be taken against them for alleged contempt of court. And in Srinagar, the Chief Judicial Magistrate issued a bailable warrant against the producer of Nikaah on the charge that the film was produced with the intent to disrespect the laws of a minority community. In recent years, Shekhar Kapoor's Bandit Queen and Mira Nair's Kamasutra have been subject to severe censorship. Besides, there are pressure groups that bring their opinions to bear on the kind of films that ought to be exhibited. They halt the screening of films by force, or take their complaints to the courts.

❑